Quality assurance of pharmaceuticals

A compendium of guidelines
and related materials

Volume 1

Quality assurance of pharmaceuticals

A compendium of guidelines
and related materials

Volume 1

World Health Organization
Geneva
1997

WHO Library Cataloguing in Publication Data

Quality assurance of pharmaceuticals: a compendium of guidelines and related materials: volume 1.
1. Drug and narcotic control 2. Drug industry—standards
3. Legislation, Drug 4. Quality control 5. Guidelines
ISBN 92 4 154504 6   (NLM Classification: QV 33)

The World Health Organization welcomes requests for permission to reproduce or translate its publications, in part or in full. Applications and enquiries should be addressed to the Office of Publications, World Health Organization, Geneva, Switzerland, which will be glad to provide the latest information on any changes made to the text, plans for new editions, and reprints and translations already available.

© **World Health Organization 1997**

Publications of the World Health Organization enjoy copyright protection in accordance with the provisions of Protocol 2 of the Universal Copyright Convention. All rights reserved.

The designations employed and the presentation of the material in this publication do not imply the expression of any opinion whatsoever on the part of the Secretariat of the World Health Organization concerning the legal status of any country, territory, city or area or of its authorities, or concerning the delimitation of its frontiers or boundaries.

The mention of specific companies or of certain manufacturers' products does not imply that they are endorsed or recommended by the World Health Organization in preference to others of a similar nature that are not mentioned. Errors and omissions excepted, the names of proprietary products are distinguished by initial capital letters.

Much of the material reproduced in this publication is extracted from the reports of the WHO Expert Committee on Specifications for Pharmaceutical Preparations. These reports contain the collective views of an international group of experts and do not necessarily represent the decisions or the stated policy of the World Health Organization.

Printed in England
95/10460 – Clays – 8000

Contents

Introduction   1

    National drug regulation   2
    Product assessment and registration   3
    Good manufacturing practices and inspection   6
    Distribution   7
    The international pharmacopoeia and related activities   7
    Basic tests   9
    Laboratory services   10
    International trade in pharmaceuticals   12
    Counterfeit products   15
    Training   15
    Conclusion   17

1. National drug regulation

    Guiding principles for small national drug regulatory authorities   18

2. Product assessment and registration

    Guidelines for the assessment of herbal medicines   31
    Stability of drug dosage forms   37
    Guidelines for stability testing of pharmaceutical products
        containing well established drug substances in conventional
        dosage forms   46
    Multisource (generic) pharmaceutical products: guidelines on
        registration requirements to establish interchangeability   62

3. Distribution

    Quality assurance in pharmaceutical supply systems   105

4. *The international pharmacopoeia* and related activities

Guidance for those preparing or commenting on monographs for preparations to be included in *The international pharmacopoeia*	116
Validation of analytical procedures used in the examination of pharmaceutical materials	119
General guidelines for the establishment, maintenance, and distribution of chemical reference substances	124
General recommendations for the preparation and use of infrared spectra in pharmaceutical analysis	136
List of available International Chemical Reference Substances	142
List of available International Infrared Reference Spectra	148

5. Basic tests

Collaboration within the basic test programme	150

6. Laboratory services

National laboratories for drug quality surveillance and control	154
Good laboratory practices in governmental drug control laboratories	162
Sampling procedure for industrially manufactured pharmaceuticals	175

7. International trade in pharmaceuticals

Guidelines for implementation of the WHO Certification Scheme on the Quality of Pharmaceutical Products Moving in International Commerce	187
World Health Assembly resolution WHA50.3: Guidelines on the WHO Certification Scheme on the Quality of Pharmaceutical Products Moving in International Commerce	209
Guidelines on import procedures for pharmaceutical products	210

8. Counterfeit products

Observations and recommendations on counterfeit drugs	220

9. Training

Training programme in drug analysis	227
Places of training in drug quality control offered by the International Federation of Pharmaceutical Manufacturers Associations	235

Introduction

The quality of pharmaceuticals has been a concern of the World Health Organization (WHO) ever since its inception. The setting of global standards is requested in Article 2 of the WHO Constitution which cites as one of the Organization's functions that it should "develop, establish and promote international standards with respect to food, biological, pharmaceutical and similar products".

Every government allocates a substantial proportion of its total health budget to drugs. This proportion tends to be greatest in developing countries, where it may exceed 40%.

Without assurance that these drugs are relevant to priority health needs and that they meet acceptable standards of quality, safety and efficacy, any health service is evidently compromised. In developed countries considerable administrative and technical effort is directed to ensuring that patients receive effective drugs of good quality. It is crucial to the objective of health for all that a reliable system of drug control be brought within the reach of every country.

The supply of essential drugs of good quality was identified as one of the prerequisites for the delivery of health care at the International Conference on Primary Health Care in Alma-Ata in 1978. Similarly, the Conference of Experts on the Rational Use of Drugs, held in Nairobi in 1985, and WHO's Revised Drug Strategy, adopted by the World Health Assembly in May 1986, identified the effective functioning of national drug regulation and control systems as the only means to assure safety and quality of medicines. Yet the World Health Assembly continues to express great concern about the quality, safety and efficacy of medicines, particularly those products or active pharmaceutical substances imported into, or produced in, developing countries. In recent years counterfeit products have infiltrated certain markets in disquieting proportions. Since the founding of WHO, the World Health Assembly has adopted many resolutions requesting the Organization to develop international standards, recommendations and instruments to assure the quality of medicines, whether produced and traded nationally or internationally.

In response to these resolutions, the WHO Expert Committee on Specifications for Pharmaceutical Preparations, which was originally created to prepare *The international pharmacopoeia*, has made numerous recommendations relevant to quality assurance and control. Most of these recommendations, even if they were made several years ago, are still valid. Thus far, however, most have been available only as separate sets of recommendations contained in annexes to various WHO Technical Reports. The recommendations are essential to all concerned with the quality assurance of medicines, but separate publication over a period of years made it difficult to recognize them as complementary parts of a comprehensive system of quality assurance.

To provide easy access to this information, the appropriate annexes are being reproduced in the two volumes of this publication. They are supplemented with other material relevant to the quality assurance of pharmaceuticals, some already issued in the form of WHO documents. The information is not necessarily presented in chronological order of original issue. Instead it is presented in logical sequence as a series of administrative instruments and technical elements of an overall quality assurance system. Readers should bear in mind that, in certain previously published texts, reference is made to WHO guidelines and other documents that have since been updated. Some of these updated texts are themselves included in the compendium and others are mentioned in this introductory section or listed inside the back cover of the book. All material relating specifically to good manufacturing practices (GMP) and inspection of pharmaceutical manufacturers will appear in Volume 2 of this publication. The actual standards for analytical controls are contained in *The international pharmacopoeia*. Other relevant publications include *Basic tests for pharmaceutical substances* and *Basic tests for pharmaceutical dosage forms*.

WHO has addressed not only pharmaceutical aspects of the quality of medicines, but also the intrinsic safety and efficacy of pharmacologically active substances. Advice on this has been published in the reports of the WHO Expert Committee on Essential Drugs, the *WHO model prescribing information* series, the *WHO pharmaceuticals newsletter*, and the quarterly *WHO drug information*. From there relevant information is carried over into the regularly updated United Nations *Consolidated list of products whose consumption and/or sale have been banned, withdrawn, severely restricted or not approved by governments*.

National drug regulation

The existence and functioning of a comprehensive drug regulatory system supported by legislation is a prerequisite for an overall quality assurance system. The first duty of a national regulatory authority is to register pharmaceutical products, thus defining the pharmaceutical market in the country. Only when this has been done will it be possible to distinguish between legally traded products and illegal and counterfeit ones.

The WHO Expert Committee on Specifications for Pharmaceutical Preparations addressed this issue in its thirty-first report and adopted guiding principles for small national drug regulatory authorities. These guiding principles, later endorsed by the World Health Assembly in resolution WHA47.17, are reproduced in **Chapter 1**. The text gives advice on how to organize national drug regulatory activities. The first section is devoted to general considerations such as the scope of drug control, basic responsibilities, licensing functions, product licences, manufacturers' and distributors' licences, new drug assessments, authorization of clinical trials, terms of reference of the regulatory authority, powers of enforcement, technical competence, advisory bodies and independence of operation.

The second and third sections of Chapter 1 address the administrative and technical aspects of the product registration or licensing process and give advice on the setting of priorities and on implementation by stages. It is anticipated that, once the initial drug registrations have been made, the registration process can be administered effectively if due advantage is taken of the WHO Certification Scheme on the Quality of Pharmaceutical Products Moving in International Commerce, and prudence is exercised when accepting new chemical entities. It is recommended that developing countries do not register a new chemical entity before it has been on the market for at least five years in a country with a sophisticated drug regulatory system that includes post-marketing surveillance, unless the chemical entity presents a real therapeutic advance in combating a major endemic disease. If this approach is respected, the major work of the registration process will be the pharmaceutical evaluation of products that have not been registered in the country of export or that have been produced locally.

In some countries with large public sector procurement of essential drugs, major challenges will be to coordinate drug registration and procurement, making sure that only duly registered products are purchased. This is the only way to take real advantage of favourably priced generic products. If the purchase of generic products is allowed regardless of their registration status, there is no guarantee of the products' quality with regard to stability and bioavailability, since pharmacopoeial specifications do not necessarily address these features.

A model software package for computer-assisted drug registration has been developed by WHO's Division of Drug Management and Policies in collaboration with the Health System Information Unit of the Pan American Health Organization, and has now been field-tested in several countries. It can be obtained from the Division of Drug Management and Policies, WHO, 1211 Geneva 27, Switzerland.

Product assessment and registration

The WHO Expert Committee on Specifications for Pharmaceutical Preparations has on several occasions discussed and adopted guidelines and other texts concerned with the assessment of pharmaceutical products and with registration requirements.

Herbal medicines

At its thirty-fourth meeting, the Expert Committee adopted guidelines for the assessment of herbal medicines. These guidelines, reproduced in **Chapter 2**, have been widely distributed to WHO Member States and were discussed at the Sixth International Conference of Drug Regulatory Authorities (ICDRA), held in Ottawa in October 1991. Their utility has been widely recognized.

Stability of pharmaceutical products

The problem of stability of pharmaceuticals has been addressed a number of times by the WHO Expert Committee on Specifications for Pharmaceutical Preparations. The introduction to this subject in the thirty-first report of the Expert Committee reads as follows:

> Inadequate storage and distribution of pharmaceutical products can lead to their physical deterioration and chemical decomposition, resulting in reduced activity and, occasionally, in the formation of toxic degradation products. Degradation is particularly likely to occur under tropical conditions of high ambient temperature and humidity; and it is not widely recognized that, because of the potential for chemical interaction between the active ingredients and excipients, drug dosage forms can be more vulnerable to degradation than pure drug substances.
>
> The stability of a specific product is thus dependent, in a large measure, on its formulation, and its expiry date should be determined on the basis of stability studies carried out by the manufacturer. Studies undertaken with a view to determining the stability of a product under temperate conditions, however, do not necessarily provide a reliable indication of its shelf-life in tropical climates. In such cases, additional proof of stability should be requested from the manufacturer, who should assume responsibility for formulating a product that is stable under the climatic conditions prevailing in the countries of destination. Relevant information should be specifically requested by the national regulatory authority in the importing country within the context of the WHO Certification Scheme ... It is obviously impossible to obtain satisfactory assurances when a product is purchased through an intermediary if its provenance is unknown to the purchaser. For domestically produced products, the regulatory authority should evaluate stability data furnished by the manufacturer. The procurement agencies and the pharmacists responsible for drug distribution should ensure that they are supplied with adequate information concerning the proper storage and handling of each product.

Specific guidelines on the stability of drug dosage forms were annexed to the Expert Committee's report and are contained in Chapter 2. They provide a comprehensive statement on both the technical aspects of the subject and the responsibilities that devolve upon the manufacturer and all agencies and individuals responsible for the product throughout the distribution chain up to the time of the drug's administration or delivery to the patient. The thirty-first report of the Expert Committee explains:

> Within the distribution chain, the labelled expiry date on a pharmaceutical product has a dual significance: after this date, no formal assurance is provided regarding the condition of the product; and the manufacturer may no longer have legal liability for it. The Committee agreed that the use of time-expired stock should be entertained only in the most exceptional circumstances, when to withhold the stock would have serious consequences for patients. In every instance, the proposal to release such a product must be channelled through a pharmacist or other professional experienced in quality assurance and, when appropriate, referred to the competent authority, which must decide on the necessity for analysis and the period of time during which the product may be used, having regard to all relevant circumstances. Doctors and other health professionals using the product may need to be alerted to the situation. Procurement procedures should be reviewed and, if necessary, modified to prevent such situations arising in the future.

Guidelines for stability testing of pharmaceutical products containing well established drug substances in conventional dosage forms were adopted by the WHO Expert Committee on Specifications for Pharmaceutical Preparations at its thirty-fourth meeting, and are reproduced in Chapter 2. Recognizing that stability testing represents the evaluation of a pharmaceutical formulation in its final container, the Expert Committee emphasized that the same fundamental approach should be used for all products irrespective of whether the active ingredient was an established drug substance. Where sufficient information was already available on the chemical stability of the active ingredient, however, this could be taken into account. The availability of these guidelines was considered to be of special importance since they include advice on the stability testing of products for use in the more extreme climatic conditions found in many developing countries.

WHO has arranged for the conduct of accelerated stability studies on substances in the WHO Model List of Essential Drugs and has also sent out questionnaires to identify the products most likely to present stability problems. The accelerated stability studies are discussed in the twenty-eighth report of the WHO Expert Committee on Specifications for Pharmaceutical Preparations. For newly introduced substances much information on stability is available, since in many countries this information is a mandatory requirement for registration of a new product and for determining expiry dates. By contrast, little information has been published on the degradation of long-established pharmaceutical substances (except for obviously unstable products) and, in many cases, their behaviour when exposed to extreme climatic conditions is uncertain.

For this reason, accelerated stability studies were carried out on long-established essential drug substances under standardized conditions (e.g. 30 days' exposure to air at a temperature of 50 °C and a relative humidity of 100%). The appearance of degradation products was detected by thin-layer chromatography, supplemented (as necessary) by spectrophotometry, fluorescence reactions, high-performance liquid chromatography and chemical determinations. The substances were additionally exposed to a temperature of 70 °C under the same humidity conditions for a further 3–5 days. Negative results provided conclusive proof of the stability of the substance even under highly adverse conditions. All tests were carried out with light excluded since it is easy to protect substances from light during storage.

A document entitled "Accelerated stability studies of widely used pharmaceutical substances under simulated tropical conditions" (WHO/PHARM/86.529) contains the results of these accelerated stability studies and is available on request from the Quality Assurance unit, Division of Drug Management and Policies, WHO, 1211 Geneva 27, Switzerland.

Interchangeability of multisource (generic) pharmaceutical products

The final text in Chapter 2 provides guidance on registration requirements to establish the interchangeability of multisource (generic) pharmaceutical products. In adopting these guidelines at its thirty-fourth meeting, the WHO Expert Committee on Specifications for Pharmaceutical Preparations was pleased to note that they had already been adapted for local use by a number of WHO Member States and that positive feedback had been received especially with regard to the flexibility and clarity of the guidance. The guidelines were designed to allow a step-by-step approach tailored to the stage of development of a particular registration system and the needs and priorities of the national health authorities. They were intended to assist drug regulatory authorities and international organizations involved in the procurement of pharmaceutical products, and to provide manufacturers with an indication of the data required. It was recognized that these guidelines were a first step: they would need to be supported by training and advice on implementation.

Good manufacturing practices and inspection

The guidelines approved by the WHO Expert Committee on Specifications for Pharmaceutical Preparations on good manufacturing practices (GMP) for pharmaceutical products will be reproduced in Volume 2 of this compendium, together with supplementary guidelines for biological products, the validation of manufacturing processes and the manufacture of investigational pharmaceutical products for clinical trials in humans and of herbal medicinal products. This publication will also contain guidelines on the inspection of pharmaceutical manufacturers and of drug distribution channels.

Distribution

The Twenty-eighth World Health Assembly, in resolution WHA28.66, enumerated a number of objectives relating to regulatory control of drugs. In consequence, in its twenty-seventh report, the WHO Expert Committee on Specifications for Pharmaceutical Preparations discussed the various elements of quality assurance in pharmaceutical supply systems (see **Chapter 3**).

Although parts of the elements described in Chapter 3 have been incorporated into or expanded in the guidelines for small national drug regulatory authorities, the text still provides a succinct review of quality assessment and assurance, premarketing quality assessment, and drug surveillance during marketing.

Pharmacists play an important role in the distribution of pharmaceuticals and must ensure that the service provided to patients is of appropriate quality. Guidelines on good pharmacy practice have been prepared by the International Pharmaceutical Federation in collaboration with WHO to encourage national pharmaceutical organizations to focus the attention of pharmacists in the community and hospital pharmacy sector on developing the elements of their services to meet changing circumstances. They provide a framework within which each country can set standards relevant to its own aspirations and needs.

The guidelines were presented in April 1997 to the WHO Expert Committee on Specifications for Pharmaceutical Preparations and will be included as an annex to the Committee's report. Copies of the text can be obtained from the Regulatory Support unit, Division of Drug Management and Policies, WHO, 1211 Geneva 27, Switzerland.

The international pharmacopoeia and related activities

The international pharmacopoeia provides internationally acceptable standards for the potency, purity and quality of pharmaceutical products moving in international commerce. These standards are available for adoption by Member States in accordance with Articles 21(d) and 23 of the Constitution of the World Health Organization and resolution WHA3.10 of the Third World Health Assembly.

Many national or regional pharmacopoeias rely increasingly on complex techniques of analysis that require expensive equipment and highly trained personnel. Such methods are inapplicable, however, in countries lacking these resources. For the most part, these methods merely permit analyses to be carried out more rapidly than by classical chemical methods.

Whereas earlier editions of *The international pharmacopoeia* had relied heavily on material taken from certain national pharmacopoeias, the third edition, of which four volumes have been published so far, aims to accommodate the needs of developing countries by offering sound quality standards for essential drugs on the basis (wherever possible) of classical procedures. Volume 1, published in 1979, describes general methods of analysis. Volumes 2 and 3, published in 1981 and 1988 respectively, contain quality specifications mainly for essential drug substances included in WHO's Model List of Essential Drugs. Volume 4 (1994) includes monographs on pharmaceutical substances, widely used excipients and dosage forms of essential drugs. Volume 5 (in preparation) will contain several new general requirements and additional test methods for substances and dosage forms, and a revised procedure for high-performance liquid chromatography. The volume will also contain specifications for the determination of more than 35 pharmaceutical substances and some 20 finished preparations in tablet form.

The role and objectives of *The international pharmacopoeia* are thus to a large extent to provide an alternative to some widely used national and regional pharmacopoeias that include sophisticated testing methods. Of course, if laboratory facilities permit use of advanced analytical methods, it is logical to analyse products according to the modern methods of such pharmacopoeias. Indeed, products may often be labelled as conforming to these pharmacopoeias. But where sophisticated testing is not possible, *The international pharmacopoeia* still allows verification of the quality of a product.

In its twenty-eighth report, the WHO Expert Committee on Specifications for Pharmaceutical Preparations summarized the functions and characteristics of *The international pharmacopoeia* and commented: "*Inter alia*, the production of *The international pharmacopoeia* helps to advance the setting of pharmacopoeial standards at national level, in that it fosters a valuable exchange of experiences gained in a wide variety of countries". At its thirty-fifth meeting, the Committee recommended that manufacturers in exporting countries be encouraged to use *The international pharmacopoeia* and to indicate such use in product information.

The international pharmacopoeia is developed in close collaboration with members of the WHO Expert Advisory Panel on the International Pharmacopoeia and Pharmaceutical Preparations, other specialists from government authorities, industry, the academic world and WHO Collaborating Centres. **Chapter 4** contains guidance for those preparing or commenting on monographs for inclusion in *The international pharmacopoeia*.

Analytical procedures used to control the quality of pharmaceutical substances and dosage forms must be adequately validated. Guidelines on validation, endorsed by the WHO Expert Committee on Specifications for Pharmaceutical Preparations, are included in Chapter 4. Since the extent to which validation is necessary is determined by the purpose of the analysis, judgement on the extent to which the guidelines need to be applied must be made on a case-by-case basis. These guidelines are directed primarily to the examination of chemical and physicochemical attributes, but many of the general principles are also applicable to microbiological and biological procedures.

Reference materials

Whenever necessary, monographs included in *The international pharmacopoeia* rely on the use of reference materials. These are provided either in the form of International Chemical Reference Substances and Melting-point Reference Substances or as International Infrared Reference Spectra. Chapter 4 provides general guidelines for the establishment, maintenance and distribution of chemical reference substances. These include a section on the need for national and/or regional collections of secondary reference materials that have been calibrated against International Chemical Reference Substances. The chapter also contains recommendations for the preparation and use of infrared spectra in pharmaceutical analysis.

The guidelines on reference substances reproduced in Chapter 4 were published in 1982. These guidelines were revised in 1996 in the light of developments in analytical chemistry and international collaboration and to take into account established practice in the use of chemical reference substances for pharmacopoeial purposes. The revised guidelines are not intended to be specific to International Chemical Reference Substances, but are general guidelines for all bodies issuing chemical reference substances, and give advice on the establishment of both primary and secondary reference substances. The revised text was presented in April 1997 to the WHO Expert Committee on Specifications for Pharmaceutical Preparations and will be included as an annex to the Committee's report. Copies can be obtained from the Quality Assurance unit, Division of Drug Management and Policies, WHO, 1211 Geneva 27, Switzerland.

Some 180 International Chemical Reference Substances and some 60 International Infrared Reference Spectra have been produced and are listed in Chapter 4. Information is also provided on how to obtain them. The establishment of International Chemical Reference Substances and International Infrared Reference Spectra is continuing and new lists will be annexed to the report of the thirty-fifth meeting of the WHO Expert Committee on Specifications for Pharmaceutical Preparations.

A general list of reference substances for pharmacopoeial analysis is issued by the Quality Assurance unit, Division of Drug Management and Policies, WHO, 1211 Geneva 27, Switzerland, and is updated yearly. It provides current information on the availability and sources of reference substances. Most of these substances are prepared and issued by regional/national pharmacopoeial commissions or regional/national quality control laboratories on behalf of drug regulatory authorities. Each substance is generally established for a specific analytical purpose as defined by the issuing body. Use for any other purpose becomes the responsibility of the user and a suitable caution is included in the accompanying information sheet.

Basic tests

Simplified or basic tests for pharmaceutical substances have been published in *Basic tests for pharmaceutical substances* in 1986 and *Basic tests for pharmaceutical dosage forms* in 1991. In 1994, the WHO Expert Committee on Specifications for

Pharmaceutical Preparations suggested that the scope of the next publication on basic tests should be extended to include additional information on, and references to, other simple test methodologies. These are considered a valuable tool for primary screening and could play an important part in identifying counterfeit and spurious products. The third volume in the series of basic tests, which is in preparation for publication, will therefore refer to collections of simple tests other than those published by WHO. It will also contain details of basic tests for 23 additional pharmaceutical substances, 4 medicinal plant materials and 58 dosage forms. The substances covered by basic tests are mainly those included in WHO's Model List of Essential Drugs.

In its twenty-eighth report, the WHO Expert Committee on Specifications for Pharmaceutical Preparations stated: "Basic tests are not, in any circumstances, intended to replace the requirements of pharmacopoeial monographs. The latter give an assurance of quality whereas basic tests merely confirm the identity".

Basic tests do not need to be carried out by fully qualified pharmacists or chemists, but they should be performed by persons who have some understanding of analytical chemistry, such as required in courses for pharmaceutical assistants.

It is thus acknowledged that basic tests have a clearly defined but limited role. They have gained importance as screening tests to identify falsely labelled, spurious and counterfeit drugs.

Basic tests are developed in close collaboration with experts from all over the world and are tried in various laboratories to ensure their global applicability. Guidance on collaboration within the basic test programme, including a protocol for the development and verification of basic tests, was given in the twenty-ninth report of the WHO Expert Committee on Specifications for Pharmaceutical Preparations and is contained in **Chapter 5**.

Laboratory services

National laboratories for drug quality surveillance and control

An independent drug quality control laboratory is an indispensable element of a national drug quality assurance system, and is particularly important nowadays in the light of infiltration of distribution channels by counterfeit products. Laboratories are still missing in many developing countries. The reason for this is partly that, in the absence of any guidance on the basic requirements for such a laboratory, it was assumed for a long time that the costs would be so exorbitant that it would be beyond the resources of most developing countries.

In its twenty-ninth report, the WHO Expert Committee on Specifications for Pharmaceutical Preparations stated that every country, regardless of its stage of development, should consider investment in an independent national drug quality control laboratory. The Expert Committee made recommendations directed to the many developing countries that have not yet created such a facility and do not have the resources to maintain a comprehensive system of control.

It should be recognized, in particular, that:

— simple procedures, such as tablet disintegration tests, are frequently of critical importance in eliminating seriously substandard preparations;
— a small laboratory directed by a competent, discerning individual will provide a persuasive deterrent to negligent or fraudulent manufacturing practices;
— the availability of complex automated equipment accelerates but does not necessarily raise the standard of analytical work. Moreover, such equipment performs reliably only when it is expertly maintained. Its operation may require the use of highly purified and expensive reagents.

Chapter 6 contains proposed models for a first-stage laboratory for drug surveillance, and a medium-size drug control laboratory. It provides advice on capabilities, premises, staff and equipment as well as on the scope of activities, factors influencing size and location of a laboratory, and the implementation of control laboratory projects. Even the smaller of the two model laboratories provides for the full pharmacopoeial analysis of more that 75% of WHO's Model List of Essential Drugs in accordance with the methods provided for in *The international pharmacopoeia*.

A document containing current prices for laboratory equipment is regularly updated and is available on request from the Quality Assurance unit, Division of Drug Management and Policies, WHO, 1211 Geneva 27, Switzerland.

Good practices for quality control laboratories

To complement its advice on setting up governmental drug control laboratories, the WHO Expert Committee on Specifications for Pharmaceutical Preparations included in its thirtieth report guidelines on good practices in governmental drug control laboratories. These, reproduced in Chapter 6, deal with management and operational issues affecting governmental drug control laboratories which analyse products for registration or during post-marketing surveillance. The scope of the guidelines ranges from organizational structure and staffing to advice on routines and management, documentation requirements, and the evaluation of test results. The sections on analytical work are primarily concerned with chemical and physicochemical analyses rather than with microbiological, pharmacological or other specialized test methods. The practices outlined are not fully applicable to quality control laboratories in manufacturing establishments, where test procedures and documentation may be different.

The guidelines are intended to be illustrative rather than prescriptive and need to be adapted to differing local circumstances such as the size of the laboratory. Alternative approaches to management are acceptable, provided that reliability of operations remains assured. In small laboratories many of the responsibilities lie with one qualified analyst, but the principles of management and operation are the same.

Sampling procedure for industrially manufactured pharmaceuticals

Since analytical control procedures are often performed on only a small portion of the material under consideration, it is vital to ensure that the sample tested is reasonably representative of the whole batch or consignment. Many of the operations described in the guidelines on good laboratory practices in governmental drug control laboratories require the use of sound sampling procedures. It is for this reason that, in its thirty-first report, the WHO Expert Committee on Specifications for Pharmaceutical Preparations provided guidelines for sampling procedures for industrially manufactured pharmaceuticals. These are reproduced in Chapter 6.

No single sampling plan is applicable to all situations. Different considerations and methodologies apply to in-process control, to batch release by manufacturers, to routine control of consignments within the distribution chain, and to spot-sampling carried out by purchasers or government inspectors.

The guidelines on sampling procedures are intended primarily for use by national drug regulatory authorities and governmental procurement agencies, but the general principles and much of the advice are also applicable to manufacturers and wholesalers.

International trade in pharmaceuticals

WHO Certification Scheme on the Quality of Pharmaceutical Products Moving in International Commerce

The WHO Certification Scheme on the Quality of Pharmaceutical Products Moving in International Commerce was developed in response to concern raised in the World Health Assembly about import of substandard products into developing countries in the 1960s. The Certification Scheme is based on the concept of sharing of responsibilities between three partners. The pharmaceutical manufacturer in the exporting country has to produce in accordance with good manufacturing practices, the drug regulatory authority of the exporting country has to inspect the manufacturing plant to confirm that it complies with good manufacturing practices, and the drug regulatory authority of the importing country has to request from its counterpart in the exporting country information on the regulatory status of the product it intends to import and confirmation that the manufacturer complies with standards of good manufacturing practices. In normal circumstances the certified information issued by the drug regulatory authority in the exporting country, as provided for under the WHO Certification Scheme, reaches the drug regulatory authority of the importing country via the manufacturer, exporter or importer and is used as the basis for drug registration in the importing country. When there are problems or queries the Certification Scheme provides for a channel for direct communication between the regulatory authorities in the importing and exporting countries.

Some countries do not yet have effectively functioning drug registration systems. In such situations the procurement agency has to operate an unofficial de facto registration system in order to assure the quality of products it intends to purchase and makes use of the provisions of the Certification Scheme before importing a new pharmaceutical formulation. Provision of information as provided for under the Certification Scheme should be a precondition when tenders are submitted.

Where a legally based national drug registration system exists, all procurement agencies must comply with the law and limit their procurement to duly registered products. In the case of favourable conditions for a product not yet registered in the country, the procurement agency should submit all necessary information to the registration body. This may speed up the registration process for public sector procurement agencies, provided all elements necessary to guarantee quality have been properly and positively evaluated.

The Certification Scheme was first recommended by the World Health Assembly in 1969 in resolution WHA22.50. A revised version was recommended in 1975 in resolution WHA28.65. The Certification Scheme was evaluated in the 1980s and a further revised and expanded version was recommended to WHO Member States by the World Health Assembly in resolution WHA41.18 of 1988. The Scheme now includes provision of approved product information, certification of veterinary products when administered to food-producing animals, and certification of starting materials in so far as they are subject to regulatory control in the country of export. Certification of starting materials, and particularly of active pharmaceutical ingredients, has become of particular relevance as many developing countries now produce the dosage forms themselves and are therefore more concerned to import raw materials of good quality. Parallel to this, there has been a shift in the production of active drug substances to developing countries, especially the more industrially advanced ones.

A country wishing to participate in the Certification Scheme must notify WHO of its intention to do so. The country must define both the extent to which it wishes to participate and the authority competent to issue and/or receive information as provided for in the Scheme. As of 1 January 1997, 140 of the 190 WHO Member States had informed the Organization officially of their intention to participate.

In order to facilitate the use of the Certification Scheme, the World Health Assembly endorsed provisional guidelines in 1992 in resolution WHA45.29. These guidelines, which deal with certification of pharmaceutical products, were refined following field trials in a number of WHO Member States and discussion during the sixth and seventh biennial International Conferences of Drug Regulatory Authorities. The revised guidelines were adopted by the WHO Expert Committee on Specifications for Pharmaceutical Preparations and published in its thirty-fourth report. Separate guidelines on certification of active pharmaceutical ingredients are under development.

Chapter 7 contains the text of the revised guidelines for implementing the WHO Certification Scheme on the Quality of Pharmaceutical Products Moving in International Commerce. It also reproduces Resolution WHA50.3, adopted by the World Health Assembly in May 1997, which endorses the guidelines and urges Member States to implement them. A regularly updated list of Member States participating in the Scheme can be obtained from Regulatory Support, Division of Drug Management and Policies, WHO, 1211 Geneva 27, Switzerland, together with the addresses of the competent authorities of participating countries and details of any significant reservations expressed by countries regarding their participation in the Scheme.

Import procedures

Chapter 7 also contains guidelines on import procedures for pharmaceutical products, which take into account the needs of, and resources available in, developing countries. They are intended to provide a framework for the effective control of pharmaceutical products at specified ports of entry and a basis for collaboration between the various interested parties.

Arrangements for independent analysis of drug samples

In the case of disputes arising from an unanticipated adverse reaction to a drug or from physical signs of deterioration in the product, a country may need to turn to a foreign laboratory for analytical confirmation of a presumed defect. The solution should be first sought at the regional level, through the respective WHO Regional Office. Regional or subregional testing laboratories have been or are being established in the WHO Regions of Africa, the Americas and the Eastern Mediterranean. Exceptionally, an impartial retesting in a national laboratory of a European country may be arranged through WHO in Geneva. It should be noted, however, that in this case analyses will be expensive (over US$ 300 for a full pharmacopoeial testing) and may take one or two months (or more), depending on the workload of the laboratory approached. It is hoped that these arrangements can be extended to all products covered by the WHO Certification Scheme on the Quality of Pharmaceutical Products Moving in International Commerce and that, when such analyses have undisputed implications for public health, directors of the testing laboratories will have discretionary authority to undertake them at reduced cost or even free of charge.

Counterfeit products

Counterfeit pharmaceutical products present a new and serious threat to health care delivery. The alert was first given during the Conference of Experts on the Rational Use of Drugs, held in Nairobi in November 1985. In 1988, the Forty-first World Health Assembly adopted a resolution (WHA41.16) requesting governments and pharmaceutical manufacturers "to cooperate in the detection and prevention of the increasing incidence of the export or smuggling of falsely labelled, spurious, counterfeited or substandard pharmaceutical preparations" and requesting the Director-General "to initiate programmes for the prevention and detection of the export, import and smuggling of falsely labelled, spurious, counterfeited or substandard pharmaceutical preparations, and to cooperate with the Secretary-General of the United Nations in cases when the provisions of the international drug treaties are violated". A joint WHO/International Federation of Pharmaceutical Manufacturers Associations workshop on counterfeit drugs was organized in Geneva in April 1992. The observations and recommendations published in the report of the workshop are contained in **Chapter 8**. Apart from the need for coordination and exchange of information between all interested parties, the recommendations stress the need for overall regulatory control through the setting up and strengthening of national drug regulatory and control authorities.

In 1995 a project was started to develop means to combat counterfeit drugs. Guidelines on drug inspection and the analysis of suspect samples have been prepared and a model training course on the application of these guidelines has been developed. A global workshop will be held at the end of 1997 to consider progress made and plan further activities.

Training

The establishment and development of pharmaceutical manufacturing facilities and national quality control laboratories in developing countries call for relevant training programmes for technical personnel. In particular, there is an evident need for group training of recent science and pharmacy graduates and for on-site individual training at more advanced level. The following advice on group training is taken from the twenty-ninth report of the WHO Expert Committee on Specifications for Pharmaceutical Preparations:

> Ideally, all graduate personnel should undergo a six-month period of preparatory training in practical and theoretical aspects of drug analysis. Emphasis should be on the practical approach, although some provisions should be made for discussion of the theoretical basis of the work, and the experimental programme should be developed having regard to:
>
> — the structure and organization of the model laboratories [described in Chapter 6];

— common practical problems encountered in the analysis of pharmaceutical products;
— the importance of selecting and validating appropriate analytical methods and of evaluating all results.

Following an introductory course lasting about 1 week, in which the general principles of drug quality control and analysis are presented, including an appreciation of their relevance to procurement and distribution, separate courses should be offered in chemical, microbiological, and biological control. It is important, however, that a trainee in one of these disciplines should have a general appreciation of the other aspects of control. A clear perception must be gained of all the duties and responsibilities of an analyst and of the need to institute good laboratory practice in the interests of both efficiency and safety.

Basic training in microbiological control should lay particular emphasis upon sterility testing, microbiological spoilage testing, and potency tests for antibiotics. Guidance is also required on the preparation and monitoring of culture media from locally available materials.

An introduction to biological control should be directed to pyrogen testing and other specific safety tests. Since the testing of biological products, including vaccines, blood products, and hormones, is usually undertaken in specialized institutions, this work falls outside the scope of a general introductory course.

A detailed model syllabus for such training programmes, which could be organized in many national quality control laboratories, is contained in **Chapter 9**. It covers both the practical and the theoretical aspects of drug analysis for regulatory purposes.

A primary objective is to teach students how to work efficiently and how to determine priorities for analyses so that limited resources can be used to best effect. This need is obviously most acute where facilities are most limited.

The syllabus provides for a general introduction to the objectives and principles of drug control and laboratory management, followed by separate parallel courses in chemical, microbiological and biological techniques of analysis. A six-month course is proposed for both chemical and microbiological analysis, and a course of three to four months for biological (pharmacological) techniques.

The sequence in which the subjects are listed is that in which the various analytical techniques are used in the control of specific categories of pharmaceutical raw materials and dosage forms, and it differs in this respect from the usual presentation of analytical methods.

Obviously trainees working in a first-stage laboratory, such as that described in Chapter 6, will not need practical experience in all the methods of analysis covered by the syllabus. If the training is to be used to best advantage, it is therefore important for the course organizer to obtain advance information on the facilities available to participants in their own countries.

A simpler syllabus should also be drawn up for the training of laboratory technicians and courses should be organized for laboratory managers.

On-site training of persons already employed in national quality control laboratories is available through the scheme operated under the aegis of the International Federation of Pharmaceutical Manufacturers Associations, as described in Chapter 9.

Conclusion

Recommendations and guidelines provide an essential foundation for the development and maintenance of quality assurance of pharmaceutical products. But it is personnel who are crucial to quality assurance at all levels of pharmaceutical manufacture, regulation and distribution.

Pharmacists have an important contribution to make in public health and particularly in the field of medicines. WHO meetings on the role of the pharmacist in the health care system were held in New Delhi in 1988 and in Tokyo in 1993, and the World Health Assembly, in resolution WHA47.12, has stressed the key role pharmacists can play in the rational use and quality assurance of medicines.

By virtue of their training, pharmacists can play a part in drug regulation and control, particularly in the evaluation of pharmaceutical formulations at the time of product registration, and in the licensing and inspection of pharmaceutical manufacturing plants and distribution channels. In addition to their work in central medical stores, hospitals, pharmacies and other drug outlets, trained pharmacists may also contribute to quality assurance by assisting in pharmaceutical manufacture, in drug procurement and in distribution.

While quality assurance is founded on regulations and standards, it is the people who enforce the regulations or work to comply with the standards who make the difference between quality assurance and lack of it. The assurance of quality, safety and efficacy of medicines is a continuing concern of WHO. This compilation of material is intended to assist all involved in the manufacture, regulation and distribution of pharmaceuticals to achieve these aims more effectively.

1.
National drug regulation

Guiding principles for small national drug regulatory authorities[1,2]

1.	General considerations	19
	1.1 The scope of drug control	19
	1.2 Basic responsibilities	19
	1.3 Licensing functions	19
	1.4 Product licences	20
	1.5 Manufacturers' and distributors' licences	21
	1.6 New drug assessments	21
	1.7 Authorization of clinical trials	21
	1.8 Terms of reference of the regulatory authority	22
	1.9 Powers of enforcement	22
	1.10 Technical competence	23
	1.11 Advisory bodies	23
	1.12 Independence of operation	23
2.	Administrative aspects of the licensing process	24
	2.1 Provisional registration of existing medicinal products	24
	2.2 Screening of provisionally registered products	24
	2.3 New product licences	26
	2.4 Renewal and variation of licences	26
3.	Technical aspects of the licensing process	27
	3.1 General considerations	27
	3.2 Products containing long-established chemical entities	27
	3.3 Products containing new chemical entities	28
	3.4 Herbal products	29

---

[1] *WHO Expert Committee on Specifications for Pharmaceutical Preparations. Thirty-first Report.* Geneva, World Health Organization, 1990 (WHO Technical Report Series, No. 790).
[2] Based on the report of a meeting convened by WHO in November 1987, with the following participants: Mr J. Y. Binka, Medicines Board, Medical and Health Department, Banjul, The Gambia; Dr J. L. Carrois, Cabinet International Carrois, Paris, France; Dr H. El-Sheikh, Ministry of Health, Khartoum, Sudan; Dr G. Lewandowski, Ciba-Geigy Ltd, Basle, Switzerland; Mr L. Prescod, Barbados Drug Service, St Michael, Barbados; Professor M. D. Rawlins, Department of Pharmacological Sciences, University of Newcastle-upon-Tyne, Newcastle-upon-Tyne, England; Mr J. Ruberantwari, Ministry of Health, Entebbe, Uganda; Dr P. N. Suwal, Ministry of Forest and Soil Conservation, Kathmandu, Nepal; Mr Tan Kiok K'ng, Pharmaceutical Department, Ministry of Health, Singapore; Mrs S. S. Tessema, Office of the Chief Pharmacist, Nairobi, Kenya.

3.5   Combinations of potent, therapeutically active substances   29
3.6   Generic products   29

1. General considerations

Small countries which have yet to introduce comprehensive legal provisions for drug regulation can draw from a diversity of national systems in determining their own requirements. None the less, problems in establishing drug control in developing countries have too often resulted from the adaptation of provisions successful elsewhere but of a complexity that precludes their effective implementation in the country of adoption. It is of paramount importance that legislation and administrative practices are attuned to available resources and that every opportunity is taken to obtain and use information provided by regulatory authorities in other countries on pharmaceutical products and substances moving in international commerce.

Channels of communication between national regulatory authorities are improving, as is evident from the information contained in WHO's monthly *Pharmaceuticals newsletter*, the quarterly journal *WHO drug information*, and the *United Nations Consolidated List of Products Whose Consumption and/or Sale have been Banned, Withdrawn, Severely Restricted or Not Approved by Governments*. Moreover, many difficulties inherent in storing, retrieving and analysing data that subserve the many facets of the regulatory process can now be overcome by the use of microcomputers and commercial software packages.

1.1 The scope of drug control

To be effective, a small drug regulatory authority needs to operate within the context of a defined national drugs policy and to interrelate with other interested bodies, including organizations responsible for drug procurement in the public sector and the national formulary committee, where such exists.

1.2 Basic responsibilities

The responsibilities of the regulatory authority are to ensure that all products subject to its control conform to acceptable standards of quality, safety and efficacy; and that all premises and practices employed to manufacture, store and distribute these products comply with requirements to ensure the continued conformity of the products to these standards until such time as they are delivered to the end-user.

1.3 Licensing functions

These objectives can be accomplished effectively only if a mandatory system of licensing products, manufacturers, importing agents, and distributors is in place.

A small authority has strictly limited capacity to undertake these tasks. For the assurances it requires in relation to imported pharmaceutical products and drug substances, it is vitally dependent on authoritative, reliable, and independent information generated in the exporting country. This information is most effectively obtained through the WHO Certification Scheme on the Quality of Pharmaceutical Products Moving in International Commerce.

Before a formal licensing system can become operative, it is necessary:

(a) to adopt a precise definition of a drug product and of the various categories of licence-holders;
(b) to determine the content and format of licences, both for products and for licence-holders;
(c) to detail the criteria on which licence applications will be assessed; and
(d) to provide guidance to interested parties on the content and format of licence applications, and on the circumstances in which an application for renewal, extension or variation of a licence will be required.

The definition of a drug product is commonly contingent upon the claims that are made for it. Ideally, controls need to be applied to any product that is offered for sale for administration to human beings for treating, preventing and diagnosing disease, for anaesthesia, for contraception, and for otherwise altering normal physiological functions.[1] In practice, exemptions may need to be granted to various specific categories of products in order to address priorities effectively. It might be decided as an interim measure, for example, to require licences only for products listed in a national formulary. Ultimately, however, control needs to be extended not only to all products moving in the major distribution channels, but to those formulated in pharmacies and hospital dispensaries, to herbal preparations, and to other traditional medicines entering into local commerce.

Analogous priorities may also need to be accorded to the registration of licence-holders, although the ultimate objective should be to embrace all manufacturers, importing agents, wholesalers involved in repackaging, pharmacies, and hospital dispensaries in a system that imposes upon them relevant statutory obligations.

1.4 Product licences

The issuance of product licences is pivotal to any system of drug control. The licence is a legal document that establishes the detailed composition and formulation of the product, the pharmacopoeial or other officially recognized specifications of its ingredients, its clinical interchangeability (in the case of

---

[1] Veterinary products administered to food-producing animals may also fall into this category; see the revised WHO Certification Scheme on the Quality of Pharmaceutical Products Moving in International Commerce (WHO Technical Report Series, No. 790, 1990, Annex 5).

multisource products), and its packaging, shelf-life and labelling. Of itself, this goes a long way towards establishing the assurances of quality, efficacy, and safety to which the system is directed. However, without a viable pharmaceutical inspectorate or access to an independent quality-control laboratory operating to standards that will ensure its credibility in the event of dispute, licensing provisions cannot be effectively enforced.

1.5 Manufacturers' and distributors' licences

The pharmaceutical inspectorate is responsible for ensuring that pharmaceutical products comply with conditions set out in the licence up to the time that they are delivered to the end-user. Its functions are:

(a) to establish, through periodic formal inspections and spot-checks, that all categories of licence-holder are operating in accordance with their licensed activities, prevailing standards of good manufacturing practice, and other prescribed regulations;
(b) to maintain oversight of distribution channels, either by inspection and monitoring or by arranging for pharmacopoeial analysis of selected samples, with a view to ensuring that products are not subject to unacceptable degradation during transit and storage at the periphery.

1.6 New drug assessments

Within highly evolved national drug regulatory authorities much effort is directed to establishing the efficacy and safety of new drug entities through pharmaceutical, biological, and clinical assessment and through subsequent surveillance of their performance in routine use after marketing. Premarketing assessment is dependent upon detailed multidisciplinary technical review, and postmarketing surveillance requires a highly developed health care infrastructure. Only in exceptional circumstances should a small regulatory authority contemplate allocation of scarce resources to these ends. Reliance must be placed primarily on information notified by other countries through the network of national information officers established by WHO.

1.7 Authorization of clinical trials

A small authority may occasionally need to consider an application to conduct a clinical trial of an unregistered drug in the treatment of a condition that has a high local prevalence. To provide for this contingency, the registration system should include provision for the importation of the necessary materials, subject to appropriate controls. Such trials should only take place after formal clearance has been obtained from the competent registration authority and after assurances have been obtained that they will be conducted in conformity with the principles contained in the World Medical Association's Declaration of Helsinki and the *Proposed International Guidelines for Biomedical Research Involving Human Subjects* issued by the Council for International Organizations of Medical Sciences.[1] WHO stands ready to offer independent technical advice to national authorities in these circumstances.

1.8 Terms of reference of the regulatory authority

The formal terms of reference of a national drug regulatory authority are determined by statute and regulation. Legislation relating to pharmaceutical products has developed piecemeal in many countries, and there are obvious advantages in bringing matters concerned with their regulation under one law. For example, it is important to correlate laws relating to the control of narcotic and psychotropic substances with requirements for product registration. If comprehensive overhaul of the legal system is impracticable, control within the existing framework through regulations specifically related to the registration of pharmaceutical products offers advantages of economy and time-saving. Whichever option is chosen, regulatory authorities require the flexibility to respond to changing circumstances imposed by the evolution of pharmaceutical science.

In general terms, the authority should be vested with legal powers to:

(a) issue, vary and revoke licences for pharmaceutical products on grounds of quality, safety, and efficacy;
(b) secure the subsequent safe and effective use of each product by controlling, through the terms of the licence, the content of all labelling (including package inserts, associated prescribing information and advertising) and the channels through which the product may legitimately be supplied; and
(c) inspect and license all manufacturing premises, importing agents, wholesalers and distributors, hospital dispensaries, independent pharmacies, and other retail outlets to ensure that they comply with prevailing regulations and guidelines.

1.9 Powers of enforcement

In order to implement these responsibilities the authority must command powers of enforcement backed by legal provision for penal sanction against offenders.

In establishing administrative mechanisms for decision-making, the regulatory authority should not lose necessary flexibility. In particular, it should make provision for:

---

[1] Council for International Organizations of Medical Sciences. Proposed international guidelines for biomedical research involving human subjects. Geneva, 1982 (also contains the Declaration of Helsinki as revised by the 29th World Medical Assembly, Tokyo, 1975).

(a) implementing decisions regarded as urgent in the interest of public safety; and
(b) formal consultation (usually through representative bodies) with pharmaceutical companies and other interested parties, including pharmacists, doctors, nurses, and patients.

1.10 Technical competence

A small licensing authority will rarely, if ever, undertake comprehensive independent assessments of the safety and efficacy of individual products. The administrative and technical responsibilities that fall within its ambit are essentially of a pharmaceutical nature and they are directed primarily to quality assurance. The professional staff must include members with a thorough understanding and practical experience of the different facets of this work.

The responsible officer is accountable for the professional validation and assessment of licence applications and for the administrative aspects of licensing and, as such, should be involved in determining priorities and developing a timetable for implementation of controls. These activities require administrative and clerical support and premises sufficient to handle the large volume of documentation involved with appropriate confidentiality. Efficiency of operation is enhanced when the required information can be retrieved rapidly from a computerized data base.

1.11 Advisory bodies

The responsible officer must also have access to a standing advisory committee or board of independent experts (including academic and practising health care professionals) for advice on technical issues. Consideration should also be given to the need for a multidisciplinary commission to advise on matters of general policy and administration and to ensure effective relations with bodies responsible for drug procurement in the public sector and with the national formulary committee.

1.12 Independence of operation

To retain public confidence and respect, the authority must be seen to undertake its tasks in an independent, authoritative, and impartial manner. It should be concerned exclusively with the determination of standards and the implementation of controls. Although it will need to work closely with the authority responsible for drug procurement within the public sector, it should not itself be responsible for procurement and it should remain independent and autonomous in its operational activities and decisions.

2. Administrative aspects of the licensing process

2.1 Provisional registration of existing medicinal products

Before any system of control can become effective, it is necessary to identify and catalogue all products already sold or otherwise supplied on the domestic market, in both the public and the private sectors, that qualify for control. To this end, all manufacturers and importing agencies must be given reasonable notice through official gazettes, the trade press and other media of their obligation to notify the authority by a specific date of all medicinal products that they currently distribute within the jurisdiction of the authority and that they intend to continue to supply after a duly appointed day, on which licensing requirements enter into operation. After the appointed day no medicinal product may lawfully be distributed or supplied unless its existence has been notified to the authority, and no new product may be introduced until a request for a product licence has been granted by the authority.

Effective administration of the provisional registration procedure is dependent upon:

(a) prior identification of all interested manufacturers and importers;
(b) a precise definition of a notifiable medicinal product based primarily on the labelled claims and the indications for use;
(c) the issuance of guidelines on the procedure to be followed.

Each notified product must be identified by name (either brand or generic), the names and full addresses of the manufacturer and importing agent, a description of the dosage form, its composition—including active and inactive ingredients (using international nonproprietary names where appropriate)—the therapeutic class, the indications, a copy of all labelling, including any package insert, and a copy of any relevant certificates and warranties relating to the product or its components.

2.2 Screening of provisionally registered products

A rapid screening of notified products should be undertaken at the earliest opportunity with a view to securing the withdrawal of any products which, simply on the basis of a review of their ingredients and indications, are judged not to meet admissible standards of safety. This may be achieved by the withdrawal of permission to trade in specific notified products or the issuance of regulations imposing specified restrictions on precisely defined groups of products. After this preliminary review, a set of longer-term priorities needs to be set for the definitive assessment of provisionally registered products. Consideration needs to be given to the resources required, both in manpower and information, if the review is to be adapted to a proposed time-schedule. Standards must be maintained and calls to accelerate the speed of implementation must be recognized as having resource implications.

In planning priorities, consideration must be given to:

(a) the number of provisionally registered products to be processed;
(b) the number of staff and/or consultants to be allocated to the task;
(c) the amount of relevant information available from other national authorities;
(d) the extent to which products can be reviewed in groups rather than individually;
(e) the extent to which a laissez-faire disposition can be adopted towards such products as herbal remedies and tonics that are without potent pharmacological activity and carry imprecise claims, but which satisfy an acknowledged public demand.

Considerations of safety require that particular attention be accorded to:

(a) products that either have been withdrawn or are the subject of restrictive regulatory action in other countries as notified in the *United Nations Consolidated List of Products Whose Consumption and/or Sale have been Banned, Withdrawn, Severely Restricted or Not Approved by Governments,* and in WHO's *Pharmaceuticals newsletter* to national drug regulatory authorities;
(b) products representing examples of irrational poly-pharmacy; and
(c) products for which exaggerated or spurious promotional claims are made in the labelling.

Subsequently, the review needs to be extended in a phased manner, giving priority to drugs that are widely used, listed in nationally recognized formularies, or of a particularly important therapeutic class. An adequate documentation and information retrieval system is vital for this purpose. Some traditional products and particularly herbal preparations, because of their complexity, do not lend themselves to licensing on a product-specific basis. Control is then more readily applied through consideration of individual ingredients. Several regulatory authorities have devised administrative approaches to their licensing which are based on a three-category system of classification:

(a) all herbal ingredients, save for those items classified under (b) below, which may be dispensed for a specific, named patient by practitioners of herbal medicine who do not possess a formal medical qualification;
(b) ingredients such as digitalis leaf and atropine which, because of their pharmacological potency or their toxicity, need to be subjected to prescription control; and
(c) ingredients which, as a result of widespread, long-established and apparently innocuous traditional usage, are included, often within defined permissible limits, in labelled products for which limited claims are made and which are sold directly to the public from retail outlets other than pharmacies.

2.3 New product licences

No product that is first proposed for authorization after the appointed day (see section 2.1 above) should be accorded a product licence without first having been submitted to technical assessment. Such products may not necessarily contain a new active ingredient: they may constitute a new combination of two or more established substances or they may merely represent a new dosage strength, a new dosage form, or a generic version of a pre-existing, nominally equivalent licensed product. In no case should the requirement for assessment be waived. A rationale for the formulation of every new product should invariably be provided, but the extent of the required review will vary considerably according to circumstances. The normal procedure for the authorization of a product is accomplished in three stages:

(a) the application is received from the manufacturer and is checked and assessed for completeness by the authority's technical staff;
(b) it is submitted to the competent standing committee for advice on whether or not to authorize marketing of the product;
(c) the formal administrative action to grant or refuse a licence and to settle its content is then taken by the authority.

The assessment of the product must be based primarily on its safety, quality, and efficacy, with regard to its intended use. In accordance with locally determined requirements, the assessment might also impinge upon comparative efficacy and/or safety and embrace economic factors, including price, cost-effectiveness, and other considerations determined by national policy.

For administrative convenience, the product licence should be as simple as possible. It should always describe the product by name, manufacturer and importing agent, identify the ingredients (preferably by their international nonproprietary names), and provide full details of the dosage form. It should also contain a serial number, the date of issuance of the licence, its date of expiry, and any special conditions to be observed. It is advisable to cite certain additional items in the licence for easy reference, such as shelf-life and sales category; but in other particulars it should refer to the information submitted by the licence-holder in the dated product application.

2.4 Renewal and variation of licences

Licences should never be regarded as immutable. Ideally, they should be reviewed at, say, five-year intervals. However, many national authorities do not have the capacity to undertake this task, particularly for as long as they remain engaged in the initial review of provisionally licensed products. In these circumstances many products fall to review on an *ad hoc* basis. Sometimes this is inspired by recently generated concern regarding safety. More frequently, a product attracts attention because the licence-holder has altered the formulation in some way—by changing, for instance, the source of the starting materials, the nature of the excipients, the route of synthesis of an active ingredient, or the claims made in labelling and promotional material. The precise circumstances in which licence-holders are required to apply for variations in a product licence differ from country to country. These circumstances should be clearly defined in all product licence documents, including provisional licences.

Licence-holders should be required, in all circumstances, to inform regulatory authorities immediately of unanticipated adverse effects that could possibly be associated with a licensed product and that might call for restrictive licensing action or the withdrawal of the product licence.

3. Technical aspects of the licensing process

3.1 General considerations

Although countries vary in their resources and priorities, advantage accrues from harmonizing documentary requirements to the fullest possible extent, since this simplifies registration procedures and reduces costs.

The most important starting-point for imported products is the WHO Certification Scheme on the Quality of Pharmaceutical Products Moving in International Commerce.[1] This gives basic information on composition, an assurance that the product is manufactured in accordance with good manufacturing practices in premises subject to inspection, and information on the regulatory status of the product in the country of export. A certificate, issued in compliance with the model format recommended by WHO, should be required whenever application is made to license an imported product.

3.2 Products containing long-established chemical entities

For products indicated for standard uses and that contain established ingredients, the following elements of information usually suffice as the basis both for a product licence and for a computerized data retrieval system:

— name of the product
— active ingredient(s) [by international nonproprietary name(s)]
— type of formulation
— therapeutic category
— quantitative formula (including excipients)
— quality control specifications
— indications, dosage, method of use
— contraindications, warnings, precautions
— bioavailability data (*in vitro/in vivo*)

---

[1] *WHO Expert Committee on Specifications for Pharmaceutical Preparations. Thirty-first Report.* Geneva, World Health Organization, 1990 (WHO Technical Report Series, No. 790), Annex 5.

- stability data, shelf-life
- container, packaging, labelling
- intended method of distribution:
  controlled drug; prescription item
  pharmacy sale; general sale
- manufacturer
- importer/distributor
- regulatory status in the exporting country.

If the dosage form is a novel one, such as a delayed-release tablet, or if a new route of administration is proposed, supporting data from clinical studies will be required.

3.3 Products containing new chemical entities

Considerably more extensive information is required to support a marketing application for a new drug substance in order to provide assurance of efficacy and safety as well as of quality. In particular, detailed accounts are required of:

(a) chemistry (structure, physical properties, synthesis, specification, impurities, stability characteristics);
(b) pharmacological properties (in animals, in humans);
(c) toxicological data (short and long-term studies in animals, including carcinogenicity studies);
(d) reproductive and teratological studies in animals;
(e) clinical studies.

Small regulatory authorities need to adopt caution in licensing newly developed products because they are likely not to possess the capacity to undertake the multidisciplinary assessment applied to them within large, highly evolved authorities, or to monitor their performance in use through postmarketing surveillance.

In general, a small authority is best advised to wait until this information has been generated and assessed elsewhere before authorizing such a product for use.

In the case of products intended exclusively for tropical parasitic diseases, much of this evidence may need to be built up in countries with limited resources. The expertise of the World Health Organization is at hand to offer advice in these circumstances. Once a decision is taken to authorize such a product for general use, the regulatory authority and the manufacturer share a responsibility to ensure that a monitoring mechanism is put in place to detect unanticipated reactions. A mutually acceptable plan for postmarketing surveillance should be settled in advance and included in the product licence as a condition of approval.

3.4 Herbal products

The use of herbal and other naturally occurring substances is part of the fabric of traditional medicine. Because of the complex, and sometimes imprecise nature of the ingredients they contain and the paucity of scientific information on their properties, products containing these substances, often in combination, can rarely be reviewed on a rigorously scientific basis. Where time-honoured practices do no apparent harm, there is no urgency for regulatory intervention other than to set up a system for provisional registration.

However, prolonged and apparently uneventful use of a substance offers insecure testimony of its safety. In a few instances, recently commissioned investigations of the potential toxicity of naturally occurring substances widely used as ingredients in these preparations have revealed a previously unsuspected potential for systemic toxicity, carcinogenicity and teratogenicity. Small regulatory authorities need to be quickly and reliably informed of these findings. They should also have the authority to respond promptly to such alerts, either by withdrawing or varying the licences of registered products containing the suspect substance, or by rescheduling the substance in order, for instance, to disallow its use by practitioners who are not medically qualified.

All regulatory authorities should also be alert to the practice of incorporating potent pharmacologically active compounds, such as steroids, into herbal preparations. When this is done clandestinely, it is a manifestly dangerous practice which demands immediate withdrawal of the products and a review of the manufacturer's licence.

3.5 Combinations of potent, therapeutically active substances

The justifications for formulating fixed combinations of potent, therapeutically active substances are few. All biologically active substances have a potential to induce harm as well as therapeutic benefit. The administration of two or more such substances, rather than one, increases the potential for adverse effects. Fixed-ratio combination products are consequently acceptable only when the dosage of each ingredient meets the requirements of a defined population group and when use of the combination provides a clear advantage over separate administration of the individual active compounds, in either therapeutic effect or compliance, or when it enhances safety—as in the case of multiple chemotherapy intended to reduce the emergence of resistant pathogens.

3.6 Generic products

In many countries, for reasons of economy, drugs destined for use in the public sector are purchased on open tender. This favours the use of generic products, and the practice in some countries is for tenders to be issued, bids examined, and contracts offered by the procurement authority without reference to the drug regulatory authority.

The licensing of generic products poses a challenge to all regulatory authorities, particularly when the product to be supplied is not registered in the country of origin. The need for expert assessment is accentuated because not all drug-exporting countries submit drugs intended exclusively for export to the same rigorous controls as drugs intended for the domestic market. Nominally equivalent generic products should contain the same amount of the same therapeutically active ingredients in the same dosage form and they should meet required pharmacopoeial standards. However, they are not necessarily identical and in some instances their clinical interchangeability may be in question. Differences in colour, shape and flavour, while obvious and sometimes disconcerting to the patient, are often inconsequential to the performance of the product, but differences in sensitizing potential due to the use of different excipients and differences in stability and bioavailability have obvious clinical implications. Regulatory authorities consequently need to consider not only the quality, efficacy and safety of such products, but also their interchangeability one with another and with the original innovative product. This concept of interchangeability applies not only to the dosage form but also to the instructions for use and even to the packaging specifications, when these are critical to stability and shelf-life.

Some highly evolved authorities require that every generic product must satisfy three sets of criteria of therapeutic equivalence. These relate to:

(a) manufacturing and quality control;
(b) product characteristics and labelling; and
(c) bioequivalence.

Others adopt a more pragmatic approach to the need for experimental demonstration of bioequivalence. Study of the bioavailability of a dosage form is a costly undertaking that is demanding of human resources. It is clearly not a cost-effective requirement for highly water-soluble substances, when neither precise dosage nor consistency of response is a critical consideration. In developing countries the *in vivo* bioavailability testing of all domestically manufactured products would be impracticably costly. The regulatory authority should be in a position to help local manufacturers by advising them on drugs that pose potential bioavailability problems.

In the case of imported products, assurance should be obtained through the WHO Certification Scheme on the Quality of Pharmaceutical Products Moving in International Commerce that the product has been produced in accordance with WHO's standards of good manufacturing practices and that, in the light of a full assessment, it has been authorized to be placed on the market in the country of origin.

2.
Product assessment and registration

Guidelines for the assessment of herbal medicines[1,2]

Introduction

For the purpose of these guidelines, herbal medicines are defined as follows:

> Finished, labelled medicinal products that contain as active ingredients aerial or underground parts of plants, or other plant material, or combinations thereof, whether in the crude state or as plant preparations. Plant material includes juices, gums, fatty oils, essential oils, and any other substances of this nature. Herbal medicines may contain excipients in addition to the active ingredients. Medicines containing plant material combined with chemically defined active substances, including chemically defined, isolated constituents of plants, are not considered to be herbal medicines.
>
> Exceptionally, in some countries herbal medicines may also contain, by tradition, natural organic or inorganic active ingredients which are not of plant origin.

The past decade has seen a significant increase in the use of herbal medicines. As a result of WHO's promotion of traditional medicine, countries have been seeking the assistance of the Organization in identifying safe and effective herbal medicines for use in national health care systems.

In 1991, the Director-General of WHO, in a report to the Forty-fourth World Health Assembly, emphasized the great importance of medicinal plants to the health of individuals and communities. Earlier, in 1978, the Thirty-first World Health Assembly had adopted a resolution (WHA31.33) that called on the Director-General to compile and periodically update a therapeutic classification of medicinal plants, related to the therapeutic classification of all drugs; subsequently resolution WHA40.33, adopted in 1987, urged Member States to

---

[1] *WHO Expert Committee on Specifications for Pharmaceutical Preparations. Thirty-fourth Report.* Geneva, World Health Organization, 1996 (WHO Technical Report Series, No. 863).
[2] Adapted from WHO document WHO/TRM/91.4. These guidelines were finalized at a WHO consultation in Munich, Germany, 19–21 June 1991. The request for WHO to prepare the guidelines came from the Fifth International Conference of Drug Regulatory Authorities (ICDRA) held in Paris in 1989. The finalized guidelines were presented to the Sixth ICDRA in Ottawa in 1991.

ensure quality control of drugs derived from traditional plant remedies by using modern techniques and applying suitable standards and good manufacturing practices; and resolution WHA42.43, of 1989, urged Member States to introduce measures for the regulation and control of medicinal plant products and for the establishment and maintenance of suitable standards. Moreover, the International Conference on Primary Health Care, held in Alma-Ata, USSR, in 1978, recommended, *inter alia*, the accommodation of proven traditional remedies in national drug policies and regulatory measures.

In developed countries, a resurgence of interest in herbal medicines has resulted from the preference of many consumers for products of natural origin. In addition, manufactured herbal medicines often follow in the wake of migrants from countries where traditional medicines play an important role.

In both developed and developing countries, consumers and health care providers need to be supplied with up-to-date and authoritative information on the beneficial properties, and possible harmful effects, of all herbal medicines.

The Fourth International Conference of Drug Regulatory Authorities, held in Tokyo in 1986, organized a workshop on the regulation of herbal medicines moving in international commerce. Another workshop on the same subject was held as part of the Fifth International Conference of Drug Regulatory Authorities, held in Paris in 1989. Both workshops confined their considerations to the commercial exploitation of traditional medicines through over-the-counter labelled products. The Paris meeting concluded that the World Health Organization should consider preparing model guidelines containing basic elements of legislation designed to assist those countries wishing to develop appropriate legislation and registration.

The objective of these guidelines is to define basic criteria for the evaluation of quality, safety and efficacy of herbal medicines and thereby to assist national regulatory authorities, scientific organizations and manufacturers to undertake an assessment of the documentation/submissions/dossiers in respect of such products. As a general rule in this assessment, traditional experience means that long-term use as well as the medical, historical and ethnological background of those products shall be taken into account. The definition of long-term use may vary according to the country but should be at least several decades. Therefore, the assessment should take into account a description in the medical/pharmaceutical literature or similar sources, or a documentation of knowledge on the application of a herbal medicine without a clearly defined time limitation. Marketing authorizations for similar products should be taken into account.

Prolonged and apparently uneventful use of a substance usually offers testimony of its safety. In a few instances, however, investigation of the potential toxicity of naturally occurring substances widely used as ingredients in these preparations has revealed previously unsuspected potential for systematic toxicity, carcinogenicity and teratogenicity. Regulatory authorities need to be quickly and reliably informed of these findings. They should also have the authority to respond promptly to such alerts, either by withdrawing or varying the licences of registered products containing suspect substances, or by rescheduling the substances to limit their use to medical prescription.

Assessment of quality

Pharmaceutical assessment

This should cover all important aspects of the quality assessment of herbal medicines. It should be sufficient to make reference to a pharmacopoeial monograph if one exists. If no such monograph is available, a monograph must be supplied and should be set out as in an official pharmacopoeia.

All procedures should be in accordance with good manufacturing practices.

Crude plant material

The botanical definition, including genus, species and authority, should be given to ensure correct identification of a plant. A definition and description of the part of the plant from which the medicine is made (e.g. leaf flower, root) should be provided, together with an indication of whether fresh, dried or traditionally processed material is used. The active and characteristic constituents should be specified and, if possible content limits should be defined. Foreign matter, impurities and microbial content should be defined or limited. Voucher specimens, representing each lot of plant material processed, should be authenticated by a qualified botanist and should be stored for at least a 10-year period. A lot number should be assigned and this should appear on the product label.

Plant preparations

Plant preparations include comminuted or powdered plant materials, extracts, tinctures, fatty or essential oils, expressed juices and preparations whose production involves fractionation, purification or concentration. The manufacturing procedure should be described in detail. If other substances are added during manufacture in order to adjust the plant preparation to a certain level of active or characteristic constituents or for any other purpose, the added substances should be mentioned in the manufacturing procedures. A method for identification and, where possible, assay of the plant preparation should be added. If identification of an active principle is not possible, it should be sufficient to identify a characteristic substance or mixture of substances (e.g. "chromatographic fingerprint") to ensure consistent quality of the preparation.

Finished product

The manufacturing procedure and formula, including the amount of excipients, should be described in detail. A finished product specification should be defined. A method of identification and, where possible, quantification of the plant material in the finished product should be defined. If the identification of an active principle is not possible, it should be sufficient to identify a characteristic substance or mixture of substances (e.g. "chromatographic fingerprint") to ensure consistent quality of the product. The finished product should comply with general requirements for particular dosage forms.

For imported finished products, confirmation of the regulatory status in the country of origin should be required. The WHO Certification Scheme on the Quality of Pharmaceutical Products Moving in International Commerce should be applied.

Stability

The physical and chemical stability of the product in the container in which it is to be marketed should be tested under defined storage conditions and the shelf-life should be established.

Assessment of safety

This should cover all relevant aspects of the safety assessment of a medicinal product. A guiding principle should be that, if the product has been traditionally used without demonstrated harm, no specific restrictive regulatory action should be undertaken unless new evidence demands a revised risk–benefit assessment.

A review of the relevant literature should be provided with original articles or references to the original articles. If official monograph/review results exist, reference can be made to them. However, although long-term use without any evidence of risk may indicate that a medicine is harmless, it is not always certain how far one can rely solely on long-term usage to provide assurance of innocuity in the light of concern expressed in recent years over the long-term hazards of some herbal medicines.

Reported side-effects should be documented according to normal pharmacovigilance practices.

Toxicological studies

Toxicological studies, if available, should be part of the assessment. Literature should be indicated as above.

Documentation of safety based on experience

As a basic rule, documentation of a long period of use should be taken into consideration when assessing safety. This means that, when there are no detailed toxicological studies, documented experience of long-term use without evidence of safety problems should form the basis of the risk assessment. However, even in cases of drugs used over a long period, chronic toxicological risks may have occurred but may not have been recognized. The period of use, the health disorders treated, the number of users and the countries with experience should be specified. If a toxicological risk is known, toxicity data must be submitted. The assessment of risk, whether independent of dose or related to dose, should be documented. In the latter case, the dosage specification must be an important part of the risk assessment. An explanation of the risks should be given, if possible. Potential for misuse, abuse or dependence must be documented. If long-term traditional use cannot be documented or there are doubts on safety, toxicity data should be submitted.

Assessment of efficacy

This should cover all important aspects of efficacy assessment. A review of the relevant literature should be carried out and copies provided of the original articles or proper references made to them. Research studies, if they exist, should be taken into account.

Activity

The pharmacological and clinical effects of the active ingredients and, if known, their constituents with therapeutic activity should be specified or described.

Evidence required to support indications

The indication(s) for the use of the medicine should be specified. In the case of traditional medicines, the requirements for proof of efficacy should depend on the kind of indication. For treatment of minor disorders and for non-specific indications, some relaxation in requirements for proof of efficacy may be justified, taking into account the extent of traditional use. The same considerations may apply to prophylactic use. Individual experiences recorded in reports from physicians, traditional health practitioners or treated patients should be taken into account.

Where traditional use has not been established, appropriate clinical evidence should be required.

Combination products

As many herbal remedies consist of a combination of several active ingredients, and as experience of the use of traditional remedies is often based on combination products, assessment should differentiate between old and new combination products. Identical requirements for the assessment of old and new combinations would result in inappropriate assessment of certain traditional medicines.

In the case of traditionally used combination products, the documentation of traditional use (such as classical texts of Ayurveda, traditional Chinese medicine, Unani, Siddha) and experience may serve as evidence.

An explanation of a new combination of well known substances, including effective dose ranges and compatibility, should be required in addition to the documentation of traditional knowledge of each single ingredient. Each active ingredient must contribute to the efficacy of the medicine.

Clinical studies may be required to justify the efficacy of a new ingredient and its positive effect on the total combination.

Intended use

Product information for the consumer

Product labels and package inserts should be understandable to the consumer or patient. The package information should include all necessary information on the proper use of the product.

The following elements of information will usually suffice:

- name of the product
- quantitative list of active ingredient(s)
- dosage form
- indications
  - dosage (if appropriate, specified for children and the elderly)
  - mode of administration
  - duration of use
  - major adverse effects, if any
  - overdosage information
  - contraindications, warnings, precautions and major drug interactions
  - use during pregnancy and lactation
- expiry date
- lot number
- holder of the marketing authorization.

Identification of the active ingredient(s) by the Latin botanical name, in addition to the common name in the language of preference of the national regulatory authority, is recommended.

Sometimes not all information that is ideally required may be available, so drug regulatory authorities should determine their minimal requirements.

Promotion

Advertisements and other promotional material directed to health personnel and the general public should be fully consistent with the approved package information.

Utilization of these guidelines

These guidelines for the assessment of herbal medicines are intended to facilitate the work of regulatory authorities, scientific bodies and industry in the development, assessment and registration of such products. The assessment should reflect the scientific knowledge gathered in that field. Such assessment could be the basis for future classification of herbal medicines in different parts of the world. Other types of traditional medicines in addition to herbal products may be assessed in a similar way.

The effective regulation and control of herbal medicines moving in international commerce also requires close liaison between national institutions that are able to keep under regular review all aspects of production and use of herbal medicines, as well as to conduct or sponsor evaluative studies of their efficacy, toxicity, safety, acceptability, cost and relative value compared with other drugs used in modern medicine.

Stability of drug dosage forms[1]

1. Introduction	37
2. General considerations	39
3. Responsibility of parties involved in the assurance of drug stability	41
3.1 Manufacturers	41
3.2 Drug regulatory authorities	41
3.3 Procurement agencies	42
3.4 Pharmacists and other workers in the supply system	42
4. Use of terms	42
5. Less stable drug substances	44
References	46

---

[1] *WHO Expert Committee on Specifications for Pharmaceutical Preparations. Thirty-first Report.* Geneva, World Health Organization, 1990 (WHO Technical Report Series, No. 790).

1. Introduction

For industrially manufactured pharmaceutical products, especially those entering international commerce and/or distributed in territories with adverse climatic conditions, stability poses serious problems. Adequate stability may be achieved only through the combined efforts of all parties involved in product development, manufacture, registration, national quality surveillance, distribution, and use. It was pointed out at the Conference of Experts on the Rational Use of Drugs [Nairobi, 1985 (*1*)] that "no tests or certification schemes can prevent the gradual deterioration of products passing through a storage and distribution system and subjected to prolonged heat, humidity, rough handling and careless dispensing".

The stability and expiry date of a product depend on its formulation and conclusions from stability studies carried out by the manufacturer during product development and cannot be assessed by simple analysis of the final product. Mandatory use of the WHO Certification Scheme on the Quality of Pharmaceutical Products Moving in International Commerce (*2*), which makes it possible to establish the true origin of the product and to distinguish between registered and unregistered products, can go a long way to providing assurance of product stability. The reason for this is that registration of a dosage form in the exporting country means that the formulation has been examined by an independent government authority for its pharmaceutical characteristics, including stability, based on submission of results of stability studies carried out by the manufacturer and, where applicable, of bioavailability studies. It is acknowledged, however, that stability studies conducted for temperate climates may not be fully relevant to storage and distribution in countries with extreme climatic conditions and that additional proof of stability under extreme conditions may need to be requested from the manufacturers. In the absence of registration in the exporting country buyers have to rely solely on the firm's assurance and on their own professional knowledge to assess relevant stability data submitted by the firm. When the product is purchased from a broker, the manufacturer is often not known at all. In these cases, it is virtually impossible to obtain reliable information on product stability.

In 1979 the WHO Expert Committee on Specifications for Pharmaceutical Preparations, in the text on quality assurance in the pharmaceutical supply system annexed to its report, noted that an important facet of quality assurance concerns storage. It pointed out further that "inadequate . . . storage can lead to physical deterioration and chemical decomposition, resulting in a reduction in activity . . . as well as the formation of possibly harmful degradation products" (*3*). At a later date other aspects, such as microbiological instability and impaired bioavailability, started to be considered.

The importance of factors related to storage, such as expiry dating (shelf-life), has been recognized. The Twenty-fifth World Health Assembly requested the Director-General in 1972 to undertake a study of the most feasible means of indicating, by a uniform system of marking, the limits of shelf-life of pharmaceutical products under the recommended conditions of their storage, as well as the date of manufacture and batch number (resolution WHA25.61).

In the past WHO has addressed some of the issues related to drug stability and storage. Recommendations have been formulated on the inclusion of the batch number, expiry date and date of manufacture in the text of drug labels (3–5). Results of accelerated stability studies and a manual for simplified tests permitting the detection of gross degradation of the least stable substances have been published (6).

The Organization is often asked for information and advice with regard to stability of finished pharmaceutical products. Particular interest in the issue of drug stability was expressed by many delegates at the Forty-first World Health Assembly, in 1988, during the discussion on the implementation of the revised drug strategy. The present document is an attempt to summarize basic principles in this area. It is addressed to policy-makers, health ministries, manufacturers, procurement agencies, and workers in the distribution system. It may be supplemented in future by technical advice in specific areas.

The document is concerned with industrially manufactured dosage forms and not with those prepared in the pharmacy or reconstituted in the hospital. Although many points discussed apply also to preparations of biological origin and radiopharmaceuticals, this document is not primarily intended for that purpose. The use of terms that occur most frequently in discussing these issues is explained in section 4.

2. General considerations

The most important factors that may influence the degree and rate of deterioration of drug products are the following:

(a) Environmental factors such as heat, moisture, light, oxygen and various other forms of physical stress and changes (for example, vibration or freezing).

(b) Product-related factors. These may include:

   (i) the chemical and physical properties of the active drug substance and of the pharmaceutical aids (excipients) used (for example, the presence of certain impurities, the particular polymorphic or crystal form, the particle size and the possible presence of water or other solvents);

   (ii) the dosage form and its composition;

   (iii) the manufacturing process used (including environmental conditions and technological procedures);

   (iv) the nature of the container or other packaging with which the product may be in direct contact or which may otherwise influence the stability.

All the above factors have to be considered when establishing the shelf-life of a product.

The stability of the finished product depends to a large degree upon the stability of the drug substance it contains. At the same time it should be noted that formulation and packaging may exert a positive or a negative influence on the stability of the active substance.[1] In section 5 drug substances are listed that were found to be less stable under simulated tropical conditions. All other factors being equal, finished products containing these substances require particular attention from the stability viewpoint.

For each product the shelf-life has to be established on the basis of stability testing. For practical reasons of commerce and distribution, a stated shelf-life exceeding five years is not recommended. Shorter shelf-lives may be expected for numerous active ingredients, e.g. antibiotics and vitamins, or for some types of dosage form, e.g. certain aqueous solutions, emulsions or creams. Products developed and packaged for a temperate climate may not necessarily be suitable for distribution in tropical zones.

The stability overage[2] is acceptable only in limited cases and on grounds of scientific and practical justification.

The use of time-expired drugs should be strongly discouraged. Only in exceptional cases, e.g. emergencies, should the use of such products be considered. The decision to utilize such products may be taken on a case-by-case basis by a responsible national health authority only, and then after careful weighing of all relevant factors by a competent professional. In such cases, samples of these products have to be retested against pharmacopoeial or similar standards by stability-indicating methods such as chromatography, attention also being paid to microbiological aspects. The economic loss and health hazards arising from the rejection of expired stock should be balanced against risks of impaired efficacy and safety. The availability of other appropriate medicines and/or the practicability of replenishing stocks should be taken into consideration. The eventual liability problems should be considered since the expiry date indicates the moment at which the manufacturer's liability for the product may be relinquished. Whenever feasible, such a decision should be taken after consultation with the manufacturer as well as with independent experts. When a decision is taken to use time-expired material, a new expiry date, well defined and as limited as practicable, has to be established.

---

[1] It follows that the stability of a product is producer-specific.
[2] An excess of the active drug substance in a dosage form, added at the time of manufacture to compensate for the expected loss of potency during storage.

3. Responsibility of parties involved in the assurance of drug stability

3.1 Manufacturers

As stated in *Good Practices in the Manufacture and Quality Control of Drugs* (*4*), it is the responsibility of manufacturers to ensure the quality of the drugs they produce. Similarly, they have the responsibility to develop appropriate dosage forms (including packaging) that are adequately stable under climatic conditions prevailing in the country or countries in which the preparations are intended to be used.

The manufacturer must establish the shelf-life of the product in relation to recommended storage conditions by using an appropriate stability-testing programme. Full details of the work carried out to establish the shelf-life should be made available to drug regulatory authorities. The expiry date and recommended storage conditions must be communicated to all involved in the pharmaceutical supply system and to patients; it is recommended that this information should be given on the label. When necessary, the utilization period must be determined and additionally specified on the label.

3.2 Drug regulatory authorities

Drug regulatory authorities must request adequate stability data from manufacturers in support of their claims concerning the shelf-life of registered products relevant to their countries. These data must be evaluated in the light of scientific knowledge and experience.

They should develop means to ensure that relevant information on shelf-life and storage conditions is readily available to all concerned, for example by establishing regulations on labelling. They should ensure, when inspections of manufacturing establishments are carried out in accordance with the requirements of *Good Practices in the Manufacture and Quality Control of Drugs* (*4*), that appropriate stability-testing programmes for marketed products are being followed.

Guidelines and inspections are necessary to ensure that drug products are adequately handled and stored in the pharmaceutical supply system—for example, by requiring that the temperature regimen recommended by the manufacturer is followed, that there is appropriate control of other environmental factors, that a proper system of stock rotation ("first-in-first-out" rule) is maintained, and that expired products are destroyed. More detailed consideration of such factors is to be found in publications by FIP and IFPMA (*7*) and others (*8, 9*). The importance of adequate storage facilities cannot be overemphasized. Experience in many countries proves that investment in warehouses is cost-effective. Products should be monitored by random visual inspection and where possible by laboratory testing at various stages in the distribution system (including hospital wards).

QUALITY ASSURANCE OF PHARMACEUTICALS

3.3 Procurement agencies

Procurement agencies should require sufficient information on the composition, the process of manufacture, stability, and provisions for appropriate labelling to be included in the drug procurement documents. Where possible, this information should be checked against data provided for registration purposes. In cases where the date of manufacture is not indicated on the label of a product, this information should be given in the accompanying documentation. In addition, the procurement agencies should inform potential suppliers of any extreme environmental conditions that might prevail.

3.4 Pharmacists and other workers in the supply system

Normally the supply system should be under the direct control of a pharmacist. When this is not possible, the responsible person should be under pharmaceutical supervision and have adequate training.

The responsible person should ensure that:

(a) Older stock is dispensed first and attention is paid to the expiry dates.
(b) Products are stored according to the recommended storage conditions, as stated on the label, etc.
(c) Products are observed for evidence of instability.[1]
(d) Products that are repackaged or further processed are properly handled and labelled.
(e) Products are dispensed in the proper containers with the proper closures.
(f) Patients are educated and informed concerning the proper storage and use of the products, including the disposal of outdated or excessively aged prescriptions.

4. Use of terms

The following working definitions or explanations are offered for a number of the terms used in this text.

Stability: The ability of a drug to retain its properties within specified limits throughout its shelf-life. The following aspects of stability are to be considered: chemical, physical, microbiological and biopharmaceutical.

Expiry (expiration) date: The expiry date placed on the container of a drug product designates the date up to and including which the product is expected to remain within specification if stored correctly. It is established for every batch by adding the shelf-life period to the manufacturing date.

---

[1] General requirements for drug dosage forms will be published in *The international pharmacopoeia*.

Shelf-life (expiration dating period or validity period): The period of time during which a drug product is expected, if stored correctly, to remain within specification as determined by stability studies on a number of batches of the product. The shelf-life is used to establish the expiry date of each batch.

Provisional (tentative) shelf-life: The provisional shelf-life is determined by projecting results from accelerated stability studies.

Date of manufacture: A date fixed for the individual batch, indicating the completion date of the manufacture. It is normally expressed by a month and a year. The date of the release analysis may be taken as a date of manufacture, provided that the period between the beginning of production and the release of the product is not longer than one-twentieth of the shelf-life.

Normal storage conditions: Storage in dry, well-ventilated premises at temperatures of 15–25 °C or, depending on climatic conditions, up to 30 °C. Extraneous odours, other indications of contamination, and intense light have to be excluded.

Defined storage instructions: Drug products that must be stored under defined conditions require appropriate storage instructions. Unless otherwise specifically stated, e.g. continuous maintenance of cold storage, deviation may be tolerated only during short-term interruptions, for example during local transportation.

The following instructions are recommended:

On the label	*Means:*
"Do not store over 30 °C"	from +2 °C to +30 °C
"Do not store over 25 °C"	from +2 °C to +25 °C
"Do not store over 15 °C"	from +2 °C to +15 °C
"Do not store over 8 °C"	from +2 °C to +8 °C
"Do not store below 8 °C"	from +8 °C to +25 °C
"Protect from moisture"	no more than 60% relative humidity in normal storage conditions; to be provided to the patient in a moisture-resistant container
"Protect from light"	to be provided to the patient in a light-resistant container

Stability tests: The purpose of stability tests is to obtain information in order to define the shelf-life of the pharmaceutical product in its original container and to specify storage conditions.

Accelerated (stress) stability studies: Studies designed to increase the rate of chemical or physical degradation of a drug by using exaggerated storage conditions with the purpose of monitoring degradation reactions and predicting the shelf-life under normal storage conditions. The design of accelerated studies may include elevated temperature (e.g. 37–40 °C and up to 50–55 °C), high humidity and light.

Only a provisional shelf-life may be established on the basis of these studies. Therefore, accelerated studies should always be supplemented by real-time studies under expected storage conditions.

Utilization period: A period of time during which a reconstituted preparation or the preparation in an opened multidose container can be used.

5. Less stable drug substances

The experimental conditions used to compile this list of less stable substances were the following: initial exposure for 30 days to air at 50 °C and 100% humidity; if no degradation was demonstrable after this time, the temperature was raised to 70 °C for a further period of 3–7 days. All other factors being equal, finished products containing the following substances require particular attention from the stability viewpoint.[1]

acetylsalicylic acid
aminophylline
amitriptyline hydrochloride
ammonium chloride
amphotericin B
ampicillin sodium
ampicillin trihydrate
antimony sodium tartrate
ascorbic acid

bacitracin
bacitracin zinc
benzathine benzylpenicillin
benzylpenicillin potassium
benzylpenicillin sodium
bephenium hydroxynaphthoate

calcium gluconate
calcium *para*-aminosalicylate
carbenicillin sodium

cefalexin
chloral hydrate
chloramphenicol sodium succinate
chlorphenamine hydrogen maleate
chlorpromazine hydrochloride
chlortetracycline hydrochloride
cloxacillin sodium (monohydrate)
codeine phosphate
colecalciferol

dapsone
dexamethasone sodium phosphate
dicloxacillin sodium (monohydrate)
diethylcarbamazine dihydrogen
    citrate
doxycycline hyclate

emetine hydrochloride
ephedrine
ephedrine sulfate

---

[1] For the report of the study on which this list is based, see *Accelerated stability studies of widely used pharmaceutical substances under simulated tropical conditions.* Geneva, World Health Organization, 1986 (unpublished document WHO/PHARM/86.529; available on request from Quality Assurance, Division of Drug Management and Policies, World Health Organization, 1211 Geneva 27, Switzerland).

epinephrine
epinephrine hydrogen tartrate
ergocalciferol
ergometrine hydrogen maleate
ergotamine maleate
ergotamine tartrate
ethosuximide
ethylmorphine hydrochloride

ferrous sulfate
fluphenazine decanoate
fluphenazine hydrochloride
formaldehyde solution

gentamicin sulfate
guanethidine sulfate

hexylresorcinol
hydralazine hydrochloride
hydrocortisone sodium succinate
hydroxocobalamin
hyoscyamine sulfate

imipramine hydrochloride
ipecacuanha powder
isoprenaline hydrochloride
isoprenaline sulfate

lidocaine hydrochloride

melarsoprol
mercuric oxide yellow
metrifonate

naloxone hydrochloride
neomycin sulfate
nystatin

orciprenaline sulfate
oxytetracyline hydrochloride

paromomycin sulfate
penicillamine
pethidine hydrochloride

phenobarbital sodium
phenoxymethylpenicillin
phenoxymethylpenicillin calcium
phenoxymethylpenicillin potassium
phentolamine mesilate
phenylbutazone
pilocarpine hydrochloride
pilocarpine nitrate
procainamide hydrochloride
procaine benzylpenicillin
procaine hydrochloride
procarbazine hydrochloride
promazine hydrochloride
promethazine hydrochloride
pyridoxine hydrochloride

quinine bisulfate
quinine dihydrochloride

retinol (vitamin A)

salbutamol sulfate
senna leaf
silver nitrate
sodium calcium edetate
sodium lactate
sodium nitrite
sodium *para*-aminosalicylate
sodium stibogluconate
sulfacetamide sodium
sulfadiazine sodium
sulfadimidine sodium
suxamethonium chloride

tetracaine hydrochloride
tetracycline hydrochloride
thiamine hydrochloride
thiamine mononitrate
thiopental sodium
tolbutamide

undecylenic acid

warfarin sodium

References

1. WORLD HEALTH ORGANIZATION. *The rational use of drugs. Report of the conference of experts, Nairobi. 25–29 November 1985.* Geneva, 1987.

2. WHO Technical Report Series, No. 790, 1990 (Thirty-first report of the WHO Expert Committee on Specifications for Pharmaceutical Preparations), Annex 5.

3. WHO Technical Report Series. No. 645, 1980 (Twenty-seventh report of the WHO Expert Committee on Specifications for Pharmaceutical Preparations), p. 27.

4. *WHO Official Records*, No. 226. 1975, Annex 12, Part 1.

5. WHO Technical Report Series, No. 567, 1975 (Twenty-fifth report of the WHO Expert Committee on Specifications for Pharmaceutical Preparations).

6. WORLD HEALTH ORGANIZATION. *Basic tests for pharmaceutical substances.* Geneva, 1986.

7. DÖRNER, G. ET AL. *Management of drug purchasing, storage and distribution. Manual for developing countries*, 2nd rev. ed. 1985 (available from Fédération internationale pharmaceutique (FIP), Alexanderstraat 11, 2514 JL The Hague; and from International Federation of Pharmaceutical Manufacturers Associations (IFPMA), 67 rue de St Jean, 1201 Geneva).

8. BATTERSBY, A. *How to look after a health centre store.* London, Appropriate Health Resources and Technologies Action Group, 1983.

9. *Managing drug supply.* Boston, MA, Management Sciences for Health, 1982.

Guidelines for stability testing of pharmaceutical products containing well established drug substances in conventional dosage forms[1]

General	47
Definitions	47
1. Stability testing	49
2. Intended market	51
3. Design of stability studies	52
4. Analytical methods	54
5. Stability report	55
6. Shelf-life and recommended storage conditions	55
References	56

---

[1] *WHO Expert Committee on Specifications for Pharmaceutical Preparations. Thirty-fourth Report.* Geneva, World Health Organization, 1996 (WHO Technical Report Series, No. 863).

Official, international and national guidelines	57
Appendix 1 Survey on the stability of pharmaceutical preparations included in the WHO Model List of Essential Drugs: answer sheet	58
Appendix 2 Stability testing: summary sheet	61

General

The stability of finished pharmaceutical products depends, on the one hand, on environmental factors such as ambient temperature, humidity and light, and, on the other, on product-related factors, e.g. the chemical and physical properties of the active substance and of pharmaceutical excipients, the dosage form and its composition, the manufacturing process, the nature of the container-closure system and the properties of the packaging materials.

For established drug substances in conventional dosage forms, literature data on the decomposition process and degradability of the active substance (*1*) are generally available together with adequate analytical methods. Thus, the stability studies may be restricted to the dosage forms.

Since the actual stability of a dosage form will depend to a large extent on the formulation and packaging-closure system selected by the manufacturer, stability considerations, e.g. selection of excipients, determination of their level and process development, should be given high priority in the developmental stage of the product. The possible interaction of the drug product with the packaging material in which it will be delivered, transported and stored throughout its shelf-life must also be investigated.

The shelf-life should be established with due regard to the climatic zone(s) (see section 2) in which the product is to be marketed. For certain preparations, the shelf-life can be guaranteed only if specific storage instructions are complied with.

The storage conditions recommended by manufacturers on the basis of stability studies should guarantee the maintenance of quality, safety, and efficacy throughout the shelf-life of a product. The effect on products of the extremely adverse climatic conditions existing in certain countries to which they may be exported calls for special consideration (see section 6).

To ensure both patient safety and the rational management of drug supplies, it is important that the expiry date and, when necessary, the storage conditions are indicated on the label.

Definitions

The definitions given below apply to the terms used in these guidelines. They may have different meanings in other contexts.

accelerated stability testing
Studies designed to increase the rate of chemical degradation and physical change of a drug by using exaggerated storage conditions as part of the formal stability testing programme. The data thus obtained, in addition to those derived from real-time stability studies, may be used to assess longer-term chemical effects under non-accelerated conditions and to evaluate the impact of short-term excursions outside the label storage conditions, as might occur during shipping. The results of accelerated testing studies are not always predictive of physical changes.

batch
A defined quantity of product processed in a single process or series of processes and therefore expected to be homogeneous. In continuous manufacture, the batch must correspond to a defined fraction of production, characterized by its intended homogeneity.

climatic zones
The four zones into which the world is divided based on the prevailing annual climatic conditions (see section 2).

expiry date
The date given on the individual container (usually on the label) of a drug product up to and including which the product is expected to remain within specifications, if stored correctly. It is established for each batch by adding the shelf-life period to the date of manufacture.

mean kinetic temperature
The single test temperature for a drug product corresponding to the effects on chemical reaction kinetics of a given temperature-time distribution. A mean kinetic temperature is calculated for each of the four world climatic zones according to the formula developed by Haynes (*2*). It is normally higher than the arithmetic mean temperature.

real-time (long-term) stability studies
Experiments on the physical, chemical, biological, biopharmaceutical and microbiological characteristics of a drug, during and beyond the expected shelf-life and storage periods of samples under the storage conditions expected in the intended market. The results are used to establish the shelf-life, to confirm the projected shelf-life, and to recommend storage conditions.

shelf-life
The period of time during which a drug product, if stored correctly, is expected

to comply with the specification[1] as determined by stability studies on a number of batches of the product. The shelf-life is used to establish the expiry date of each batch.

stability
The ability of a pharmaceutical product to retain its chemical, physical, microbiological and biopharmaceutical properties within specified limits throughout its shelf-life.

stability tests
A series of tests designed to obtain information on the stability of a pharmaceutical product in order to define its shelf-life and utilization period under specified packaging and storage conditions.

supporting stability data
Supplementary data, such as stability data on small-scale batches, related formulations, and products presented in containers other than those proposed for marketing, and scientific rationales that support the analytical procedures, the proposed retest period or the shelf-life and storage conditions.

utilization period
The period of time during which a reconstituted preparation or the finished dosage form in an opened multidose container can be used.

1. Stability testing

The main objectives and uses of stability testing are shown in Table 1.

Table 1. Main objectives of stability testing

Objective	Type of study	Use
To select adequate (from the viewpoint of stability) formulations and container-closure systems	Accelerated	Development of the product
To determine shelf-life and storage conditions	Accelerated and real-time	Development of the product and of the registration dossier
To substantiate the claimed shelf-life	Real-time	Registration dossier
To verify that no changes have been introduced in the formulation or manufacturing process that can adversely affect the stability of the product	Accelerated and real-time	Quality assurance in general, including quality control

---

[1] "Shelf-life specification" means the requirements to be met throughout the shelf-life of the drug product (should not be confused with "release specification").

1.1 In the development phase

Accelerated stability tests provide a means of comparing alternative formulations, packaging materials, and/or manufacturing processes in short-term experiments. As soon as the final formulation and manufacturing process have been established, the manufacturer carries out a series of accelerated stability tests which will enable the stability of the drug product to be predicted and its shelf-life and storage conditions determined. Real-time studies must be started at the same time for confirmation purposes. Suitable measures should be taken to establish the utilization period for preparations in multidose containers, especially for topical use.

1.2 For the registration dossier

The drug regulatory authority will require the manufacturer to submit information on the stability of the product derived from tests on the final dosage form in its final container and packaging. The data submitted are obtained from both accelerated and real-time studies. Published and/or recently obtained experimental supporting stability data may also be submitted, e.g. on the stability of active ingredients and related formulations.

Where the product is to be diluted or reconstituted before being administered to the patient (e.g. a powder for injection or a concentrate for oral suspension), "in use" stability data must be submitted to support the recommended storage time and conditions for those dosage forms.

With the approval of the drug regulatory authority, a tentative (provisional) shelf-life is often established, provided that the manufacturer has undertaken, by virtue of a signed statement, to continue and complete the required studies and to submit the results to the registration authority.

1.3 In the post-registration period

The manufacturer must carry out on-going real-time stability studies to substantiate the expiry date and the storage conditions previously projected. The data needed to confirm a tentative shelf-life must be submitted to the registration body. Other results of on-going stability studies are verified in the course of GMP inspections. To ensure the quality and safety of products with particular reference to degradation, national health authorities should monitor the stability and quality of preparations on the market by means of a follow-up inspection and testing programme.

Once the product has been registered, additional stability studies are required whenever major modifications are made to the formulation, manufacturing process, packaging or method of preparation. The results of these studies must be communicated to the competent drug regulatory authorities.

2. Intended market

The design of the stability testing programme should take into account the intended market and the climatic conditions in the area in which the drug products will be used.

Four climatic zones can be distinguished for the purpose of worldwide stability testing, as follows:

- Zone I: temperate.
- Zone II: subtropical, with possible high humidity.
- Zone III: hot/dry.
- Zone IV: hot/humid.

(See Schumacher P. Aktuelle Fragen zur Haltbarkeit von Arzneimitteln. [Current questions on drug stability.] *Pharmazeutische Zeitung*, 1974, 119:321-324.)

The mean climatic conditions, calculated data and derived storage conditions in these zones are summarized in Tables 2 and 3.

Since there are only a few countries in zone I, the manufacturer would be well advised to base stability testing on the conditions in climatic zone II when it is intended to market products in temperate climates. For countries where certain regions are situated in zones III or IV, and also with a view to the global market, it is recommended that stability testing programmes should be based on the conditions corresponding to climatic zone IV.

In a stability study, the effect on the product in question of variations in temperature, time, humidity, light intensity and partial vapour pressure are investigated. The effective or mean kinetic temperature therefore reflects the actual situation better than the measured mean temperature; a product kept for 1 month at 20 °C and 1 month at 40 °C will differ from one kept for 2 months at 30 °C. Moreover, the storage conditions are often such that the temperature is higher than the average meteorological data for a country would indicate.

For some dosage forms, especially liquid and semi-solid ones, the study design may also need to include subzero temperatures, e.g. −10 to −20 °C

Table 2. Mean climatic conditions: measured data in the open air and in the storage room[1]

Climatic zone	Measured data in the open air		Measured data in the storage room	
	°C	% RH	°C	% RH
I	10.9	75	18.7	45
II	17.0	70	21.1	52
III	24.4	39	26.0	54
IV	26.5	77	28.4	70

[1] RH = relative humidity.

Table 3. **Mean climatic conditions: calculated data and derived storage conditions**[1]

Climatic zone	Calculated data			Derived storage conditions (for real-time studies)	
	°C[2]	°C MKT[3]	% RH[4]	°C	% RH
I	20.0	20.0	42	21	45
II	21.6	22.0	52	25	60
III	26.4	27.9	35	30	35
IV	26.7	27.4	76	30	70

[1] Based on: Grimm W. Storage conditions for stability testing in the EC, Japan and USA; the most important market for drug products. *Drug development and industrial pharmacy*, 1993, 19:2795–2830.
[2] Calculated temperatures are derived from measured temperatures, but all measured temperatures of less than 19 °C were set equal to 19 °C.
[3] MKT = mean kinetic temperature (see p. 48).
[4] RH = relative humidity.

(freezer), freeze–thaw cycles or temperatures in the range 2–8 °C (refrigerator). For certain preparations it may be important to observe the effects caused by exposure to light.

3. Design of stability studies

Stability studies on a finished pharmaceutical product should be designed in the light of the properties and stability characteristics of the drug substance as well as the climatic conditions of the intended market zone. Before stability studies of dosage forms are initiated, information on the stability of the drug substance should be sought, collected and analysed. Published information on stability is available on many well established drug substances.

3.1 Test samples

For registration purposes, test samples of products containing fairly stable active ingredients are taken from two different production batches; in contrast, samples should be taken from three batches of products containing easily degradable active ingredients or substances on which limited stability data are available. The batches to be sampled should be representative of the manufacturing process, whether pilot plant or full production scale. Where possible, the batches to be tested should be manufactured from different batches of active ingredients.

In on-going studies, current production batches should be sampled in accordance with a predetermined schedule. The following sampling schedule is suggested:

— one batch every other year for formulations considered to be stable, otherwise one batch per year;

PRODUCT ASSESSMENT AND REGISTRATION

— one batch every 3–5 years for formulations for which the stability profile has been established, unless a major change has been made, e.g. in the formulation or the method of manufacture.

Detailed information on the batches should be included in the test records, namely the packaging of the drug product, the batch number, the date of manufacture, the batch size, etc.

3.2 Test conditions

3.2.1 Accelerated studies

An example of conditions for the accelerated stability testing of products containing relatively stable active ingredients is shown in Table 4.

For products containing less stable drug substances, and those for which limited stability data are available, it is recommended that the duration of the accelerated studies for zone II should be increased to 6 months.

Alternative storage conditions may be observed, in particular, storage for 6 months at a temperature of at least 15 °C above the expected actual storage temperature (together with the appropriate relative humidity conditions). Storage at higher temperatures may also be recommended, e.g. 3 months at 45–50 °C and 75% relative humidity (RH) for zone IV.

Where significant changes (see below) occur in the course of accelerated studies, additional tests at intermediate conditions should be conducted, e.g. 30 ± 2 °C and $60 \pm 5\%$ RH. The initial registration application should then include a minimum of 6 months' data from a 1-year study.

A significant change is considered to have occurred if:

— the assay value shows a 5% decrease as compared with the initial assay value of a batch;
— any specified degradation product is present in amounts greater than its specification limit;
— the pH limits for the product are no longer met;
— the specification limits for the dissolution of 12 capsules or tablets are no longer met;

Table 4. Example of conditions for accelerated stability testing of products containing relatively stable active ingredients

Storage temperature (°C)	Relative humidity (%)	Duration of studies (months)
Zone IV – For hot climatic zones or global market:		
40 ± 2	75 ± 5	6
Zone II – For temperate and subtropical climatic zones:		
40 ± 2	75 ± 5	3

— the specifications for appearance and physical properties, e.g. colour, phase separation, caking, hardness, are no longer met.

Storage under test conditions of high relative humidity is particularly important for solid dosage forms in semi-permeable packaging. For products in primary containers designed to provide a barrier to water vapour, storage conditions of high relative humidity are not necessary. As a rule, accelerated studies are less suitable for semi-solid and heterogeneous formulations, e.g. emulsions.

3.2.2 Real-time studies

The experimental storage conditions should be as close to the projected actual storage conditions in the distribution system as practicable (see Table 3). For registration purposes, the results of studies of at least 6 months' duration should be available at the time of registration. However, it should be possible to submit the registration dossier before the end of this 6-month period. Real-time studies should be continued until the end of the shelf-life.

3.3 Frequency of testing and evaluation of test results

In the development phase and for studies in support of an application for registration, a reasonable frequency of testing of products containing relatively stable active ingredients is considered to be:

— for accelerated studies, at 0, 1, 2, 3 and, when appropriate, 6 months;
— for real-time studies, at 0, 6 and 12 months, and then once a year.

For on-going studies, samples may be tested at 6-month intervals for the confirmation of the provisional shelf-life, or every 12 months for well established products. Highly stable formulations may be tested after the first 12 months and then at the end of the shelf-life. Products containing less stable drug substances and those for which stability data are available should be tested every 3 months in the first year, every 6 months in the second year, and then annually.

Test results are considered to be positive when neither significant degradation nor changes in the physical, chemical and, if relevant, biological and microbiological properties of the product have been observed, and the product remains within its specification.

4. Analytical methods

A systematic approach should be adopted to the presentation and evaluation of stability information, which should include, as necessary, physical, chemical, biological and microbiological test characteristics.

All product characteristics likely to be affected by storage, e.g. assay value or potency, content of products of decomposition, physicochemical properties (hardness, disintegration, particulate matter, etc.), should be determined; for solid or semi-solid oral dosage forms, dissolution tests should be carried out.

Test methods to demonstrate the efficacy of additives, such as antimicrobial agents, should be used to determine whether such additives remain effective and unchanged throughout the projected shelf-life.

Analytical methods should be validated or verified, and the accuracy as well as the precision (standard deviations) should be recorded. The assay methods chosen should be those indicative of stability. The tests for related compounds or products of decomposition should be validated to demonstrate that they are specific to the product being examined and are of adequate sensitivity.

A checklist similar to that used in the WHO survey on the stability of pharmaceutical preparations included in the WHO Model List of Essential Drugs (Appendix 1) can be used to determine the other stability characteristics of the product.

5. Stability report

A stability report must be established for internal use, registration purposes, etc., giving details of the design of the study, as well as the results and conclusions.

The results should be presented as both a table and a graph. For each batch, the results of testing both at the time of manufacture and at different times during storage should be given. A standard form should be prepared in which the results for each pharmaceutical preparation can be summarized (see Appendix 2).

The stability of a given product, and therefore the proposed shelf-life and storage conditions, must be determined on the basis of these results.

6. Shelf-life and recommended storage conditions

Shelf-life is always determined in relation to storage conditions. If batches of a product have different stability profiles, the shelf-life proposed should be based on the stability of the least stable, unless there are justifiable reasons for doing otherwise.

The results of stability studies, covering the physical, chemical, biological, microbiological and biopharmaceutical quality characteristics of the dosage form, as necessary, are evaluated with the objective of establishing a tentative shelf-life. Statistical methods are often used for the interpretation of these results. Some extrapolation of real-time data beyond the observed range, when accelerated studies support this, is acceptable.

A tentative shelf-life of 24 months may be established provided the following conditions are satisfied:

— the active ingredient is known to be stable (not easily degradable);
— stability studies as outlined in section 3.2 have been performed and no significant changes have been observed;

- supporting data indicate that similar formulations have been assigned a shelf-life of 24 months or more;
- the manufacturer will continue to conduct real-time studies until the proposed shelf-life has been covered, and the results obtained will be submitted to the registration authority.

Products containing less stable active ingredients and formulations not suitable for experimental studies on storage at elevated temperature (e.g. suppositories) will need more extensive real-time stability studies. The proposed shelf-life should then not exceed twice the period covered by the real-time studies.

After the stability of the product has been evaluated, one of the following recommendations as to storage conditions can be prominently indicated on the label:

- store under normal storage conditions[1]
- store between 2 and 8 °C (under refrigeration, no freezing);
- store below 8 °C (under refrigeration);
- store between −5 and −20 °C (in a freezer);
- store below −18 °C (in a deep freezer).

Normal storage conditions have been defined by WHO (3) as: "storage in dry well-ventilated premises at temperatures of 15–25 °C or, depending on climatic conditions, up to 30 °C. Extraneous odours, contamination, and intense light have to be excluded."

These conditions may not always be met, bearing in mind the actual situation in certain countries. "Normal conditions" may then be defined at the national level. Recommended storage conditions must be determined in the light of the conditions prevailing within the country of designated use.

General precautionary statements, such as "protect from light" and/or "store in a dry place", may be included, but should not be used to conceal stability problems.

If applicable, recommendations should also be made as to the utilization period and storage conditions after opening and dilution or reconstitution of a solution, e.g. an antibiotic injection supplied as a powder for reconstitution.

References

1. *Accelerated stability studies of widely used pharmaceutical substances under simulated tropical conditions.* Geneva, World Health Organization, 1986 (unpublished document WHO/PHARM/86.529 available on request from Division of Drug Management and Policies, World Health Organization, 1211 Geneva 27, Switzerland).

2. HAYNES JD. World wide virtual temperatures for product stability testing. *Journal of pharmaceutical sciences*, 1971, 60:927–929.

---

[1] This statement may not always be required for products intended for areas with a temperate climate.

3. *WHO Expert Committee on Specifications for Pharmaceutical Preparations. Thirty-first report.* Geneva, World Health Organization, 1990 (WHO Technical Report Series, No. 790).

Official, international and national guidelines

Arbeitsgemeinschaft für Pharmazeutische Verfahrenstechnik e.V.

Arbeitsgemeinschaft für Pharmazeutische Verfahrenstechnik e.V. Richtlinie und Kommentar [Guidelines and commentary]. *Pharmazeutische Industrie*, 1985, **47**(6): 627–632.

European Community

Stability test on active ingredients and finished products. Note for guidance concerning the application of Part 1, Section F. Annex to Directive 75/318. In: *The rules governing medicinal products in the European Community Vol. 1, the rules governing medicinal products for human use in the European Community (III/3574/92)*. Brussels, EEC Office for Official Publications of the European Community, 1991:50.

European Organization for Quality Control

Cartwright AC. *The design of stability trials (memorandum and conclusions)*. London, European Organization for Quality Control, Section for Pharmaceutical and Cosmetic Industries, 1986.

Food and Drug Administration, USA

Guidelines for stability studies for human drugs and biologics. Rockville, MD, Center for Drugs and Biologics, Office of Drug Standards, Food and Drug Administration, 1987.

Expiration dating and stability testing for human drug products. Inspection technical guide. Rockville, MD, Food and Drug Administration, 1985, No. 41.

Former German Democratic Republic

Testing of medicaments. *International digest of health legislation*, 1987, **38**(2): 309–316. (For original reference, see: First regulations of 1 December 1986 for the implementation of the Medicaments Law. Testing, authorization, and labelling of medicaments intended for use in human medicine. *Gesetzblatt der Deutschen Demokratischen Republik*, Part 1, 10 December 1986, **37**:479–483.)

Pharmacopoeia of the German Democratic Republic, English version. Berlin, 1988:99 (AB DDR 85).

International Conference on Harmonisation

Stability testing of new drug substances and products. Harmonised tripartite guideline. 1993 (available from ICH Secretariat, c/o IFPMA, 30 rue de St-Jean, 1211 Geneva, Switzerland).

Japan

Draft policy to deal with stability data required in applying for approval to manufacture (import) drugs and draft guidelines for stability studies. Tokyo, Pharmaceutical Affairs Bureau, Ministry of Health and Welfare, 1990.

Pharmaceutical Inspection Convention

Stability of pharmaceutical products: collected papers given at a seminar, Salzburg, 9–11 June 1976 (available from the Secretariat to the Convention for the Mutual Recognition of Inspections in Respect of the Manufacture of Pharmaceutical Products, c/o EFTA Secretariat, 9–11 rue de Varembé, 1202 Geneva, Switzerland).

Appendix 1. Survey on the stability of pharmaceutical preparations included in the WHO Model List of Essential Drugs: answer sheet

A checklist similar to that shown here can be used to determine the stability characteristics of a product.

Name of reporting person   Address   Country
                                                         Climatic zone

---

NAME OF ESSENTIAL DRUG:

Description of product

Dosage form
1. tablet   coated ☐   uncoated ☐
2. capsule   hard ☐   soft ☐
3. injection   liquid ☐   powder ☐
4. oral liquid   solution ☐   suspension ☐
5. topical semi-solid   cream ☐   ointment ☐
6. eye preparations   liquid ☐   semi-solid ☐
7. other (please state)

Packaging (material and type)
1. glass   bottle ☐   vial ☐   ampoule ☐
2. plastic   bottle ☐   vial ☐   ampoule ☐
3. paper   box ☐   bag ☐   ☐
4. metal   ☐

PRODUCT ASSESSMENT AND REGISTRATION

    5. blister pack ☐
    6. other (please state)

State of packaging   intact ☐   damaged ☐

Storage conditions
    according to the manufacturer's indications?   yes ☐   no ☐

Shelf-life (if available)
    claimed by the manufactuer   ...... years   ...... months
    percentage elapsed when tested   ...... %

Source of product tested
    1. manufactured in country of use ☐
    2. imported from neighbouring country/countries ☐
    3. imported from distant country/countries ☐

Problems encountered

Occurrence
1. very frequent ☐
2. occasional, but important ☐
3. rare ☐

Pharmacopoeial non-compliance
1. identification ☐
2. assay ☐
3. purity tests ☐
4. other pharmacopoeial test(s) ☐

Organoleptic
1. change of colour ☐
2. visible changes, i.e. capping, cracking, foam ☐
3. inhomogeneous appearance ☐
4. crystallization ☐
5. particles, turbidity, precipitation ☐
6. sedimentation, caking, agglomeration ☐
7. smell, i.e. gas formation ☐
8. rancidity ☐
9. phase separation of emulsion ☐
10. other interaction with packaging material ☐
11. other (please state)

Microbial
1. Microorganisms visible ☐
2. tests for bacteria positive ☐
3. tests for fungi positive ☐
4. tests for pyrogens positive ☐
5. other (please state)

Additional information

Date :

Instructions

1. The answer sheet is to be completed for drug products mentioned in the following list of essential drugs for which you have experienced stability problems:

    acetylsalicylic acid   benzylpencillin
    aminophylline
    ampicillin   chloramphenicol

chloroquine	nifedipine
chlorpromazine	
	paracetamol
epinephrine	phenoxymethylpenicillin
ergometrine	propranolol
ethinylestradiol	
	spironolactone
glyceryl trinitrate	sulfamethoxazole + trimethoprim
	suxamethonium bromide
ibuprofen	
indometacin	tetracycline
isosorbide dinitrate	thiamine
methyldopa	warfarin

2. A separate answer sheet should be completed for each of the above preparations in a specific finished dosage form, e.g. one for tetracycline capsules and another for tetracycline ointment.

   Also applicable for other categories such as packaging material, source of drug product, etc.

3. Climatic zones (Schumacher P. Aktuelle Fragen zur Haltbarkeit von Arzneimitteln. [Current questions on drug stability.] *Pharmazeutische Zeitung*, 1974, 119: 321–324):

   zone I   – temperate
   zone II – subtropical with possible high humidity
   zone III – hot and dry
   zone IV – hot and moist.

Appendix 2. Stability testing: summary sheet

An example of a form in which the results of stability testing can be presented is shown below. A separate form should be completed for each pharmaceutical preparation tested.

Accelerated/real-time studies

Name of drug product ....
Manufacturer ....
Address ....

Active ingredient (INN) ....
Dosage form ....
Packaging ....

Batch number	Date of manufacture	Expiry date
1	../../19..	../../19..
2	../../19..	../../19..
3	../../19..	../../19..
Shelf-life	... years(s)	... month(s)

Batch size   Type of Batch (experimental, pilot plant, production)
1 ....
2 ....
3 ....
Samples tested (per batch) ....

Storage/test conditions:
    Temperature ..... °C   Humidity ..... %
    Light   ..... cd

Results

1. Chemical findings ....
   ....
2. Microbiological and biological findings ....
   ....
3. Physical findings ....
   ....
4. Conclusions ....
   ....

Responsible officer .... Date ../../19..

Multisource (generic) pharmaceutical products: guidelines on registration requirements to establish interchangeability[1]

Introduction — 63

Glossary — 64

Part One. Regulatory assessment of interchangeable multisource pharmaceutical products — 66
1. General considerations — 66
2. Multisource products and interchangeability — 67
3. Technical data for regulatory assessment — 68
4. Product information and promotion — 69
5. Collaboration between drug regulatory authorities — 69
6. Exchange of evaluation reports — 69

Part Two. Equivalence studies needed for marketing authorization — 69
7. Documentation of equivalence for marketing authorization — 69
8. When equivalence studies are not necessary — 70
9. When equivalence studies are necessary and types of studies required — 71
   - *In vivo* studies — 71
   - *In vitro* studies — 72

Part Three. Tests for equivalence — 72
10. Bioequivalence studies in humans — 74
    - Subjects — 75
    - Design — 76
    - Studies of metabolites — 78
    - Measurement of individual isomers for chiral drug substance products — 78
    - Validation of analytical procedures — 78
    - Reserve samples — 78
    - Statistical analysis and acceptance criteria — 79
    - Reporting of results — 80
11. Pharmacodynamic studies — 80
12. Clinical trials — 82
13. *In vitro* dissolution — 82

Part Four. *In vitro* dissolution tests in product development and quality control — 83

---

[1] *WHO Expert Committee on Specifications for Pharmaceutical Preparations. Thirty-fourth Report.* Geneva, World Health Organization, 1996 (WHO Technical Report Series, No. 863).

PRODUCT ASSESSMENT AND REGISTRATION

Part Five. Clinically important variations in bioavailability leading to non-approval of the product   84

Part Six. Studies needed to support new post-marketing manufacturing conditions   85

Part Seven. Choice of reference product   85

Authors   85

References   87

Appendix 1
Examples of national requirements for *in vivo* equivalence studies for drugs included in the WHO Model List of Essential Drugs (Canada, Germany and the USA, December 1994)   88

Appendix 2
Explanation of symbols used in the design of bioequivalence studies in humans, and commonly used pharmacokinetic abbreviations   103

Appendix 3
Technical aspects of bioequivalence statistics   104

Introduction

Multisource (generic) drug products must satisfy the same standards of quality, efficacy and safety as those applicable to the originator's product. In addition, reasonable assurance must be provided that they are, as intended, clinically interchangeable with nominally equivalent market products.

With some classes of product, obviously including parenteral formulations of highly water-soluble compounds, interchangeability is adequately assured by the implementation of good manufacturing practices (GMP) and evidence of conformity with relevant pharmacopoeial specifications. For other classes of product, including many biologicals, such as vaccines, animal sera, products derived from human blood and plasma, and products manufactured by biotechnology, the concept of interchangeability raises complex considerations that are not addressed here, and these products will consequently not be considered. However, for most nominally equivalent pharmaceutical products (including most solid oral dosage forms), a demonstration of therapeutic equivalence can and should be carried out, and should be included in the documentation submitted with the application for marketing authorization.

During the International Conference of Drug Regulatory Authorities (ICDRA) held in Ottawa, Canada, in 1991 and again in The Hague, The Netherlands, in 1994, regulatory officials supported the proposal that WHO should develop global standards and requirements for the regulatory assessment, marketing authorization and quality control of interchangeable multisource (generic) pharmaceutical products. On the basis of these suggestions, WHO convened three consultations during 1993 and 1994 in Geneva which led to the formulation of the present guidelines. Participants at the consultations included representatives of drug regulatory authorities, the universities, and the pharmaceutical industry, including the generic industry.

The objective of these guidelines is not only to provide technical guidance to national drug regulatory authorities and to drug manufacturers on how such assurance can be provided, but also to create an awareness that in some instances failure to assure interchangeability can prejudice the health and safety of patients. This danger has recently been highlighted in a joint statement by the WHO Tuberculosis Programme and the International Union against Tuberculosis and Lung Disease. This states, *inter alia*, that "studies of fixed-dose combinations containing rifampicin have shown that in some of the preparations the rifampicin was poorly absorbed or not absorbed at all". Fixed-dosage combinations containing rifampicin must therefore be "demonstrably bioavailable".

Highly developed national drug regulatory authorities now routinely require evidence of bioavailability for a very large majority of solid oral dosage forms, including those contained in the WHO Model List of Essential Drugs. WHO will assist small regulatory authorities, for whom these guidelines are primarily intended, in determining relevant policies and priorities – in relation to both locally manufactured and imported products – by compiling and maintaining a list of preparations that are known to have given rise to incidents indicative of clinical inequivalence. It will also work to promote a technical basis for assuring the interchangeability of multisource products within both an international and a national context by proposing the establishment of international reference materials as comparators for bioequivalence testing.

These guidelines apply to the marketing of pharmaceutical products intended to be therapeutically equivalent and thus interchangeable (generics) but produced by different manufacturers. They should be interpreted and applied without prejudice to the obligations incurred through existing international agreements on trade-related aspects of intellectual property rights (*1*).

Glossary

The definitions given below apply specifically to the terms used in this guide. They may have different meanings in other contexts.

bioavailability

The rate and extent of availability of an active drug ingredient from a dosage form as determined by its concentration–time curve in the systemic circulation or by its excretion in urine.

bioequivalence

Two pharmaceutical products are bioequivalent if they are pharmaceutically equivalent and their bioavailabilities (rate and extent of availability), after administration in the same molar dose, are similar to such a degree that their effects can be expected to be essentially the same.

dosage form

The form of the completed pharmaceutical product, e.g. tablet, capsule, elixir, injection, suppository.

therapeutic equivalence

Two pharmaceutical products are therapeutically equivalent if they are pharmaceutically equivalent and after administration in the same molar dose their effects, with respect to both efficacy and safety, will be essentially the same, as determined from appropriate studies (bioequivalence, pharmacodynamic, clinical or *in vitro* studies).

generic product

The term "generic product" has somewhat different meanings in different jurisdictions. In this document, therefore, use of this term is avoided as much as possible, and the term "multisource pharmaceutical product" (see definition below) is used instead. Generic products may be marketed either under the nonproprietary approved name or under a new brand (proprietary) name. They may sometimes be marketed in dosage forms and/or strengths different from those of the innovator products. However, where the term "generic product" has had to be used in this document, it means a pharmaceutical product, usually intended to be interchangeable with the innovator product, which is usually manufactured without a licence from the innovator company and marketed after the expiry of patent or other exclusivity rights.

innovator pharmaceutical product

Generally, the innovator pharmaceutical product is that which was first authorized for marketing (normally as a patented drug) on the basis of documentation of efficacy, safety and quality (according to contemporary requirements). When drugs have been available for many years, it may not be possible to identify an innovator pharmaceutical product.

interchangeable pharmaceutical product

An interchangeable pharmaceutical product is one which is therapeutically equivalent to a reference product.

multisource pharmaceutical products

Multisource pharmaceutical products are pharmaceutically equivalent products that may or may not be therapeutically equivalent. Multisource pharmaceutical products that are therapeutically equivalent are interchangeable.

pharmaceutical equivalence

Products are pharmaceutical equivalents if they contain the same amount of the same active substance(s) in the same dosage form; if they meet the same or comparable standards; and if they are intended to be administered by the same route. However, pharmaceutical equivalence does not necessarily imply therapeutic equivalence as differences in the excipients and/or the manufacturing process can lead to differences in product performance.

reference product

A reference product is a pharmaceutical product with which the new product is intended to be interchangeable in clinical practice. The reference product will normally be the innovator product for which efficacy, safety and quality have been established. Where the innovator product is not available, the product which is the market leader may be used as a reference product, provided that it has been authorized for marketing and its efficacy, safety and quality have been established and documented.

Part One. Regulatory assessment of interchangeable multisource pharmaceutical products

1. General considerations

The national health authorities (national drug regulatory authorities) should ensure that all pharmaceutical products subject to their control are in conformity with acceptable standards of quality, safety and efficacy, and that all premises and practices employed in the manufacture, storage and distribution of these products comply with GMP standards so as to ensure the continued conformity of the products with these requirements until such time as they are delivered to the end user.

These objectives can be accomplished effectively only if a mandatory system of marketing authorization for pharmaceutical products and the licensing of their manufacturers, importing agents and distributors exists and adequate resources are available for implementation. Health authorities in countries with limited resources are less able to perform these tasks. To assure the quality of imported pharmaceutical products and drug substances, they are therefore dependent on authoritative, reliable, and independent information from the drug regulatory authority of the exporting country. This information, including information on the regulatory status of a pharmaceutical product, and the manufacturer's compliance with GMP (*2*) in the exporting country, is most effectively obtained through the WHO Certification Scheme on the Quality of Pharmaceutical Products Moving in International Commerce [see pp. 187–209], which provides a channel of communication between the regulatory authorities in the importing and exporting countries (see World Health Assembly resolutions WHA41.18 and WHA45.29).

The essential functions and responsibilities of a drug regulatory authority have been further elaborated by WHO in the guiding principles for small national drug regulatory authorities (3, 4).

2. Multisource products and interchangeability

Economic pressures often favour the use of generic products, and this can sometimes result in the purchase on contract of such products by procurement agencies without prior licensing by the appropriate drug regulatory authority. However, all pharmaceutical products, including generic products, should be used in a country only after approval by that authority. Equally, pharmaceutical products intended exclusively for export should be subjected by the regulatory authority of the exporting country to the same controls and marketing authorization requirements with regard to quality, safety and efficacy as those intended for the domestic market in that country.

Nominally equivalent interchangeable (generic) pharmaceutical products should contain the same amount of the same therapeutically active ingredients in the same dosage form and should meet required pharmacopoeial standards. However, they are usually not identical, and in some instances their clinical interchangeability may be in question. Although differences in colour, shape and flavour are obvious and sometimes disconcerting to the patient, they are often without effect on the performance of the pharmaceutical product. However, differences in sensitizing potential due to the use of different excipients, and differences in stability and bioavailability, could have obvious clinical implications. Regulatory authorities consequently need to consider not only the quality, efficacy and safety of such pharmaceutical products, but also their interchangeability. This concept of interchangeability applies not only to the dosage form but also to the instructions for use and even to the packaging specifications, when these are critical to stability and shelf-life.

Regulatory authorities should therefore require the documentation of a generic pharmaceutical product to meet three sets of criteria relating to:

— manufacture (GMP) and quality control;
— product characteristics and labelling; and
— therapeutic equivalence (see Part Two).

Assessment of equivalence will normally require an *in vivo* study, or a justification that such a study is not required in a particular case. Types of *in vivo* studies include bioequivalence studies, pharmacodynamic studies, and comparative clinical trials (see sections 10–12). In selected cases, *in vitro* dissolution studies may be sufficient to provide some indication of equivalence (see section 13). The regulatory authority should be in a position to help local manufacturers by advising them on drugs that pose potential bioavailability problems so that *in vivo* studies are therefore required.

Examples of national requirements for *in vivo* studies for drugs included in the WHO Model List of Essential Drugs are given in Appendix 1.

3. Technical data for regulatory assessment

For pharmaceutical products indicated for standard, well established uses and containing established ingredients, the following information, *inter alia*, should be provided in the documentation submitted with the application for marketing authorization and for inclusion in a computerized data retrieval system:

— the name of the product;
— the active ingredient(s) (designated by their international nonproprietary name(s)), their source, and a description of the manufacturing methods and the in-process controls;
— the type of dosage form;
— the route of administration;
— the main therapeutic category;
— a complete quantitative formula with justification and the method of manufacture of the dosage form in accordance with WHO GMP (*2*);
— quality control specifications for the starting materials, intermediates and final dosage form product, together with a validated analytical method;
— the results of batch testing together with the batch number and date of manufacture, including, where appropriate, the batch(es) used in bioequivalence studies;
— the indications, dosage and method of use;
— the contraindications, warnings, precautions and drug interactions;
— use in pregnancy and in other special groups of patients;
— the adverse effects;
— the effects and treatment of overdosage;
— equivalence data (comparative bioavailability, pharmacodynamic or clinical studies and comparative *in vitro* dissolution tests);
— stability data, proposed shelf-life, and recommended storage conditions;
— the container, packaging and labelling, including the proposed product information;
— the proposed method of distribution, e.g. as a controlled drug or a prescription item, and whether the product is intended for pharmacy sale or for general sale;
— the manufacturer and the licensing status (date of most recent inspection, date of licence and the authority that issued the licence);
— the importer/distributor;
— the regulatory status in the exporting country and, where available, summary of regulatory assessment documents from the exporting country, as well as the regulatory status in other countries.

If the dosage form is a novel one intended to modify drug delivery, e.g. a prolonged-release tablet, or if a different route of administration is proposed, supporting data, including clinical studies, will normally be required.

4. Product information and promotion

The product information intended for prescribers and end users should be available for all generic products authorized for marketing, and the content of this information should be approved as a part of the marketing authorization. It should be updated in the light of current information. The wording and illustrations used in the subsequent promotion of the product should be fully consistent with this approved product information. All promotional activities should satisfy the WHO ethical criteria for medicinal drug promotion (see World Health Assembly resolution WHA41.17, 1988).

5. Collaboration between drug regulatory authorities

Bilateral or multilateral collaboration between drug regulatory authorities assists countries with limited resources. Sharing responsibilities in assessment and increasing mutual cooperation provide a wider spectrum of expertise for evaluation. Harmonization of the registration requirements for generics of the various drug regulatory authorities can accelerate the approval process. Furthermore, an agreed mechanism of quality assurance in relation to the assessment work of collaborating agencies is vital.

6. Exchange of evaluation reports

When a company applies for marketing authorization in more than one country, the exchange of evaluation reports between drug regulatory authorities on the same product from the same manufacturer can accelerate sound decision-making at the national level. Such an exchange should take place only subject to the agreement of the company concerned. Appropriate measures for safeguarding data confidentiality must be taken.

Part Two. Equivalence studies needed for marketing authorization

7. Documentation of equivalence for marketing authorization

Pharmaceutically equivalent multisource pharmaceutical products must be shown to be therapeutically equivalent to one another in order to be considered interchangeable. Several test methods are available for assessing equivalence, including:

- Comparative bioavailability (bioequivalence) studies in humans, in which the active drug substance or one or more metabolites is measured in an accessible biological fluid such as plasma, blood or urine.

- Comparative pharmacodynamic studies in humans.
- Comparative clinical trials.
- *In vitro* dissolution tests.

The applicability of each of these four methods is discussed in subsequent sections of these guidelines and special guidance is provided on assessing bioequivalence studies. Other methods have also been used to assess bioequivalence, e.g. bioequivalence studies in animals, but are not discussed here because they have not been accepted worldwide.

The acceptance of any test procedure in the documentation of the equivalence of two pharmaceutical products by a drug regulatory authority depends on many factors, including the characteristics of the active drug substance and the drug product, and the availability of the resources necessary for the conduct of a specific type of study. Where a drug produces meaningful concentrations in an accessible biological fluid, such as plasma, bioequivalence studies are preferred. Where a drug does not produce measurable concentrations in such a fluid, comparative clinical trials or pharmacodynamic studies may be necessary to document equivalence. *In vitro* testing, preferably based on a documented *in vitro/in vivo* correlation, may sometimes provide some indication of equivalence between two pharmaceutical products (see section 13).

Other criteria that indicate when equivalence studies are, or are not, necessary are discussed in sections 8 and 9 below.

8. When equivalence studies are not necessary

The following types of multisource pharmaceutical products are considered to be equivalent without the need for further documentation:

(a) products to be administered parenterally (e.g. by the intravenous, intramuscular, subcutaneous or intrathecal route) as aqueous solutions that contain the same active substance(s) in the same concentration(s) and the same excipients in comparable concentrations;

(b) solutions for oral use that contain the active substance in the same concentration and do not contain an excipient that is known or suspected to affect gastrointestinal transit or absorption of the active substance;

(c) gases;

(d) powders for reconstitution as a solution when the solution meets either criterion (a) or criterion (b) above;

(e) otic or ophthalmic products prepared as aqueous solutions that contain the same active substance(s) in the same concentration(s) and essentially the same excipients in comparable concentrations;

(f) topical products prepared as aqueous solutions that contain the same active substance(s) in the same concentration(s) and essentially the same excipients in comparable concentrations;

(g) inhalation products or nasal sprays that are administered with or without essentially the same device, are prepared as aqueous solutions, and contain the same active substance(s) in the same concentration(s) and essentially the same excipients in comparable concentrations. Special *in vitro* testing should be required to document comparable device performance of the multisource inhalation product.

For requirements (e), (f) and (g) above, it is incumbent on the applicant to demonstrate that the excipients in the multisource product are essentially the same as, and are present in concentrations comparable to, those in the reference product. If this information about the reference product cannot be provided by the applicant, and the drug regulatory authority does not have access to these data, *in vivo* studies should be performed.

9. When equivalence studies are necessary and types of studies required

Except for the cases listed in section 8, it is recommended in these guidelines that documentation of equivalence should be requested by registration authorities for multisource pharmaceutical products. In such documentation, the product should be compared with the reference pharmaceutical product. Studies must be carried out using the formulation intended for marketing (see also Part Seven).

In vivo studies

For certain drugs and dosage forms, *in vivo* documentation of equivalence, through either a bioequivalence study, a comparative clinical pharmacodynamic study, or a comparative clinical trial, is regarded as especially important. Examples include:

(a) oral immediate-release pharmaceutical products with systemic action when one or more of the following criteria apply:
   (i) indicated for serious conditions requiring assured therapeutic response;
   (ii) narrow therapeutic window/safety margin; steep dose–response curve;
   (iii) pharmacokinetics complicated by variable or incomplete absorption or absorption window, non-linear pharmacokinetics, presystemic elimination/high first-pass metabolism >70%;
   (iv) unfavourable physicochemical properties, e.g. low solubility, instability, metastable modifications, poor permeability;
   (v) documented evidence for bioavailability problems related either to the drug itself or to drugs of similar chemical structure or formulation;
   (vi) high ratio of excipients to active ingredients;
(b) non-oral and non-parenteral pharmaceutical products designed to act by systemic absorption (e.g. transdermal patches, suppositories);
(c) sustained-release and other types of modified-release pharmaceutical products designed to act by systemic absorption;
(d) fixed combination products (*4*) with systemic action;

(e) non-solution pharmaceutical products for non-systemic use (oral, nasal, ocular, dermal, rectal, vaginal, etc.) and intended to act without systemic absorption. The concept of bioequivalence is then not applicable, and comparative clinical or pharmacodynamic studies are required to prove equivalence. This does not, however, exclude the potential need for drug concentration measurements in order to assess unintended partial absorption.

For the first four types of pharmaceutical products, plasma concentration measurements over time (bioequivalence) are normally sufficient proof of efficacy and safety. For the last type, as already pointed out, the bioequivalence concept is not applicable, and comparative clinical or pharmacodynamic studies are required to prove equivalence.

In vitro studies

For certain drugs and dosage forms (see also section 13), equivalence may be assessed by means of *in vitro* dissolution testing. This may be considered acceptable for example for:

(a) drugs for which *in vivo* studies (see above) are not required;
(b) different strengths of a multisource formulation, when the pharmaceutical products are manufactured by the same manufacturer at the same manufacturing site, and:
 — the qualitative composition of the different strengths is essentially the same;
 — the ratio of active ingredients to excipients for the different strengths is essentially the same or, for low strengths, the ratio between the excipients is the same;
 — an appropriate equivalence study has been performed on at least one of the strengths of the formulation (usually the highest strength unless a lower strength is chosen for reasons of safety); and
 — in the case of systemic availability, pharmacokinetics have been shown to be linear over the therapeutic dose range.

Although these guidelines are concerned primarily with the registration requirements for multisource pharmaceutical products, it should be noted that *in vitro* dissolution testing may also be suitable for use in confirming that product quality and performance characteristics have remained unchanged following minor changes in formulation or manufacture after approval (see Part Six).

Part Three. Tests for equivalence

The bioequivalence studies, pharmacodynamic studies and clinical trials should be carried out in accordance with the provisions and prerequisites for a clinical trial, as outlined in the guidelines for good clinical practice for trials on pharmaceutical products (5) (see box), with GMP (2) and with good laboratory practice (GLP) (6).

1. Provisions and prerequisites for a clinical trial

1.1 Justification for the trial

It is important for anyone preparing a trial of a medicinal product in humans that the specific aims, problems and risks or benefits of a particular clinical trial be thoroughly considered and that the chosen options be scientifically sound and ethically justified.

1.2 Ethical principles

All research involving human subjects should be conducted in accordance with the ethical principles contained in the current version of the Declaration of Helsinki. Three basic ethical principles should be respected, namely justice, respect for persons, and beneficence (maximizing benefits and minimizing harms and wrongs) or non-maleficence (doing no harm), as defined by the current revision of the International Ethical Guidelines for Biomedical Research Involving Human Subjects[1] or the laws and regulations of the country in which the research is conducted, whichever represents the greater protection for subjects. All individuals involved in the conduct of any clinical trial must be fully informed of and comply with these principles.

1.3 Supporting data for the investigational product

Pre-clinical studies that provide sufficient documentation of the potential safety of a pharmaceutical product for the intended investigational use are a prerequisite for a clinical trial. Information about manufacturing procedures and data from tests performed on the actual product should establish that it is of suitable quality for the intended investigational use. The pharmaceutical, pre-clinical and clinical data should be appropriate to the phase of the trial, and the amount of supporting data should be appropriate to the size and duration of the proposed trial. In addition, a compilation of information on the safety and efficacy of the investigational product obtained in previous and ongoing clinical trials is required for planning and conducting subsequent trials.

1.4 Investigator and site(s) of investigation

Each investigator should have appropriate expertise, qualifications and competence to undertake the proposed study. Prior to the clinical trial, the investigator(s) and the sponsor should establish an agreement on the protocol, standard operating procedures (SOP), the monitoring and auditing of the trial, and the allocation of trial-related responsibilities. The trial site should be adequate to enable the trial to be conducted safely and efficiently.

1.5 Regulatory requirements

Countries in which clinical trials are performed should have regulations governing the way in which these studies can be conducted. The pre-trial agreement between the sponsor and investigator(s) should designate the

---

[1] These guidelines are updated regularly by the Council for International Organizations of Medical Sciences (CIOMS).

> parties responsible for meeting each applicable regulatory requirement (e.g. application to or notification of the trial to the relevant authority, amendments to the trial protocol, reporting of adverse events and reactions, and notifications to the ethics committee). All parties involved in a clinical trial should comply fully with the existing national regulations or requirements. In countries where regulations do not exist or require supplementation, relevant government officials may designate, in part or in whole, these Guidelines as the basis on which clinical trials will be conducted. The use of these Guidelines should not prevent their eventual adaptation into national regulations or laws. Neither should they be used to supersede an existing national requirement in countries where the national requirement is more rigorous.
>
> ## 2. The protocol
>
> The clinical trial should be carried out in accordance with a written protocol agreed upon and signed by the investigator and the sponsor. Any change(s) subsequently required must be similarly agreed on and signed by the investigator and sponsor and appended to the protocol as amendments.
>
> The protocol, appendices and any other relevant documentation should state the aim of the trial and the procedures to be used; the reasons for proposing that the trial should be undertaken on humans; the nature and degree of any known risks; the groups from which it is proposed that trial subjects be selected; and the means for ensuring that they are adequately informed before they give their consent.
>
> The protocol, appendices and other relevant documentation should be reviewed from a scientific and ethical standpoint by one or more (if required by local laws and regulations) review bodies (e.g. institutional review board, peer review committee, ethics committee or drug regulatory authority), constituted appropriately for this purpose and independent of the investigator(s) and sponsor.
>
> For additional information, see the guidelines for good clinical practice for trials on pharmaceutical products (5), from which the above text has been taken.

10. Bioequivalence studies in humans

Bioequivalence studies are designed to compare the *in vivo* performance of a test multisource pharmaceutical product with that of a reference pharmaceutical product. A common design for a bioequivalence study involves the administration of the test and reference products on two occasions to volunteer subjects, the second administration being separated from the first by a wash-out period of duration such as to ensure that the drug given in the first treatment is entirely eliminated before the second treatment is administered. Just before administration and for a suitable period afterwards, blood and/or urine samples are collected and assayed for the concentration of the drug substance and/or one or more metabolites. The rise and fall of these concentrations over time in each subject in the study provide an indication of how the drug substance is released from the test and reference products and absorbed into the body. To allow comparisons between the two products, these blood (including plasma or serum) and/or urine concentration–time curves are used to calculate certain bioequivalence metrics of interest. Commonly used metrics include the area under the blood (plasma or serum) concentration–time curve (AUC) and the peak concentration. These are calculated for each subject in the study and the resulting values compared statistically. Details of the general approach are given below.

Subjects

Selection of subjects

The subject population for bioequivalence studies should be as homogeneous as possible; studies should therefore generally be performed with healthy volunteers so that variability, other than in the pharmaceutical products concerned, is reduced. Clear criteria for inclusion/exclusion should be established. If possible, subjects should be of both sexes; however, the risk to women will need to be considered on an individual basis and, if necessary, they should be warned of any possible dangers to the fetus if they should become pregnant. They should normally be in the age range 18–55 years and of weight within the normal range according to accepted life tables. Subjects should preferably be non-smokers and without a history of alcohol or drug abuse. If smokers are included, they should be identified as such. Volunteers should be screened for suitability by means of standard laboratory tests, a medical history, and a physical examination. If necessary, special medical investigations may be carried out before and during studies, depending on the pharmacology of the drug being investigated.

If the aim of the bioequivalence study is to address specific questions (e.g. bioequivalence in a special population), the selection criteria will have to be adjusted accordingly.

Genetic phenotyping
Phenotyping and/or genotyping of subjects may be considered for safety reasons.

Patients versus healthy volunteers
If the active substance is known to have adverse effects and the pharmacological effects or risks are considered unacceptable for healthy volunteers, it may be necessary to use patients under treatment instead. This alternative should be explained by the sponsor.

Monitoring the health of subjects during the study
During the study, the health of volunteers should be monitored so that the onset of side-effects, toxicity, or any intercurrent disease may be recorded, and appropriate measures taken. Health monitoring before, during and after the study must be carried out under the supervision of a qualified medical practitioner licensed in the jurisdiction in which the study is conducted.

Design

General study design

The study should be designed so that the test conditions are such as to reduce intra- and intersubject variability and avoid biased results. Standardization of exercise, diet, fluid intake and posture, and restriction of the intake of alcohol, caffeine, certain fruit juices, and drugs other than that being studied in the period before and during the study are important in order to minimize the variability of all the factors involved except that of the pharmaceutical product(s) being tested.

A cross-over design with randomized allocation of volunteers to each leg is the first choice for bioequivalence studies. Study design should, however, depend on the type of drug, and other designs may be more appropriate in certain cases, e.g. with highly variable drugs and those with a long half-life. In cross-over studies, a wash-out period between the administration of the test product and that of the reference product of more than five times the half-life of the dominant drug is usual, but special consideration will need to be given to extending this period if active metabolites with longer half-lives are produced, and also under certain other circumstances.

The administration of the test product should be standardized, i.e. the time of day for ingestion and the volume of fluid (150 ml is usual) should be specified. Test products are usually administered in the fasting state.

Parameters to be assessed

In bioavailability studies, the shape of, and the area under, the plasma concentration curve, or the profile of cumulative renal excretion and excretion rate are commonly used to assess the extent and rate of absorption. Sampling points or periods should be chosen such that the time–concentration profile is adequately defined so as to allow the calculation of relevant parameters. From the primary results, the bioavailability parameters desired, e.g. AUC_∞, AUC_t, C_{max}, t_{max}, Ae_∞, Ae_t, dAe/dt, or any other necessary parameters, are derived (see Appendix 2). The method of calculating AUC-values should be specified. AUC_∞ and C_{max} are considered to be the most useful parameters for the assessment of bioequivalence. For urine excretion data, the corresponding parameters are Ae_∞ and dAe/dt_{max}. For additional information, $t_{1/2}$ and MRT can be calculated, and for steady-state studies, AUC_τ, and the per cent peak–trough fluctuation. The exclusive use of modelled parameters is not recommended unless the pharmacokinetic model has been validated for the active substance and the products.

Additional considerations for complicated drugs

For drugs which would cause unacceptable pharmacological effects (e.g. serious adverse events) in volunteers or where the drug is toxic or particularly potent or the trial necessitates a high dose, cross-over or parallel-group studies in patients may be required.

Drugs with long half-lives may require a parallel design or the use of truncated area under curve (AUC$_t$) data or a multidose study. The truncated area should cover the absorption phase.

For drugs for which the rate of input into the systemic circulation is important, more samples may have to be collected around the time t_{max}.

Multidose studies may be helpful in assessing bioequivalence for:
— drugs with non-linear kinetics (including those with saturable plasma protein binding);
— drugs for which the assay sensitivity is too low to cover a large enough portion of AUC$_\infty$;
— drug substance combinations, if the ratio of the plasma concentration of the individual drug substances is important;
— controlled-release dosage forms;
— highly variable drugs.

Number of subjects
The number of subjects required for a sound bioequivalence study is determined by the error variance associated with the primary parameters to be studied (as estimated from a pilot experiment, from previous studies or from published data), by the significance level desired, and by the deviation from the reference product compatible with bioequivalence, safety and efficacy. It should be calculated by appropriate methods (see p. 79) and should not normally be smaller than 12. In most studies, 18–24 subjects will be needed (7–9). The number of subjects recruited should always be justified.

Investigational products
The products (samples) used in bioequivalence studies for registration purposes should be identical to the projected commercial pharmaceutical product. For this reason, not only the composition and quality characteristics (including stability) but also the methods of manufacture should be those to be used in future routine production runs.

Samples should ideally be taken from industrial-scale batches. When this is not feasible, pilot- or small-scale production batches may be used provided that they are not less than one-tenth (10%) of the size of the expected full-scale production batches.

It is recommended that the potency and *in vitro* dissolution characteristics of the test and reference pharmaceutical products should be ascertained before an equivalence study is performed. The content of active drug substance(s) in the two products should not differ by more than ±5%. If the potency of the reference material deviates by more than 5% from that corresponding to the declared content of 100%, this difference may be used subsequently to dose-normalize certain bioavailability metrics in order to facilitate comparisons between the test and reference pharmaceutical products.

Studies of metabolites

The use of metabolite data in bioequivalence studies requires careful consideration. The evaluation of bioequivalence will generally be based on the measured concentrations of the pharmacologically active drug substance and its active metabolite(s), if present. If it is impossible to measure the concentration of the active drug substance, that of a major biotransformation product may be measured instead, while measurement of the concentration of such a product is essential if the substance studied is a prodrug. If urinary excretion (rate) is measured, the product determined should represent a major fraction of the dose. Although measurement of a major active metabolite is usually acceptable, that of an inactive metabolite can only rarely be justified.

Measurement of individual isomers for chiral drug substance products

A non-stereoselective assay is currently acceptable for bioequivalence studies. Under certain circumstances, however, assays that distinguish between the enantiomers of a chiral drug substance may be appropriate.

Validation of analytical procedures

All analytical procedures must be well characterized, fully validated and documented, and satisfy the relevant requirements as to specificity, accuracy, sensitivity and precision. Knowledge of the stability of the active substance and/or biotransformation product in the sample material is a prerequisite for obtaining reliable results (*10*). It should be noted that:

— validation comprises both before-study and within-study phases;
— validation must cover the intended use of the assay;
— the calibration range must be appropriate to the study samples;
— if an assay is to be used at different sites, it must be validated at each site and cross-site comparability established;
— an assay which is not in regular use requires sufficient revalidation to show that it is performed according to the original validated procedures; the revalidation study must be documented usually as an appendix to the study report;
— within a given study, the use of two or more methods to assay samples in the same matrix over a similar calibration range is strongly discouraged;
— if different studies are to be compared, the samples from these studies have been assayed by different methods, and the methods cover a similar concentration range and the same matrix, they should be cross-validated.

The results of validation should be reported.

Reserve samples

Sufficient samples of each batch of the pharmaceutical products used in the

PRODUCT ASSESSMENT AND REGISTRATION

studies, together with a record of their analyses and characteristics, must be kept for reference purposes under appropriate storage conditions as specified by national regulations. At the specific request of the competent authorities, these reserve samples may be handed over to them so that they can recheck the products.

Statistical analysis and acceptance criteria

General consideration

The primary concern in bioequivalence assessment is to limit the risk (α) of a false declaration of equivalence to that which the regulatory authorities are willing to accept.

The statistical methods of choice at present are the two one-sided tests procedure *(11)* and the derivation of a parametric or non-parametric $100(1-2\alpha)\%$ confidence interval for the quotient μ_T/μ_R of the test and reference pharmaceutical products. The value of α is set at 5%, leading, in the parametric case, to the shortest (conventional) 90% confidence interval based on an analysis of variance or, in the non-parametric case, to the 90% confidence interval *(12, 13)*.

The statistical procedures should be specified before data collection starts (see Appendix 3), and should lead to a decision scheme which is symmetrical with respect to the two formulations, i.e. it should lead to the same decision whether the new formulation is compared with the reference product or vice versa.

Concentration and concentration-related quantities e.g. AUC and C_{max}, should be analysed after logarithmic transformation, but t_{max} will usually be analysed without such transformation.

For t_{max}, normally descriptive statistics should be given. If t_{max} is to be subjected to a statistical analysis, this should be based on non-parametric methods. Other parameters may also be evaluated by non-parametric methods, when descriptive statistics should be given that do not require specific distributional assumptions, e.g. medians instead of means.

The assumptions underlying the design or analysis should be addressed, and the possibility of differing variations in the formulations should be investigated. This covers the investigation of period effects, sequence or carry-over effects, and homogeneity of variance.

The impact of outlying observations on the conclusions should be reviewed. Medical or pharmacokinetic explanations for such observations should be sought.

Acceptance ranges

For AUC, the 90% confidence interval should generally be within the acceptance range 80–125%. For drugs with a particularly narrow therapeutic range, the AUC acceptance range may need to be smaller; this should be justified clinically.

C_{max} does not characterize the rate of absorption particularly well in many cases, but there is no consensus on any other concentration-based parameter which might be more suitable. The acceptance range for C_{max} may be wider than that for AUC (see Appendix 3).

Reporting of results

The report on a bioequivalence study should give the complete documentation of its protocol, conduct and evaluation in compliance with the guidelines on good clinical practice (GCP) for trials on pharmaceutical products (5). The responsible investigator(s) should sign the respective section(s) of the report. The names and affiliations of the responsible investigator(s), the site of the study and the period of its execution should be stated. The names and batch numbers of the pharmaceutical products used in the study, as well as the composition(s) of the tests product(s), should also be given. The analytical validation report should be attached. The results of *in vitro* dissolution tests should be provided. In addition, the applicant for registration should submit a signed statement confirming that the test product is identical with the pharmaceutical product submitted.

All results should be clearly presented. The procedure for calculating the parameters used (e.g. AUC) from the raw data should be stated. Deletion of data should be justified. If results are calculated using pharmacokinetic models, the model and the computing procedure used should be justified. Individual plasma concentration–time curves should be drawn on a linear/linear scale, and may also be shown on a linear/log scale. All individual data and results should be given, including those for any subjects who have dropped out of the trial. Drop-out and withdrawal of subjects should be reported and accounted for. Test results on representative samples should be included.

The statistical report should be sufficiently detailed to enable the statistical analyses to be repeated, if necessary. If the statistical methods applied deviate from those specified in the trial protocol, the reasons for the deviations should be stated.

11. Pharmacodynamic studies

Pharmacodynamic measurements in healthy volunteers or patients may be used for establishing equivalence between two pharmaceutical products. This may be necessary if the drug and/or its metabolite(s) in plasma or urine cannot be determined quantitatively with sufficient accuracy and sensitivity. Furthermore, pharmacodynamic studies in humans are required if measurements of drug concentrations cannot be used as surrogate end-points for the demonstration of the efficacy and safety of the particular pharmaceutical product; this applies, for example, to topical products where it is not intended that the drug should be absorbed into the systemic circulation.

If pharmacodynamic studies are used, the conditions under which they are performed must be as rigorously controlled as those of bioequivalence studies, and the requirements of the guidelines for good clinical practice (GCP) for trials on pharmaceutical products (5) must be satisfied.

The following requirements must be taken into account in planning, conducting and assessing the results of a study intended to demonstrate equivalence by means of measurements of pharmacodynamic drug responses:

— the response measured should be a pharmacological or therapeutic effect relevant to the claims of efficacy and/or safety;
— the methodology must be validated for precision, accuracy, reproducibility and specificity;
— neither the test nor the reference product should produce a maximum response in the course of the study, since it may be impossible to distinguish differences between formulations given in doses that produce maximum or near-maximum effects; investigation of dose–response relationships may be a necessary part of the design;
— the response should be measured quantitatively under double-blind conditions and be recordable by means of a suitable instrument on a repetitive basis to provide a record of the pharmacodynamic events which are substitutes for plasma concentrations; where such measurements are not possible, recordings on visual analogue scales may be used, and where the data are limited to qualitative (categorized) measurements, appropriate special statistical analysis will be required;
— non-responders should be excluded from the study by prior screening, and the criteria whereby responders and non-responders are identified must be stated in the protocol;
— where an important placebo effect can occur, allowance for this effect should be made in the study design by including placebo treatment as a third phase in that design;
— the underlying pathology and natural history of the condition should be considered in the study design, and information on the reproducibility of baseline conditions should be available;
— where a cross-over design is not appropriate, a parallel group study design should be chosen.

In studies in which continuous variables can be recorded, the time course of the intensity of the drug action can be described in the same way as in a study in which plasma concentrations are measured, and parameters can be derived which describe the area under the effect–time curve, the maximum response and the time when that response occurred.

The statistical methods for the assessment of the outcome of the study are, in principle, the same as those outlined for bioequivalence studies. However, a correction should be made for the potential non-linearity of the relationship between the dose and the area under the effect–time curve, based on the outcome of a dose–response study. However, it should be noted that the conventional acceptance range as applied for bioequivalence assessment is usually too large and therefore not appropriate; for this reason, it should be defined on a case-by-case basis and described in the protocol.

12. Clinical trials

For certain drugs and dosage forms (see example (e), p. 72) plasma concentration time-profile data are not suitable for use in assessing equivalence between two formulations. While pharmacodynamic studies can sometimes be an appropriate tool for establishing equivalence (see section 11), in other instances this type of study cannot be performed because of a lack of meaningful and measurable pharmacodynamic parameters; a comparative clinical trial must then be performed in order to demonstrate equivalence between two formulations. In such a clinical trial, the same statistical principles will apply as in bioequivalence studies. The number of patients to be included in the study will depend on the variability of the target parameters and the acceptance range, and is usually much higher than that required in bioequivalence studies.

The methodology to be used in establishing equivalence between pharmaceutical products by means of a clinical trial in patients in which there is a therapeutic end-point has not yet been discussed as extensively as that used in bioequivalence trials. However, the following are important and need to be defined in the protocol:

(a) The target parameters; these are usually relevant clinical end-points from which the intensity and the onset, if applicable and relevant, of the response can be derived.

(b) The size of the acceptance range; this must be defined on a case-by-case basis, taking into consideration the specific clinical conditions, for example the natural course of the disease, the efficacy of available treatments and the chosen target parameter. In contrast to bioequivalence studies (where a conventional acceptance range is used), the size of the acceptance range in clinical trials cannot be based on a general consensus on all the therapeutic classes and indications.

(c) The statistical method used; this is currently the confidence interval approach, the main concern being to rule out the possibility that the test product is inferior to the reference pharmaceutical product by more than the specified amount. A one-sided confidence interval (for efficacy and/or safety) may therefore be appropriate. The confidence intervals can be derived by either parametric or non-parametric methods.

Where appropriate, a placebo leg should be included in the design, and it is sometimes appropriate to include safety end-points in the final comparative assessments.

13. *In vitro* dissolution

Comparative *in vitro* dissolution studies may be useful in the documentation of equivalence between two multisource pharmaceutical products. However, because of the many limitations associated with the use of *in vitro* dissolution in the documentation of equivalence it is recommended in these guidelines that its application for this purpose should be kept to a minimum. *In vitro* dissolution testing as the sole documentation of equivalence is therefore not applicable to the drugs and dosage forms listed as examples (a)–(e) on pp. 71–72, but should be reserved for rapidly dissolving drug products.[1] When the multisource test and reference products both dissolve with sufficient rapidity (e.g. >80% in 15 minutes), their *in vivo* equivalence may be presumed. Approval of multisource formulations by the use of comparative *in vitro* dissolution studies should be based on the generation of comparative dissolution profiles rather than single-point dissolution tests, as described in various pharmacopoeial compendia and other publications. Multiple dissolution test conditions and physiologically relevant media are recommended.

Part Four. *In vitro* dissolution tests in product development and quality control

In vitro dissolution tests are useful in product development and in monitoring the batch-to-batch consistency of the manufacturing process following approval of marketing. Such tests are also used to check the consistency of the release characteristics of a dosage form during storage. Dissolution testing may also provide a useful check on a number of characteristics of the dosage form, including:

— the particle size distribution, state of hydration, crystal form and other solid state properties of the active ingredients;
— the mechanical properties of the dosage form itself (water content, resistance to crushing force for tablets, integrity of the shell for capsules and coated tablets, etc.).

When used in product quality control, information on *in vitro* dissolution should be provided in the documentation submitted with the application for marketing authorization. *In vitro* dissolution tests and quality control specifications should be based either on suitable compendial specifications or on the *in vitro* performance of the test batches used to generate material for the equivalence study. Where sufficient full-scale process validation batches are not prepared in the immediate post-approval period, several batches (two or three are recommended) of the test product should be manufactured in the preapproval period in accordance with standard, consistent, well documented procedures. Two of these batches should contain at least 100 000 units or 10% of the intended

---

[1] Where a drug substance and drug product do not dissolve with sufficient rapidity, as noted above, *in vitro* dissolution methods may still be used to document equivalence using appropriately validated dissolution methodology including an *in vitro/in vivo* correlation. Such methodology should be derived from the development and application of specifications and statistical methods to define non-equivalence. This may require formulations with different *in vivo* performance characteristics. With such formulations, discriminatory *in vitro* dissolution tests for use in equivalence studies may be developed. With these additional requirements, however, a standard *in vivo* bioequivalence study as described in section 7 may be preferable.

production batch, whichever is larger. The third, if prepared, may be smaller (e.g. 25 000 units). The use of smaller batches should be justified. Material from these test batches is used to provide material both for dissolution studies and for equivalence testing. Physiologically relevant media and test conditions should be used for dissolution tests on these batches. When selecting the test methods to be used, it is recommended that widely used compendial methods ("paddle" and "basket") should be used initially and other methods ("flow-through cell", etc.) tried if these fail to demonstrate sufficient discriminatory power. Dissolution profiles are recommended, even when a single-point compendial dissolution test is available. For immediate-release pharmaceutical products, a single-point dissolution test may be used for quality control purposes. Specifications for the dissolution performance of batches subsequently manufactured will be based on the results of the dissolution tests performed on the test batches. While it is undisputed that the value of dissolution testing will be increased if the test results can be shown by *in vivo* studies to reflect important changes in formulation and/or the manufacturing process, the practical problems involved are still under discussion. It is not recommended that the dissolution specification should be made less stringent on the basis of the performance of the test batches beyond the point where equivalence between the test material used in the equivalence study and production batches subsequently manufactured can no longer be assumed.

The following data should be recorded and included in the documentation submitted with the application for marketing authorization:

(a) comparative dissolution results for the test and reference pharmaceutical products after intervals appropriate for the products and conditions under investigation (a minimum of three sampling times is normal);
(b) for each sampling time, the observed data, individual values, the range and the coefficient of variation (relative standard deviation).

Part Five. Clinically important variations in bioavailability leading to non-approval of the product

A new formulation of bioavailability outside the acceptance range as compared with an existing pharmaceutical product is by definition not interchangeable. A marketing authorization for a formulation of lower bioavailability may not be approved because of efficacy concerns. In contrast, a formulation of higher bioavailability ("suprabioavailability") may not be approved because of safety concerns. There are then the following two options:

1. The suprabioavailable dosage form, if reformulated so as to be bioequivalent to the existing pharmaceutical product, could be accepted as interchangeable with that product. This may not be ideal, however, as dosage forms of lower bioavailability tend to be variable in performance.
2. A dosage form of increased bioavailability in which the content of active

substance has been appropriately reduced could be accepted as a new (improved) dosage form, but this decision would normally need to be supported by clinical trial data. Such a pharmaceutical product must not be accepted as interchangeable with the existing pharmaceutical product, and would normally become the reference product for future interchangeable pharmaceutical products. The name of the new pharmaceutical product should be such as to preclude confusion with the older approved pharmaceutical product(s).

Part Six. Studies needed to support new post-marketing manufacturing conditions

With all pharmaceutical products, when post-marketing changes are made, extensive *in vitro* and/or *in vivo* testing may be required. Such changes may be in: (i) formulation; (ii) site of manufacture; (iii) manufacturing process; and (iv) manufacturing equipment. The types and extent of the further testing required will depend on the magnitude of the changes made. If a major change is made, the product might then become a new pharmaceutical product, if the national regulatory authorities so decide.

Part Seven. Choice of reference product

The innovator pharmaceutical product is usually the most logical reference product for related generics because, in general, its quality will have been well assessed and its efficacy and safety will have been securely established in clinical trials and post-marketing monitoring schemes. There is, however, currently no global agreement on the selection of reference products, which are selected at national level by the drug regulatory authority. Either the most widely used "leading" pharmaceutical product in the market or the product that was first approved in that market is normally chosen. It is therefore possible that significant differences may exist between the reference products adopted in different countries.

This being so, consideration needs to be given to the feasibility of developing reference products on a global basis. Representative bodies of the pharmaceutical industry and other interested parties should be invited to collaborate in the preparation, maintenance and international acceptance of a system of international reference standards for pharmaceutical products of defined quality and bioavailability.

Authors

The guidelines were developed during three meetings convened by the Division of Drug Management and Policies, World Health Organization, Geneva, Switzerland, on 18–19 February 1993, 23–27 August 1993, and 23–26 August 1994, attended by the following people:

Professor J.-M. Aiache, University of Clermont-Ferrand, Clermont-Ferrand, France

Dr Andayaningsih, Ministry of Health, Jakarta, Indonesia

Dr N. Aoyagi, National Institute of Health Sciences, Tokyo, Japan

Dr E. Beyssac, University of Clermont-Ferrand, Clermont-Ferrand, France

Professor D. Birkett, Flinders Medical Centre, Bedford Park, Australia

Dr D. Blois, International Federation of Pharmaceutical Manufacturers Associations (IFPMA), Geneva, Switzerland

Professor H. Blume, International Pharmaceutical Federation (FIP), Eschborn, Germany

Professor A. Bondani, General Directorate for the Control of Health Inputs, Mexico City, Mexico

Miss M. Cone, International Federation of Pharmaceutical Manufacturers Associations (IFPMA), Geneva, Switzerland

Mr M. N. Dauramanzi, Drugs Control Council, Harare, Zimbabwe

Mr T. Fushimi, Ministry of Health and Welfare, Tokyo, Japan

Professor U. Gundert-Remy (*Chairman*), Department of Clinical Pharmacology, University of Göttingen, Göttingen, Germany

Dr C. G. Guyer, Food and Drug Administration, Rockville, MD, USA

Professor F. D. Juma, University of Nairobi, Nairobi, Kenya

Professor G. Kreutz, Federal Institute for Drugs and Medicinal Devices, Berlin, Germany

Dr L. Lacy, International Federation of Pharmaceutical Manufacturers Associations (IFPMA), Geneva, Switzerland

Dr I. J. McGilveray, Drugs Directorate, Ottawa, Canada

Dr O. Morin, International Federation of Pharmaceutical Manufacturers Associations (IFPMA), Geneva, Switzerland

Dr R. Nedich, Generic Pharmaceutical Industry Association, Washington, DC, USA

Dr A. Nijkerk, European Generic Medicines Association, Brussels, Belgium

Dr H. P. Osterwald, European Generic Medicines Association, Brussels, Belgium

Professor T. L. Paál, National Institute of Pharmacy, Budapest, Hungary

Dr R. N. Patnaik, Food and Drug Administration, Rockville, MD, USA

Dr J. M. Peón, General Directorate for the Control of Health Inputs. Mexico City, Mexico

Miss M.-C. Pickaert, International Federation of Pharmaceutical Manufacturers Associations (IFPMA), Geneva, Switzerland

Professor L. Rägo, State Agency of Medicines, Tartu, Estonia

Dr B. Rosenkranz, International Federation of Pharmaceutical Manufacturers Associations (IFPMA), Geneva, Switzerland

Dr H. Scheinin, Turku University Central Hospital, Turku, Finland

Mr N. Uemura, Ministry of Health, Tokyo, Japan

Professor B. Vrhovac, University Hospital Medical School, Zagreb, Croatia

Dr R. L. Williams, Food and Drug Administration, Rockville, MD, USA

Secretariat (WHO, Geneva, Switzerland)

Dr J. F. Dunne, Director, Division of Drug Management and Policies

Dr J. Idänpään-Heikkilä, Associate Director, Division of Drug Management and Policies

References

1. Annex 1C. Article 39. In: *Marrakesh Agreement Establishing the World Trade Organization*. Marrakesh, GATT, 1994.

2. Good manufacturing practices for pharmaceutical products. In: *WHO Expert Committee on Specifications for Pharmaceutical Preparations. Thirty-second report*. Geneva, World Health Organization, 1992:14–79 (WHO Technical Report Series, No. 823).

3. *WHO Expert Committee on Specifications for Pharmaceutical Preparations. Thirty-first report*. Geneva, World Health Organization, 1990:64–79 (WHO Technical Report Series, No. 790).

4. *The use of essential drugs. Model List of Essential Drugs (Seventh List). Fifth report of the WHO Expert Committee*. Geneva, World Health Organization, 1992:62–74 (WHO Technical Report Series, No. 825).

5. Guidelines for good clinical practice (GCP) for trials on pharmaceutical products. In: *The use of essential drugs. Sixth report of the WHO Expert Committee*. Geneva, World Health Organization, 1995:97–137 (WHO Technical Report Series, No. 850).

6. Good laboratory practices in governmental drug control laboratories. In: *WHO Expert*

Committee on Specifications for Pharmaceutical Preparations. Thirtieth report. Geneva, World Health Organization. 1987: 20–35 (WHO Technical Report Series, No. 748).

7. Diletti E, Hauschke D, Steinijans VW. Sample size determination for bioequivalence assessment by means of confidence intervals. *International journal of clinical pharmacology, therapy and toxicology*, 1991, **29**:1–8.

8. Hauschke D et al. Sample size determination for bioequivalence assessment using a multiplicative model. *Journal of pharmacokinetics and biopharmaceutics*, 1992, **20**:559–563.

9. Phillips KE. Power of two one-sided tests procedure in bioequivalence. *Journal of pharmacokinetics and biopharmaceutics*, 1990, **18**:137–144.

10. Conference report on analytical methods validation: bioavailability, bioequivalence and pharmacokinetic studies. *Journal of pharmaceutical sciences*, 1992, **81**:309–312.

11. Schuirmann DJ. A comparison of the two one-sided tests procedure and the power approach for assessing the equivalence of average bioavailability. *Journal of pharmacokinetics and biopharmaceutics*, 1987, **15**:657–680.

12. Hauschke D et al. A distribution-free procedure for the statistical analysis of bioequivalence studies. *International journal of clinical pharmacology, therapy and toxicology*, 1990, **28**:72–78.

13. Hollander M, Wolfe DA. *Nonparametric statistical methods.* New York, John Wiley, 1973:35–38.

Appendix 1. Examples of national requirements for *in vivo* equivalence studies for drugs included in the WHO Model List of Essential Drugs (Canada, Germany and the USA, December 1994)

General

National requirements for equivalence studies for specific drug products differ from country to country. National requirements for equivalence studies of a specific drug product can be based on any of the following:

— case-by-case study;
— criteria established by a national advisory committee; or
— application of the national regulatory guidelines.

A list of examples is presented in Table 1. It is intended to be illustrative only, in accordance with the guidelines, and does not represent a formal recommendation.

The list is based on substances and products included in the WHO Model List of Essential Drugs (*1*), but only includes essential drugs for which *in vivo* studies are required because of the nature of the dosage form. Some dosage forms, e.g. solutions and injections, have therefore been omitted from the list as they have not been identified as requiring studies in one of the three countries covered.

Examples of decisions on criteria taken by national authorities

Canada
At present, demonstration of bioequivalence is required for those drugs which are not considered to have been marketed in Canada for their intended purpose(s) for sufficient time and in sufficient quantity to establish safety and efficacy (new drugs). Bioequivalence may be demonstrated by comparative bioequivalence studies or by clinical studies including, where applicable, acceptable surrogate models. Scientific criteria, similar to those of the European Community and Australia, are being developed for deciding in which situations *in vivo* demonstration of bioequivalence is required for drugs that are not new.

Germany
Over the past years, the National Advisory Committee has taken the decision on the need for a comparative bioavailability/bioequivalence study as a requirement for marketing authorization. These decisions have been based on published data for the drug substance and its dosage form, and on the use of an algorithm. Details of the algorithm, the criteria and the resulting decisions have been published in the German Federal Register. In certain circumstances, the regulatory authority takes decisions on a case-by-case basis.

USA
Drug products introduced before 1938 in the USA do not require approval for marketing and therefore no *in vivo* equivalence study is needed. The majority of drug products, other than solution dosage forms, approved between 1938 and 1962, and known to have potential bioavailability problems, require *in vivo* equivalence studies. Generally, drug products approved after 1962, with the exception of solution dosage forms, also require *in vivo* equivalence studies.

Table 1. Examples of national requirements for equivalence studies[1]

Drug substance	Dosage form	Canada	Germany	USA
acetazolamide	tablet, 250 mg	+b	+b	+b
acetylsalicylic acid	suppository, 50–150 mg	?	+b	–
	tablet, 100–500 mg	–	+b	–

[1] +: *in vivo* studies required; +b: bioequivalence studies; +p: pharmacodynamic studies; +c: clinical trials; –: no *in vivo* studies required; ?: decision on the type of *in vivo* studies pending; O: no information available, no final decision taken, or not available on national market. See also pp. 72–83.

Table 1 (continued)

Drug substance	Dosage form	Canada	Germany	USA
albendazole	tablet, 200 mg	○	+b	○
allopurinol	tablet, 100 mg	+b	+b	+b
aluminium hydroxide	oral suspension, 320 mg/5 ml	–	+p	–
	tablet, 500 mg	–	+p	–
amiloride hydrochloride	tablet, 5 mg	+b	–	+b
aminobenzoic acid	cream	?	+p+c	–
	gel	?	+p+c	–
	lotion	?	+p+c	–
aminophylline	tablet, 100 mg, 200 mg	?	○	+b
amitriptyline hydrochloride	tablet, 25 mg	?	+b	+b
amoxicillin	capsule, 250 mg, 500 mg	+b	+b	+b
	powder for oral suspension, 125 mg/5 ml	+b	+b	+b
	tablet, 250 mg, 500 mg	+b	+b	+b
ascorbic acid	tablet, 50 mg	–	?	–
atenolol	tablet, 50 mg, 100 mg	+b	–	+b
atropine sulfate	solution (eye drops), 0.1%, 0.5%, 1%	○	+c	–
	tablet, 1 mg	○	?	○
azathioprine	tablet, 50 mg	+b	+b	+b
bacitracin zinc	ointment, 500 IU + neomycin sulfate, 5 mg/g	○	+c	–
beclometasone dipropionate	inhalation, 50 µg/dose	?	+p+c	+p
benzathine benzylpenicillin	powder for injection, 1.44 g of benzylpenicillin (=2.4 million IU) in 5-ml vials	○	–	+b

Table 1 (continued)

Drug substance	Dosage form	Canada	Germany	USA
benznidazole	tablet, 100 mg	○	+b	○
benzoic acid	cream, 6% + salicylic acid, 3%	–	+p+c	○
	ointment, 6% + salicylic acid, 3%	–	+p+c	–
benzoyl peroxide	cream, 5%	–	+p+c	–
	lotion, 5%	–	+p+c	–
benzyl benzoate	lotion, 25%	–	+p+c	○
betamethasone valerate	cream, 0.1% of betamethasone	+p	+p+c	+p
	ointment, 0.1% of betamethasone	+p	+p+c	+p
biperiden hydrochloride	tablet, 2 mg	+b	+b	+b
calamine	lotion	–	+p+c	–
calcium folinate	tablet, 15 mg	+b	○	+b
captopril	tablet, 25 mg	+b	–	+b
carbamazepine	tablet, 100 mg, 200 mg	+b	+b	+b
carbidopa	tablet, 10 mg + levodopa, 100 mg	+b	+b	+b
	25 mg + levodopa, 250 mg	+b	+b	+b
chloramphenicol	capsule, 250 mg	?	+b	+b
chloramphenicol palmitate	oral suspension, 150 mg of chloramphenicol/5 ml	?	+b	+b
chloramphenicol sodium succinate	oily suspension, injection, 0.5 g of chloramphenicol/ml in 2-ml ampoule	○	+b	○
chloroquine hydrochloride	injection, 40 mg of chloroquine/ml in 5-ml ampoule	○	–	–
chloroquine phosphate	tablet, 150 mg of chloroquine	○	+b	–

Table 1 (continued)

Drug substance	Dosage form	Canada	Germany	USA
chloroquine sulfate	tablet, 150 mg of chloroquine	○	+b	○
chlorphenamine hydrogen maleate	tablet, 4 mg	–	?	–
chlorpromazine hydrochloride	tablet, 100 mg	?	+b	+b
ciclosporin	capsule, 25 mg	+b	+b	+b
cimetidine	tablet, 200 mg	+b	–	+b
ciprofloxacin hydrochloride	tablet, 250 mg of ciprofloxacin	+b	+b	+b
clofazimine	capsule, 50 mg, 100 mg	○	+b	+b
clomifene citrate	tablet, 50 mg	+b	+b	+b
clomipramine hydrochloride	capsule, 10 mg, 25 mg	+b	○	+b
cloxacillin sodium	capsule, 500 mg of cloxacillin	?	+b	+b
codeine phosphate	tablet, 10 mg, 30 mg	○	–	–
colchicine	tablet, 500 µg	?	+b	–
cyclophosphamide	tablet, 25 mg	+b	+b	+b
dapsone	tablet, 50 mg, 100 mg	?	+b	+b
desmopressin acetate	nasal spray, 10 µg/metered dose	+b+p	+p+c	?
dexamethasone	tablet, 500 µg, 4 mg	?	?	+b
diazepam	scored tablet, 2 mg, 5 mg	+b	–	+b
diethylcarbamazine dihydrogen citrate	tablet, 50 mg	○	+b	+b
digitoxin	tablet, 50 µg, 100 µg	?	+b	–
digoxin	tablet, 62.5 µg, 250 µg	?	+b	–

Table 1 (continued)

Drug substance	Dosage form	Canada	Germany	USA
diloxanide furoate	tablet, 500 µg	○	+b	○
dimercaprol	injection, in oil, 50 mg/ml in 2-ml ampoule	+b+c	+b[1]	–
dioxybenzone	cream	?	+p+c	○
	lotion	?	+p+c	○
	gel	?	+p+c	○
dithranol	ointment, 0.1–2%	–	+p+c	–
doxycycline hyclate	capsule, 100 mg of doxycycline	+b	+b	+b
	tablet, 100 mg of doxycycline	+b	+b	+b
ergocalciferol	capsule, 1.25 mg (50 000 IU)	○	+b	–
	tablet, 1.25 mg (50 000 IU)	○	+b	–
ergometrine hydrogen maleate	tablet, 200 µg	?	+b	–
ergotamine tartrate	tablet, 2 mg	○	+b	–
erythromycin ethylsuccinate	capsule, 250 mg of erythromycin	?	+b	+b
	powder for oral suspension, 125 mg of erythromycin	?	+b	+b
	tablet, 250 mg of erythromycin	?	+b	+b
erythromycin stearate	capsule, 250 mg of erythromycin	?	+b	+b
	powder for oral suspension, 125 mg of erythromycin	?	+b	+b
	tablet, 250 mg of erythromycin	?	+b	+b
ethambutol hydrochloride	tablet, 100–400 mg	+b	+b	+b

[1] "Depot" preparation for injection.

Table 1 (continued)

Drug substance	Dosage form	Canada	Germany	USA
ethinylestradiol	tablet, 50 µg	+b	+b	+b
	tablet, 30 µg + levonorgestrel, 150 µg	+b	+b	+b
	tablet, 50 µg + levonorgestrel, 250 µg	+b	+b	+b
	tablet, 35 µg + norethisterone, 1.0 mg	+b	+b	+b
ethosuximide	capsule, 250 mg	?	+b	+b
etoposide	capsule, 100 mg	+b	+b	+b
ferrous sulfate	tablet, 60 mg of Fe	–	○	–
	tablet, 60 mg of Fe + folic acid, 250 µg	–	○	–
flucytosine	capsule, 250 mg	+b	+b	+b
fludrocortisone acetate	tablet, 100 µg	+b	+b	+b
fluorouracil	ointment, 5%	+c	+p+c	?
fluphenazine decanoate	injection, 25 mg in 1-ml ampoule	?	+b[1]	–
fluphenazine enantate	injection, 25 mg in 1-ml ampoule	?	+b[1]	–
folic acid	tablet, 5 mg, 1 mg	+b	+b	–
	tablet, 250 µg + ferrous sulfate, 60 mg of Fe	–	+b	–
furosemide	tablet, 40 mg	+b	+b	+b
gentamicin sulfate	solution (eye drops), 0.3%	+c	+p+c	–
glyceryl trinitrate	tablet (sublingual), 500 µg	?	+b	–
griseofulvin	capsule, 125 mg, 250 mg	?	+b	+b
	tablet, 125 mg, 250 mg	?	+b	+b

[1] "Depot" preparation for injection.

Table 1 (continued)

Drug substance	Dosage form	Canada	Germany	USA
haloperidol	tablet, 2 mg, 5 mg	+b	–	+b
hydralazine hydrochloride	tablet, 25 mg, 50 mg	o	+b	–
hydrochlorothiazide	tablet, 25 mg, 50 mg	?	–	+b
hydrocortisone acetate	cream, 1%	o	+p+c	–
	ointment, 1%	o	+p+c	–
	suppository, 25 mg	o	+p+c	?
ibuprofen	tablet, 200 mg	+b	–	+b
idoxuridine	eye ointment, 0.2%	o	+p+c	+c
	solution (eye drops) 0.1%	o	–	–
indometacin	capsule, 25 mg	+b	–	+b
	tablet, 25 mg	+b	–	o
insulin: insulin (soluble)	injection, 40 IU/ml in 10-ml vial,	+b	–	+b+p
	80 IU/ml in 10-ml vial,	+b	–	+b+p
	100 IU/ml in 10-ml vial	+b	–	+b+p
insulin zinc suspension	injection, 40 IU of insulin/ml in 10-ml vial	+b	o	+b+p
	80 IU of insulin/ml in 10-ml vial	+b	o	+b+p
insulin (intermediate-acting)	100 IU of insulin/ml in 10-ml vial	+b	–	+b+p
isophane insulin	injection, 40 IU of insulin/ml in 10-ml vial	+b	+b	+b+p
	80 IU of insulin/ml in 10-ml vial	+b	+b	+b+p
	100 IU of insulin/ml in 10-ml vial	+b	+b	+b+p
iodized oil	capsule, 200 mg	?	o	o
iopanoic acid	tablet, 500 mg	o	o	–
iron dextran	injection, 50 mg of Fe/ml in 2-ml ampoule	+c	–	+b+p

Table 1 (continued)

Drug substance	Dosage form	Canada	Germany	USA
isoniazid	tablet, 100–300 mg	+b	+b	–
	tablet, 100 mg + rifampicin, 150 mg	○	+b	+b
	tablet, 150 mg + rifampicin, 300 mg	○	+b	+b
	tablet, 100 mg + thioacetazone, 50 mg	○	+b	○
	tablet, 300 mg + thioacetazone, 150 mg		+b	○
isosorbide dinitrate	tablet (sublingual), 5 mg	+b	+b	+b
ivermectin	scored tablet, 6 mg	○	+b	○
ketoconazole	oral suspension, 100 mg/ 5 ml	+b	+b	+b
	tablet, 200 mg	+b	+b	+b
levamisole hydrochloride	tablet, 50 mg, 150 mg	+b	+b	+b
levodopa	tablet, 100 mg + carbidopa, 10 mg	+b	+b	+b
	250 mg + carbidopa, 25 mg	+b	+b	+b
levonorgestrel	tablet, 150 µg + ethinylestradiol, 30 µg	+b	+b	+b
	tablet, 250 µg + ethinylestradiol, 50 µg	+b	+b	+b
levothyroxine sodium	tablet, 50 µg, 100 µg	?	+b	–
lithium carbonate	capsule, 300 mg	+b	+b	+b
	tablet, 300 mg	+b	+b	+b
mebendazole	chewable tablet, 100 mg	+b	+b	+b+c
medroxyprogesterone acetate (depot)	injection, 150 mg/ml in 1-ml vial,	?	+b	+b
	injection, 50 mg/ml in 3-ml vial	?	+b	+b

Table 1 (continued)

Drug substance	Dosage form	Canada	Germany	USA
mefloquine hydrochloride	tablet, 250 mg	+b	+b	+b
mercaptopurine	tablet, 50 mg	+c+b	+b	+b
methionine (DL-)	tablet, 250 mg	?	?	–
methotrexate sodium	tablet, 2.5 mg of methotrexate	+b+c	+b	+b
methyldopa	tablet, 250 mg	?	+b	+b
metoclopramide hydrochloride	tablet, 10 mg of metoclopramide	+b	–	+b
metrifonate	tablet, 100 mg	○	+b	○
metronidazole	suppository, 500 mg, 1 g	○	+b	○
	tablet, 200–500 mg	+b	+b	+b
metronidazole benzoate	oral suspension, 200 mg of metronidazole/5 ml	○	+b	○
mexenone	cream	○	+p+c	○
	lotion	○	+p+c	○
	gel	○	+p+c	○
miconazole nitrate	cream, 2%	+c	+p+c	+c
	ointment, 2%	+c	+p+c	+c
morphine sulfate	tablet, 10 mg	○	+b	–
nalidixic acid	tablet, 500 mg	+b	+b	+b
neomycin sulfate	ointment, 5 mg + bacitracin zinc, 500 IU/g	○	+p+c	–
neostigmine bromide	tablet, 15 mg	?	?	–
niclosamide	chewable tablet, 500 mg	○	+b	+b
nicotinamide	tablet, 50 mg	–	?	–
nifedipine	capsule, 10 mg	+b	+b	+b
	tablet, 10 mg	+b	+b	○

Table 1 (continued)

Drug substance	Dosage form	Canada	Germany	USA
nifurtimox	tablet, 30 mg, 120 mg, 250 mg	○	+b	○
nitrofurantoin	tablet, 100 mg	?	+b	+b
norethisterone	tablet, 350 µg, 5 mg	+b	+b	○
	tablet, 1.0 mg + ethinylestradiol, 35 µg	+b	+b	○
norethisterone enantate	oily solution, 200 mg/ml in 1-ml ampoule	?	+b	○
nystatin	lozenge, 100 000 IU	+	?	+b
	tablet, 100 000 IU, 500 000 IU	○	–	–
oxamniquine	capsule, 250 mg	○	+b	+b
oxybenzone	cream	–	+p+c	+c
	gel	–	+p+c	+c
	lotion	–	+p+c	+c
paracetamol	suppository, 100 mg	+b	–	○
	tablet, 100–500 mg	–	–	○
penicillamine	capsule, 250 mg	+b	–	+b
	tablet, 250 mg	+b	–	+b
permethrin	lotion, 1%	–	+p+c	+c
pethidine hydrochloride	tablet, 50 mg, 100 mg	○	+b	–
phenobarbital	tablet, 15–100 mg	–	○	–
phenoxymethyl-penicillin potassium	powder for oral suspension, 250 mg of phenoxymethyl-penicillin/5 ml	○	+b	+b
	tablet, 250 mg of phenoxymethylpenicillin	?	+b	+b
phenytoin sodium	capsule, 25 mg, 100 mg	+b	+b	+b
	tablet, 25 mg, 100 mg	+b	+b	○
phytomenadione	tablet, 10 mg	+b	○	+b

Table 1 (continued)

Drug substance	Dosage form	Canada	Germany	USA
pilocarpine hydrochloride	solution (eye drops), 2%, 4%	○	+p+c	–
pilocarpine nitrate	solution (eye drops), 2%, 4%	○	+p+c	○
piperazine adipate	tablet, 500 mg of piperazine hydrate	–	○	○
piperazine citrate	tablet, 500 mg of piperazine hydrate	–	○	+b
podophyllum resin	solution, topical, 10–25%	○	+p+c	–
potassium iodide	tablet, 60 mg	–	–	–
praziquantel	tablet, 150 mg, 600 mg	○	+b	+b
prednisolone	solution (eye drops), 0.5% tablet, 1 mg, 5 mg	○ ?	+p+c +b	○ +b
primaquine diphosphate	tablet, 7.5 mg of primaquine, 15 mg of primaquine	?	+b	–
procainamide hydrochloride	tablet, 250 mg, 500 mg	+b	+b	+b
procaine benzylpenicillin	powder for injection, 1 g (= 1 million IU), 3 g (= 3 million IU)	? ○	–	+b +b
procarbazine hydrochloride	capsule, 50 mg	+c+b	+b	+b
proguanil hydrochloride	tablet, 100 mg	○	+b	○
promethazine hydrochloride	tablet, 10 mg, 25 mg	?	+b	+b
propranolol hydrochloride	tablet, 10 mg, 20 mg, 40 mg, 80 mg	+b	+b	+b
propyliodone	oily suspension, 500–600 mg/ml in 20-ml ampoule	○	○	–
propylthiouracil	tablet, 50 mg	?	–	+b

Table 1 (continued)

Drug substance	Dosage form	Canada	Germany	USA
pyrantel embonate	oral suspension, 50 mg of pyrantel/ml	○	+b	+b
	chewable tablet, 250 mg of pyrantel	○	+b	○
pyrazinamide	tablet, 500 mg	+b	+b	+b
pyridostigmine bromide	tablet, 60 mg	+b	?	+b
pyridoxine hydrochloride	tablet, 25 mg	–	?	–
pyrimethamine	tablet, 25 mg + sulfadoxine, 500 mg	+b	+b	+b
quinidine sulfate	tablet, 200 mg	?	+b	+b
quinine bisulfate	tablet, 300 mg of quinine	+b	+b	–
quinine sulfate	tablet, 300 mg of quinine	?	+b	–
reserpine	tablet, 100 µg, 250 µg	?	+b	+b
retinol palmitate	capsule, 200 000 IU (110 mg) of retinol	–	?	○
	sugar-coated tablet, 10 000 IU of retinol	–	?	○
riboflavin	tablet, 5 mg	–	?	–
rifampicin	capsule, 150 mg, 300 mg	+b	+b	+b
	tablet, 150 mg, 300 mg	+b	+b	+b
	tablet, 150 mg + isoniazid, 100 mg	○	+b	+b
	300 mg + isoniazid, 150 mg	○	+b	+b
salbutamol sulfate	inhalation (aerosol), 100 µg of salbutamol per dose	?,+p	+p+c	+p
	respirator solution for use in nebulizers, 5 mg/ml	?,+p	+p+c	–
	tablet, 2 mg, 4 mg of salbutamol	+b	+b	+b

Table 1 (continued)

Drug substance	Dosage form	Canada	Germany	USA
salicylic acid	cream, 3% + benzoic acid, 6%	–	+p+c	○
	ointment, 3% + benzoic acid, 6%	–	+p+c	–
	solution, topical, 5%	–	+p+c	○
silver nitrate	solution (eye drops), 1%	○	+p+c	–
silver sulfadiazine	cream, 1% in 500-g container	+c	+p+c	+c
sodium cromoglicate	inhalation, 20 mg/dose	? or +c	+p+c	+p+c
sodium fluoride	tablet, 500 µg	–	–	–
sodium valproate	enteric coated tablet, 200 mg, 500 mg	+b	+b	+b
spironolactone	tablet, 25 mg	+b	+b	+b
sulfadimidine	tablet, 500 mg	○	+b	○
sulfadoxine	tablet, 500 mg + pyrimethamine, 25 mg	+b	+b	+b
sulfamethoxazole	oral suspension 200 mg + trimethoprim, 40 mg/5 ml	+b	+b	+b
	tablet, 100 mg + trimethoprim, 20 mg	+b	+b	+b
	400 mg + trimethoprim, 80 mg	+b	+b	+b
sulfasalazine	tablet, 500 mg	+b	+b	+b
tamoxifen citrate	tablet, 10 mg of tamoxifen, 20 mg of tamoxifen	+b	+b	+b
testosterone enantate	injection, 200 mg in 1 ml ampoule	?	+b	–
tetracaine hydrochloride	solution (eye drops), 0.5%	○	+p+c	–
tetracycline hydrochloride	capsule, 250 mg	?	+b	+b
	tablet, 250 mg	?	+b	+b
	eye ointment, 1%	?	+p+c	–

Table 1 (continued)

Drug substance	Dosage form	Canada	Germany	USA
thiamine hydrochloride	tablet, 50 mg	–	?	–
thioacetazone	tablet, 50 mg + isoniazid, 100 mg	○	+b	○
	150 mg + isoniazid, 300 mg	○	+b	○
tolbutamide	tablet, 500 mg	+b	+b	+b
trimethoprim	oral suspension, 40 mg + sulfamethoxazole, 200 mg/5 ml	+b	+b	+b
	tablet, 100 mg, 200 mg	+b	+b	+b
	tablet, 20 mg + sulfamethoxazole, 100 mg	+b	+b	+b
	80 mg + sulfamethoxazole, 400 mg	+b	+b	+b
tropicamide	solution (eye drops), 0.5%	○	+p+c	–
verapamil hydrochloride	tablet, 40 mg, 80 mg	+b	+b	+b
warfarin sodium	tablet, 1 mg, 2 mg, 5 mg	?	+b	+b
zinc oxide	cream	–	+p+c	–
	ointment	–	+p+c	–

Reference

1. *The use of essential drugs. Sixth report of the WHO Expert Committee.* Geneva, World Health Organization, 1995 (WHO Technical Report Series, No. 850).

Appendix 2. Explanation of symbols used in the design of bioequivalence studies in humans, and commonly used pharmacokinetic abbreviations

C_{max}	The observed maximum or peak concentration of drug (or metabolite) in plasma, serum or whole blood.
C_{min}	The minimum plasma concentration.
C_{max}-ratio	The ratio of the geometric means of the test and reference C_{max} values.
C_{av}	The average plasma concentration.
AUC	The area under the curve for drug (or metabolite) concentration in plasma (or serum or whole blood) against time. The value of AUC may be that for a specific period, e.g. AUC from zero to 12 hours is shown as AUC_{12}.
AUC_t	AUC from zero to the last quantifiable concentration.
AUC_∞	AUC from zero to infinity, obtained by extrapolation.
AUC_τ	AUC over one dosing interval (τ) under steady-state conditions.
AUC-ratio	The ratio of the geometric means of the test and reference AUC values.
Ae	The cumulative urinary recovery of parent drug (or metabolite). The value of Ae may be that for a specific period, e.g. Ae from zero to 12 hours is shown as Ae_{12}.
Ae_t	Ae from zero to the last quantifiable concentration.
Ae_∞	Ae from zero to infinite time, obtained by extrapolation.
Ae_τ	Ae over one dosing interval under steady-state conditions.
dAe/dt	The rate of urinary excretion of parent drug (or metabolite).
t_{max}	The time after administration of the drug at which C_{max} is observed.
t_{max}-diff	The difference between the arithmetic means of the test and reference t_{max} values.
$t_{1/2}$	The plasma (serum, whole blood) half-life.
MRT	The mean residence time.
μ_T	Average bioavailability of the test product.
μ_R	Average bioavailability of the reference product.

Appendix 3. Technical aspects of bioequivalence statistics

The pharmacokinetic characteristics to be tested, the test procedure and the norms to be maintained should be specified beforehand in the protocol. A *post hoc* change in the methods specified for the statistical evaluation is acceptable only if adherence to the protocol would preclude a meaningful evaluation and if such a change in procedure has been fully justified.

Concentration-dependent data such as AUC and C_{max} should be log transformed before statistical analysis in order to satisfy the fundamental assumption underlying analysis of variance that effects in the model act in an additive rather than a multiplicative manner.

Acceptance ranges for main characteristics

AUC-ratio
The 90% confidence interval for this measure of relative bioavailability should lie within a bioequivalence range of 80–125% (see p. 79). If the therapeutic range is particularly narrow, the acceptance range may need to be reduced. A larger acceptance range may be acceptable if clinically appropriate.

C_{max}-ratio
This measure of relative bioavailability is inherently more variable than, for example, the AUC-ratio, and a wider acceptance range may be appropriate. The range used should be justified, taking into account safety and efficacy considerations.

t_{max}-diff
Statistical evaluation of t_{max}, makes sense only if there is a clinically relevant claim for rapid release or action, or signs of a relation to adverse effects. The non-parametric 90% confidence interval for this measure of relative bioavailability should lie within a clinically relevant range.

3.
Distribution

Quality assurance in pharmaceutical supply systems[1]

1.	Introduction and general considerations	105
2.	Elements of quality assessment and assurance	108
	2.1 Legal base	108
	2.2 Regulatory elements	108
	2.2.1 General	108
	2.2.2 Governmental drug control agencies	109
	2.3 Technical elements	110
	2.3.1 Quality specifications	110
	2.3.2 Basic tests	111
	2.3.3 Requirements for good manufacturing practices	111
3.	Pre-marketing quality assessment	112
	3.1 Drug notification, authorization and registration	112
	3.2 Drug nomenclature	113
4.	Drug quality surveillance during marketing	113
	4.1 Quality surveillance during manufacture	113
	4.2 Quality surveillance of imported drugs	114
	4.2.1 WHO Certification Scheme	114
	4.2.2 Procedures at ports of entry	114
	4.3 Quality surveillance during distribution	114
References		115

1. Introduction and general considerations

In its twenty-sixth report (*1*), the WHO Expert Committee on Specifications for Pharmaceutical Preparations expressed the opinion that a comprehensive review of quality assurance in pharmaceutical supply systems might be of value

---

[1] *WHO Expert Committee on Specifications for Pharmaceutical Preparations. Twenty-seventh Report.* Geneva, World Health Organization, 1980 (WHO Technical Report Series, No. 645).

for national programmes in the regulatory control of drugs[1] and suggested that a suitable document should be prepared. The document should refer to international problems in the field of drug quality assurance and should include a consideration of related major WHO programmes. Since a lack of resources in certain areas might prevent the application of a comprehensive system of drug quality assurance, the Committee considered that the document should also recommend the course of action that might be taken to assure the quality of drugs being supplied under such conditions.

The present document is an attempt to provide an outline of the elements involved in the development of national programmes concerned with the regulatory control of drug quality in pharmaceutical supply systems. It is intended primarily for use by the appropriate health authorities of Member States that are establishing or expanding their national drug quality assessment system.

It is necessary for each country to develop and maintain a drug quality assessment system, which should form an integral part of a national drug control system, designed to prevent the production, export, import, and distribution of ineffective, harmful or poor-quality drugs. Such a system must be based on appropriate legislation and be supervised by a suitably qualified and properly empowered authority, supported by inspection and laboratory services. Because of the wide variations that exist in pharmaceutical supply systems the organization of quality assessment and assurance has to be adapted to meet existing conditions. The subsequent sections of this document deal with various aspects of the system in depth, where this is appropriate. The subject-matter is, however, general in nature and the suggestions contained herein can be modified to meet local needs.

In the present document the term "quality" retains the meaning given to it in the twenty-second report of the WHO Expert Committee on Specifications for Pharmaceutical Preparations (3), which stated:

> The suitability of drugs for their intended use is determined by (a) their efficacy weighed against safety to health according to label claim or as promoted or publicized and (b) their conformity to specifications regarding identity, strength, purity, and other characteristics.
>
> Although these two groups of factors may be considered separately, they are, to some degree, interdependent.
>
> In order to ensure that all batches of a given drug are equally efficacious and safe, it is essential to establish adequate specifications for the

---

[1] For the purposes of this document the definition of the term "drug" is identical to that given in "Good practices in the manufacture and quality control of drugs" (2, Annex 1):
"Any substance or mixture of substances that is manufactured, sold, offered for sale, or represented for use in (1) the treatment, mitigation, prevention, or diagnosis of disease, an abnormal physical state, or the symptoms thereof in man or animal; or (2) the restoration, correction, or modification of organic functions in man or animal".

drug and its dosage forms. The desired quality can then be achieved by strict adherence to these specifications. In fact, once their efficacy and safety have been established, the quality of drugs available in commerce is judged by identifying them and by determining their strength, purity, and other characteristics.

It is considered that in the assessment of the quality of imported drugs, especially in countries that are heavily dependent on pharmaceutical products produced abroad, an increasing role should be played by the WHO Certification Scheme on the Quality of Pharmaceutical Products Moving in International Commerce (4), and the importing countries should make greater use of it. Further details concerning the operation of the scheme are given in section 4.2.1.

It is generally accepted that the manufacturer (including the firms packaging and labelling drugs) and the distributor (including importers, wholesalers, and retail and hospital pharmacists) should be responsible for the quality of the products they manufacture or distribute. Nevertheless, this does not release other persons involved in the process of distribution of pharmaceutical products, including physicians and other health personnel, from their obligation to be vigilant and to contribute, by virtue of their experience, to the assurance of drug quality.

An important facet of quality assurance concerns the packaging and storage of drugs. Adequate specifications for containers and directions for proper packaging and storage are indispensable to prevent or diminish the loss of quality caused by handling during shipment from the manufacturer or importer, storage at ports of entry, or movement in the chain of distribution through the wholesale distribution channels to the final outlet. Inadequate packaging and storage can lead to physical deterioration and chemical decomposition, resulting in a reduction in activity and, therefore, of therapeutic efficacy, as well as the formation of possibly harmful degradation products.

The factors which concern the efficacy and safety of drugs are mentioned in this document only to the extent to which they interface with the quality notion as expressed above. Pertinent elements of pre-marketing quality assessment are discussed in some detail in section 3. A discussion of the problems of bioavailability of drugs may be found in the report of a WHO Scientific Group on the Bio-availability of Drugs: Principles and Problems (5).

Aspects such as directions for use and other information given on labels or in package inserts, including storage requirements, may have quality implications but are not discussed. The present document is primarily concerned with the quality assessment of pharmaceutical products. Additional requirements specifically applicable to biological products (such as vaccines, toxoids and antisera) are given in a number of recommendations adopted by the WHO Expert Committee on Biological Standardization or other WHO expert groups. (See, for example, the report of a WHO Expert Group on Requirements for Biological Substances: Manufacturing Establishments and Control

Laboratories ... (*6*), and the twenty-second report of the Expert Committee on Biological Standardization, Annex 3: "Development of a national control laboratory for biological substances ..."(*7*).)

2. Elements of quality assessment and assurance

The area of quality assessment and assurance includes the legal base and regulatory and technical elements.

2.1 Legal base

Drug quality assessment and assurance should have an adequate legal framework forming an integral part of general drug legislation. All regulatory and technical elements of quality assessment and assurance require the provision of legal powers to undertake these activities and to prescribe norms. The enabling legislation should provide the necessary authority to develop particular regulations in connexion with quality assurance during the manufacture, importation and distribution of pharmaceutical products and, in some cases, pharmaceutical raw materials. Additional regulations governing the practice of pharmacy, which form part of health legislation, may also be relevant here.

The responsibility for the development of guides, norms, and administrative regulations may frequently be assigned to a drug control agency. Wide differences in legal approaches exist between countries according to whether the administrative structure is centralized or decentralized. It is, however, possible in the case of a decentralized system to establish legislation that permits the sharing of responsibility, and the coordination of all activities in the quality assessment of pharmaceutical supply systems.

2.2 Regulatory elements

2.2.1 General

The regulatory elements of a quality assessment system include a central administrative entity, inspection services and drug quality control laboratories.

Regulatory implementation of quality assessment requires a legal base, as mentioned in section 2.1, giving authority to a designated agency to establish and enforce quality requirements throughout the manufacturing and distribution processes.

At the manufacturing stage, the aim is to ensure that all manufacturers, whether local or foreign, comply with good manufacturing practices. At the distribution level, the aim is to ensure that the quality of all pharmaceutical products, particularly imported items, has been properly assessed and that adequate control exists over the transport, storage and rotation of supplies, including the conditions in customs, premises, warehouses, and other places in which the products are stored before reaching the final user. This also includes procedures for the recall, if necessary, of unsatisfactory products.

2.2.2 Governmental drug control agencies

To facilitate adequate national control of pharmaceutical supply systems, authority should be vested in a ministry which is responsible for health matters. This would permit the establishment of a drug control agency and the development of administrative and regulatory procedures for the control of pharmaceuticals such as drug notification, authorization or registration and for the carrying out of adequate drug quality surveillance.

Administrative and regulatory procedures based on notification, authorization or registration must provide an adequate definition or specification for each drug.

To perform drug quality surveillance, the agency needs expert staff whose training is consistent with their responsibilities. For the quality surveillance of manufacturing operations the expertise required is comparable to that described in "Good practices in the manufacture and quality control of drugs" (4).

Inspection, sampling and analysis of pharmaceutical products on the market, supplemented by information from other sources (manufacturer, distributor, other regulatory agencies and advisers, and investigations of reported defects) provides the basis for action to minimize health hazards due to poor-quality products. Study of the consolidated information provides guidance for priorities in future activities.

To perform adequately its tasks on drug quality surveillance a fully developed agency should be supported by inspection and laboratory services. Where resources are adequate, there are advantages in uniting these services in the same organization; otherwise they must be closely coordinated to maximize the efficiency of the surveillance procedures.

In countries with decentralized systems of administration the agency may be located at a central point, or it may be structured to comprise centrally coordinated regional components.

The term "agency" is capable of wide interpretation, but in the present context it is intended primarily to designate the centre of authority for drug control activities without regard to the size of the administrative organization. Alternative regulatory procedures may exist and the type and extent of control exercised will determine the resources required.

2.2.2.1 *Inspection services*. The inspection services act as the field arm of an agency by verifying that all elements within the pharmaceutical supply system comply with the regulations and that data submitted to the agency are factual. Verification by inspection includes assessment of manufacturing and distributing firms, as well as retail and dispensing outlets such as pharmacies and hospitals. There is scope for international cooperation in the field of inspection services, the activities of which are dealt with in more detail in section 4.

2.2.2.2 *Drug quality control laboratory.* A governmental drug control laboratory carries out tests and assays required to establish whether drugs conform to the specifications claimed for them. Such a laboratory may also carry out investigations on new or improved analytical methods. Its type and size will be determined by a number of factors. These include the nature of the pharmaceutical supply system, the extent of local drug production and the quantum of pharmaceutical imports, and, in addition, the availability of support from other laboratories involved in drug quality testing.

Under certain circumstances it might be useful for a group of countries to pool their efforts towards the creation of a regional control laboratory. In other circumstances, a fully established national drug control laboratory can serve neighbouring countries.

2.3 Technical elements

2.3.1 Quality specifications

Quality specifications comprise a set of properly selected standards with associated methods of analysis that may be used to assess the integrity of drugs (including dosage forms) and starting materials. Adequate specifications for a particular drug in its dosage forms for identity, purity, strength, performance and other characteristics are necessary to assure that all batches of the drug are of uniform quality. Quality can then be achieved by strict adherence to the specifications.

In the course of drug evaluation for registration, tentative dosage form specifications are developed when clinical studies have proceeded sufficiently to suggest that the dosage form is an acceptable one. They are reviewed as further experience in drug manufacture is gained. This question was discussed in Annex 5 of the twenty-fifth report of the Expert Committee on Specifications for Pharmaceutical Preparations (*2*).

Quality specifications may be either public or undisclosed in nature. The public specifications are usually contained in a pharmacopoeial monograph and are stated in terms that permit objective evaluation of product quality, not only by the manufacturer but by other interested parties also.

A pharmacopoeia normally includes the general methodology of testing, monographs on pharmaceutical raw materials, including active and inactive ingredients of pharmaceutical products, and in many cases monographs on dosage forms. A number of national pharmacopoeias are kept up to date by periodic revision. Pharmacopoeias may also be issued through the joint effort of a group of countries. The European Pharmacopoeia and the Compendium Medicamentorum are recent examples of such endeavours. The International Pharmacopoeia is issued by the World Health Organization; volume 1 of the third edition (*8*) was published in 1979. Plurinational pharmacopoeias and the International Pharmacopoeia serve to make more uniform test methodology and specifications for a particular product.

There are many specifications that either are contained in an application for an authorization or registration or exist as the manufacturer's own specifications, which are not generally subject to public disclosure. Interested parties must therefore depend on the licensing authorities or the manufacturer for assurance that these specifications are adequate and are being met. Such assurance is mentioned in the WHO Certification Scheme on the Quality of Pharmaceutical Products Moving in International Commerce (4) (see section 4.2.1) through its provision concerning batch certificates to be provided by the manufacturer.

Analytical criteria for judging drug quality, which relate to the identity, purity and strength of drugs and to the performance of dosage forms, the selection of such criteria for pharmacopoeial monographs and for manufacturer's specifications, and the relation between these two sets of quality requirements were reviewed in Annex 1 of the twenty-sixth report of the WHO Expert Committee on Specifications for Pharmaceutical Preparations (1).

The selection of methods and procedures used in specifications must be based on their utility for the purpose of quality assurance of pharmaceuticals, and progress in the development of new analytical tools requires a periodic review of the methodology. In establishing specifications full account must also be taken of various technical and economic constraints.

2.3.2 Basic tests

Simplified tests (basic tests) may serve in specific circumstances for verifying the identity of a drug and ascertaining the absence of gross degradation or contamination. They may be specially useful in situations in which well-equipped laboratories do not exist and in which full examination of drug quality according to procedures requiring special skills and equipment is not feasible. When a product fails the basic tests, it should not be used until its quality is established by a full analytical examination. Various aspects of the problem of the development and application of such tests are discussed in Annex 2 of the twenty-sixth report of the WHO Expert Committee on Specifications for Pharmaceutical Preparations (1).

2.3.3 Requirements for good manufacturing practices

The quality of pharmaceutical products depends on the correct performance of all manufacturing operations and must be built in from the beginning of the manufacturing process. The principles for quality control procedures that should be applied to drug manufacturing practices are designated "Good practices in the manufacture and quality control of drugs" (4) (see section 2.2.2). These principles are general guides which, whenever necessary, may be adapted to meet national needs, provided the established standards of drug quality are still achieved. Manufacturing establishments with a limited product line need only utilize the relevant parts of the requirements.

The requirements for good manufacturing practice indicate that the documents relating to manufacturing procedures should contain, among other necessary information, the data concerning each starting material, as well as detailed instructions for and precautions to be taken in the manufacture of the drug. If modifications due to changes in the equipment for processing or to the use of alternative types of ingredients are introduced, their influence on the quality, including the performance, of dosage forms has to be adequately evaluated.

3. Pre-marketing quality assessment

A system which serves to control the introduction of a drug to the market is a prerequisite for drug quality assessment. Quality requirements should be established by the competent health authorities (drug control agency) and these norms constitute the basis for quality assessment.

3.1 Drug notification, authorization and registration

The introduction of a drug to the market is controlled by different procedures, designated by such terms as "registration" or "licensing" in various countries. Uniform designations are given below to avoid possible confusion. The procedures thus described may be gradually evolved through discrete phases.

A notification procedure is the least resource-intensive way of obtaining information on drugs offered for sale in a country. The amount of information requested for notification may vary. It may be initially restricted to the name of the drug and of the manufacturer, and may then be expanded to include the nonproprietary names for active substances, the composition, including inactive ingredients, and the pharmacological classification.

An authorization procedure can be developed in which either all drugs or specified ones only require an authorization before they are marketed in the country. This procedure may vary in its stringency but it almost always incorporates the element of inspection of the manufacturer and the verification of product quality by analysis.

A registration procedure comprises the evaluation of data intended to prove the safety and efficacy of the drug and to determine the indications for its use. The registration may include an assessment both of the drug and of the manufacturing procedures. Pharmaceutical aspects of drug evaluation for registration are described in Annex 5 of the twenty-fifth report of the WHO Expert Committee on Specifications for Pharmaceutical Preparations (*2*). Some pertinent safety and efficacy aspects are reviewed in the report of a WHO Scientific Group on Guidelines for Evaluation of Drugs for Use in Man (*9*).

For products which have been used extensively and for which sufficient experience exists to demonstrate the safety of the active ingredient in similar types of preparation, the administrative requirements may be reduced to a declaration of manufacturing data and pharmaceutical quality specifications.

3.2 Drug nomenclature

The need to identify each pharmaceutical substance by a unique and universally applicable nonproprietary name has long been recognized. WHO is carrying out a programme on the standardization of drug nomenclature and has published International Nonproprietary Names (INN) for over 4000 pharmaceutical substances.[1] Comprehensive information on the programme can be found in the twentieth report of the WHO Expert Committee on Nonproprietary Names for Pharmaceutical Substances (*10*).

When a new drug is introduced into a country, the active ingredients should be properly identified on the label by INN or, if these are not available, by other established nonproprietary names. The names in question should also be used in all official texts.

4. Drug quality surveillance during marketing

Quality surveillance during marketing is an integral function of a drug control agency. It is undertaken by monitoring and auditing procedures involving both inspection and laboratory testing.

The places in which drugs are manufactured, stored and distributed should be known to the control authorities. This information can be obtained by requiring all manufacturers, importers and distributors to give the control authorities official notification of their planned activities before they commence operations, and to comply with any particular regulations.

Drug quality surveillance is facilitated if lists of nonproprietary names are established for all pharmaceutical substances on the market in a country, with references to trade names where applicable.

To aid the application of procedures for the recall of pharmaceutical products, it might be useful if the control authorities had knowledge of the persons responsible for marketing in each manufacturing enterprise, as well as information about the distribution mechanism and the destination of the products.

4.1 Quality surveillance during manufacture

The inspection of manufacturing facilities is required to ensure that good manufacturing practices are followed at all times. In assessing manufacture, the inspector is required to pay particular attention to raw materials, manufacturing

---

[1] INN for over 6800 pharmaceutical substances have now been published (see inside back cover for details of the latest cumulative list).

procedures, sterile operations, packaging and labelling, in-process quality control, personnel and storage facilities. Special attention should be paid to any alterations of the master formula and manufacturing procedures.

An additional mechanism of drug quality surveillance at the time of manufacture is the batch control (batch certification) of some types of drugs. According to this procedure each batch of a drug, after being declared by the manufacturer as fully conforming to quality specifications, is "put in quarantine" while a random sample is taken and analysed by a governmental drug control laboratory for confirmation of its quality. The batch is released only after a satisfactory result is obtained. Such a mechanism, which calls for a duplication of the manufacturer's control efforts by the governmental authorities, is usually restricted to specific types of drugs, such as those that are potent but highly labile. It is usually phased out once the quality level of manufacture is considered sufficiently uniform by the drug control agency.

4.2 Quality surveillance of imported drugs

4.2.1 WHO Certification Scheme

The WHO Certification Scheme on the Quality of Pharmaceutical Products Moving in International Commerce (4), when used, will provide valuable data required for pharmaceutical quality assessment of imported drugs.

The scheme permits the control authorities of importing countries to obtain information on imported drugs. In this context, it is desirable to acquire knowledge of the quality and manufacturing conditions of imported drugs similar to that which could be obtained if the product were manufactured locally. The scope of the information required may vary according to the category of the drug and the control procedure adopted in the importing country.

4.2.2 Procedures at ports of entry

At the port of entry, consignments of drugs must be stored under suitable conditions, and for as short a time as possible, to prevent deterioration. If prolonged storage is to be avoided, the proper administrative procedures must be worked out and the type of information which should accompany each shipment will have to be designated. The effective involvement of pharmaceutical officers at customs would facilitate this task.

Batch control is sometimes carried out in respect of some imported drugs and considerations similar to those mentioned in section 4.1 are pertinent here.

4.3 Quality surveillance during distribution

In the process of quality surveillance during distribution particular attention should be paid to personnel qualifications, storage facilities and transport conditions.

Every pharmaceutical product has a shelf-life during which its quality may be expected to remain within acceptable limits, but which may be seriously shortened by improper storage conditions. There is therefore a need to ensure—especially in adverse climatic conditions—that during all phases of distribution adequate conditions of storage are maintained.

For drugs that are known to have a short shelf-life, the expiry date should be stated clearly (no code being used) on all drug labels. The inclusion of expiry dates on the labelling provides a uniform system of indicating shelf-life under specified conditions of storage. In addition, the indication of the date of manufacture would further facilitate the quality surveillance of pharmaceutical products during distribution.

References

1. WHO Technical Report Series, No. 614, 1977.

2. WHO Technical Report Series, No. 567, 1975.

3. WHO Technical Report Series, No. 418, 1969.

4. WHO Official Records, No. 226, 1975, Annex 12.

5. WHO Technical Report Series, No. 536, 1974.

6. WHO Technical Report Series, No. 323, 1966.

7. WHO Technical Report Series, No. 444, 1970.

8. *The international pharmacopoeia. Third edition. Volume 1: General methods of analysis.* Geneva, World Health Organization, 1979.

9. WHO Technical Report Series, No. 563, 1975.

10. WHO Technical Report Series, No. 581, 1975.

4.
The international pharmacopoeia and related activities

Guidance for those preparing or commenting on monographs for preparations to be included in *The international pharmacopoeia*[1]

In preparing or commenting upon monographs for inclusion in *The international pharmacopoeia* experts are asked to bear in mind the role and objectives of that pharmacopoeia, which have been summarized as follows:

(a) To provide specifications on the purity and potency of essential drug substances, widely used pharmaceutical aids, and dosage forms. These specifications should be adequate to assure the safety and efficacy of these products as well as adequate reproducibility of their effects in clinical use, but they should not be unnecessarily stringent, since this would increase the cost of the products. In the case of recently introduced products, specifications should be developed to ensure compatibility with the samples for which the toxicological properties and clinical efficacy and safety were initially established.

(b) To support such specifications with readily applicable methods of testing and analysis, with attention to the facilities available within control laboratories in developing countries.

(c) To provide general methods of analysis that would be applicable not only to materials included in the pharmacopoeia but also to new products submitted for registration.

(d) To accommodate, where appropriate, a measure of flexibility into methods and requirements that will facilitate the use of *The international pharmacopoeia* on a global basis, particularly in connection with dosage forms.

(e) To present all these elements in such a manner that *The international pharmacopoeia*, or selected parts of it, can be officially adopted by any Member State of the World Health Organization.

To meet some of these aims guidance concerning monographs for drug

---

[1] *WHO Expert Committee on Specifications for Pharmaceutical Preparations. Thirty-first Report.* Geneva, World Health Organization, 1990 (WHO Technical Report Series, No. 790).

THE INTERNATIONAL PHARMACOPOEIA AND RELATED ACTIVITIES

substances has been published.[1] The additional guidelines set out below refer specifically to monographs for dosage forms.

1. Reference substances should be avoided if this is possible.

2. In cases in which infrared spectrophotometry is regarded as essential for the appropriate identification of a particular drug substance in a dosage form, an alternative series of tests should always be given. Because the process of extraction of the drug substance from the dosage form may result in a polymorphic change, appropriate instructions should be given to ensure that the extracted ingredient is converted to the form on which any reference spectrum is based.

3. In the alternative series of identification tests it is often useful to employ thin-layer chromatography (TLC), using the same solvent system as in the TLC test for related substances. This, however, requires a reference substance, and it should therefore be invoked only if it has proved essential to establish a reference substance for other purposes.

4. It is desirable that at least one colour test should be included in the identification scheme. The combination of tests proposed should provide reasonable assurance that the labelled product is adequately identified.

5. Since *The international pharmacopoeia* is intended to provide an independent challenge to dosage forms and since the analyst examining such samples may not have recourse to data obtained on the drug substance used to manufacture the dosage forms, it is considered desirable that tests should be included in the monograph for the dosage form to demonstrate freedom from undue quantities of manufacturing or degradation impurities. Tests for impurities that may arise in the synthetic process used to manufacture the drug substance serve to demonstrate that an acceptable quality of that ingredient has been used to prepare the dosage form. Tests for impurities that may arise from degradation of the drug substance, either during preparation of the dosage form or during its storage, serve to demonstrate appropriate manufacture and storage. It should be recognized, however, that the limits for impurities arising from degradation of the drug substance during manufacture of the dosage form may often need to be less stringent than those for the same degradation that apply to the drug substance itself. Limits for impurities that may arise only during synthesis should, on the other hand, be of similar stringency to those applied to the drug substance itself.

6. Wherever possible, impurities should be sought using TLC (high–low system) by applying a suitable solution prepared from the dosage form at a reasonably high loading and comparing any secondary spots obtained with the principal

---

[1] *WHO Expert Committee on Specifications for Pharmaceutical Preparations. Twenty-ninth Report.* Geneva, World Health Organization, 1984 (WHO Technical Report Series, No. 704, Annex 5).

spot in the same solution, appropriately diluted. Due regard should be paid, however, to the fact that in certain drugs the possible impurities may respond very differently to the system of visualization used. Such problems may be minimized by using, for example, fluorescent plates, which can be examined under an ultraviolet lamp having a maximum output at about 254 nm, or iodine vapours to produce coloured spots. In general, it is desirable to choose a system such that the principal spot shows an R_f value of about 0.5, although in certain cases it can be of advantage if the principal spot remains near the baseline or migrates to the solvent front, provided that secondary spots of interest are well separated.

7. Gas–liquid chromatography or high-performance liquid chromatography (HPLC) should be used only when there is full justification for doing so, i.e. where it is of particular importance to control an impurity and where no other method is reasonably available.

8. Heavy metals tests should be employed only when the dosage of the drug demands it, e.g. when quantities of 0.5 g or more are given per day over a long period, or when some other reason can be identified.

9. Where it is necessary to control the acidity or alkalinity of a preparation, pH measurement should be included if the material has inherent buffering properties; otherwise a titrimetric procedure should be recommended. In general, a test for acidity or alkalinity should be required only when the preparation being tested does not show a marked buffering effect. Such tests are, in general, only required for injectable preparations or for solutions that will come into contact with delicate membranes (such as the eye).

10. Requirements for clarity of solution should, in general, be invoked whenever the preparation, either as such or after solution, is intended to be injected or is for ocular use or when the presence of an opalescence is indicative of the presence of an impurity or of degradation. Such a test should not be included in monographs simply for the purpose of controlling the presence of mechanically introduced dirt.

11. The assay procedure employed might be stability-indicating or, if nonspecific, should be supplemented by appropriate limit tests for degradation products. It may be possible to use less accurate methods than would be necessary for the drug substance itself since specifications for dosage forms take into account not only the purity of the chemical product but also the practical facts of industrial manufacture.

12. All tests should, wherever possible, make use of reagents that are already described in *The international pharmacopoeia*. Toxic materials such as mercuric salts, benzene, reagents known to be carcinogenic, and other undesirable materials should be avoided.

13. In view of the possible use of *The international pharmacopoeia* in tropical areas, care should be taken to minimize the use of very volatile solvents, such as ether. This is of particular importance in devising mobile phases for TLC, since the composition of such phases is liable to change if volatile solvents are included.

14. Existing pharmacopoeial methods should be invoked whenever possible since these will have been examined widely, whereas new suggestions will require verification in other laboratories and the resources for this may not always be readily available.

15. Until tests for microbial contamination are developed a statement should be added to the monographs for materials of natural origin under "Additional information". Attention should be paid to the microbial purity.

Validation of analytical procedures used in the examination of pharmaceutical materials[1]

1. What is analytical validation?

Analytical monitoring of a pharmaceutical product, or of specific ingredients within the product, is necessary to ensure its safety and efficacy throughout all phases of its shelf-life, including storage, distribution, and use. Ideally, this monitoring should be conducted in accordance with specifications elaborated and validated during product development. This ensures that the quality specifications are applicable to the pharmaceutical material used to establish the biological characteristics of the active substances as well as to the marketed dosage forms. When the biomedical evaluation of the product is completed, the acceptability of all subsequent batches will be judged solely on the basis of these specifications.

The principal purpose of analytical validation is to ensure that a selected analytical procedure will give reproducible and reliable results that are adequate for the intended purpose. It is thus necessary to define properly both the conditions in which the procedure is to be used and the purpose for which it is intended. These principles apply to all procedures described in a pharmacopoeia and to non-pharmacopoeial procedures used in a manufacturing company.

These guidelines apply to procedures used to examine chemical and physicochemical attributes, but many are equally applicable to microbiological and biological procedures.

---

[1] *WHO Expert Committee on Specifications for Pharmaceutical Preparations. Thirty-second Report*. Geneva, World Health Organization, 1992 (WHO Technical Report Series, No. 823).

2. Presentation of data on analytical procedures for product registration or pharmacopoeial monographs

Any data on analytical procedures presented in support of a specification proposed for a particular ingredient (drug substance or excipient) or dosage form should be provided under three main headings:

1. *Justification for the proposed test procedure in comparison with other possible approaches.* Where an unusual procedure is proposed, its scientific basis should also be discussed. Where the procedure is being proposed to replace an existing one, comparative data should be provided.
2. *Description of a procedure giving as much detail as is deemed necessary to allow properly trained workers carry it out in a reliable manner.* The reagents required should be defined (either in detail or by reference to readily available published texts) and details concerning the availability of any reference substances required should be given. Where the procedure is based on the application of well established principles of analytical chemistry, it should not be necessary to provide formulae for the calculation of results. Where, however, the method is complex, a full formula for the calculation of results should be included, with all terms defined.
3. *Validation data.* Each analytical performance characteristic that is applicable to the particular procedure defined (see section 4) should be discussed and supported by experimental data. Where the data presented for registration purposes rely on established pharmacopoeial methods, the need for supporting validation data may be considerably reduced, on the assumption that the pharmacopoeial procedures have already been properly validated. However, evidence that the pharmacopoeial procedure is applicable to the material under test may well be required, especially for dosage forms.

3. Characteristics of analytical procedures

The characteristics that may need to be specified for analytical procedures are listed below and defined (for the purposes of this text), with an indication of how they may be determined.

Not all the characteristics are applicable to every test procedure or to every material. Much depends on the purpose for which the procedure is required. This aspect of validation is discussed in section 4.

Accuracy

The accuracy of the procedure is the closeness of the results obtained by the procedure to the true value. Accuracy may be determined by applying the procedure to samples of the material to be examined that have been prepared with quantitative accuracy. Wherever possible, these samples should contain all the components of the material, including the analyte. Samples in which the analyte has been incorporated in quantities some 10% above and below the expected range of values should also be prepared. Accuracy may also be determined by comparing the results with those obtained using an alternative procedure that has already been validated.

Precision

The precision of the procedure is the degree of agreement among individual test results. It is measured by the scatter of individual results from the mean and it is usually expressed as the standard deviation or as the coefficient of variation (relative standard deviation) when the complete procedure is applied repeatedly to separate, identical samples drawn from the same homogeneous batch of material.

Repeatability (within-laboratory variation)

This is the precision of the procedure when repeated by the same analyst under the same set of conditions (same reagents, equipment, settings, and laboratory) and within a short interval of time. The repeatability of a procedure is assessed by carrying out complete, separate determinations on separate, identical samples of the same homogeneous batch of material and thus provides a measure of the precision of the procedure under normal operating conditions.

Reproducibility

This is the precision of the procedure when it is carried out under different conditions—usually in different laboratories—on separate, putatively identical samples taken from the same homogeneous batch of material. Comparisons of results obtained by different analysts, by the use of different equipment, or by carrying out the analysis at different times can also provide valuable information.

Robustness

Robustness, or ruggedness, is the ability of the procedure to provide analytical results of acceptable accuracy and precision under a variety of conditions. It is a measure of the extent to which the results obtained from separate, putatively identical samples of the same homogeneous batch of material are influenced by changes in operational or environmental conditions but are consonant with the specifications laid down for the procedure.

Linearity and range

The linearity of an analytical procedure is its ability to produce results that are directly proportional to the concentration of analyte in the samples. The range of the procedure is an expression of the lowest and highest levels of analyte that have been demonstrated to be determinable with acceptable precision, accuracy, and linearity. These characteristics are determined by application of the procedure to a series of samples having analyte concentrations spanning the claimed range of the procedure. When the relationship between response and concentration is not linear, standardization may be provided by means of a calibration curve.

Selectivity

The selectivity or specificity of a procedure is its ability to measure the analyte in a manner that is free from interference from other components in the sample being examined (for example, impurities arising from manufacture or degradation or ingredients other than the analyte, whether these are pharmacologically active or inert). Selectivity (or lack of it) may be expressed in terms of the bias of the assay results obtained when the procedure is applied to the analyte in the presence of expected levels of other components, compared to the results obtained on the same analyte without added substances. When the other components are all known and available, selectivity may be determined by comparing the test results obtained on the analyte with and without the addition of the potentially interfering materials. When such components are either unidentified or unavailable, a measure of selectivity can often be obtained by determining the recovery of a standard addition of pure analyte to a material containing a constant level of the other components.

Sensitivity

Sensitivity is the capacity of the test procedure to record small variations in concentration. It is the slope of the calibration curve. A more general use of the term to encompass limit of detection and/or limit of quantitation should be avoided.

Limit of detection

The limit of detection is the lowest level of analyte that can be detected, but not necessarily determined in a quantitative fashion, using a specific method under the required experimental conditions. Such a limit is usually expressed in terms of a concentration of analyte (for example, in micrograms per litre) in the sample. Where the final measurement is based on an instrumental reading, due account will need to be taken of the background response (the signal-to-noise characteristics of the responses observed).

Limit of quantitation

The limit of quantitation is the lowest concentration of analyte in a sample that may be determined with acceptable accuracy and precision when the required procedure is applied. It is measured by analysing samples containing diminishing known quantities of the analyte and determining the lowest level at which acceptable degrees of accuracy and precision are attainable. Where the final assessment is based on an instrumental reading, the magnitude of background response (the signal-to-noise ratio) may need to be assessed and taken into account. In many cases the limit of quantitation is approximately twice the limit of detection.

4. What analytical characteristics are applicable in particular cases?

Not all of the characteristics referred to in section 3 will need to be considered in all cases; those applicable should be identified on a case-by-case basis. As a guide, however, the following generalizations may assist.

Methods used for the examination of pharmaceutical materials may be broadly classified as follows:

- Class A: Tests designed to establish identity, whether of bulk drug substances or of a particular ingredient in a finished dosage form.
- Class B: Methods designed to detect and quantitate impurities in a bulk drug substance or finished dosage form.
- Class C: Methods used to determine quantitatively the concentration of a bulk drug substance or of a major ingredient in a finished dosage form.
- Class D: Methods used to assess the characteristics of finished dosage forms, such as dissolution profiles and content uniformity.

Table 1 offers guidelines to the characteristics that are relevant in each case. Notwithstanding these generalizations, there will clearly be occasions when certain characteristics marked as not being required may be necessary and vice

Table 1. Characteristics that should be considered for different types of analytical procedure

	Class A	Class B		Class C	Class D
		Quantitative tests	Limit tests		
Accuracy		×		×	×[a]
Precision		×		×	×
Robustness	×	×	×	×	×
Linearity and range		×		×	×
Selectivity	×	×	×	×	×
Limit of detection	×		×		
Limit of quantitation		×			

[a] A degree of bias may be allowed.

versa. In addition, the purpose for which the submission is being made may have a bearing on the choice of characteristics and the extent to which they are specified. For example, although Classes B, C, and D are all referred to in Table 1 as requiring consideration of precision, the stringency applied may be different. For estimation of an impurity it may not be necessary to be as precise as for quantitative assessment of a bulk drug substance. By the same token, a degree of bias may be acceptable in determining the accuracy of a test for uniformity of content (Class D) that would not be permissible for a quantitative assessment of the concentration of an ingredient in a finished dosage form (Class C). Similarly, a test designed to establish the identity of a new drug entity for which no previous data have been lodged may need to be considerably more searching than tests designed to verify the identity of a long-established drug substance to be included in a pharmacopoeia.

A different emphasis may be required for pharmacopoeial as opposed to registration purposes. For example, robustness is a critical characteristic for pharmacopoeial methodology but may be less significant for a manufacturer's release specification.

General guidelines for the establishment, maintenance, and distribution of chemical reference substances[1]

1. Criteria for determining the need for the establishment of chemical reference substances 125
2. Evaluation of reference substances 127
3. Chemical and physical methods used in evaluating reference substances 127
   - 3.1 Methods useful for verifying the identity of reference substances 128
   - 3.2 Purity requirements for reference substances 128
   - 3.3 Methods used in determining the purity of reference substances 129
     - 3.3.1 Methods based on intrinsic thermodynamic properties 129
     - 3.3.2 Methods based on comparison with external standards and other methods 130
     - 3.3.3 General considerations 131
4. Handling and distribution of reference substances 131
   - 4.1 Packing and storage 131
   - 4.2 Stability and periodic re-evaluation 132
   - 4.3 Information to be supplied with reference substances 133

---

[1] *WHO Expert Committee on Specifications for Pharmaceutical Preparations. Twenty-eighth Report.* Geneva, World Health Organization, 1982 (WHO Technical Report Series, No. 681).

	4.4 Expiry of reference substances	134
	4.5 Distribution problems	135
5.	Reference materials calibrated against International Chemical Reference Substances	135
6.	Means of promoting effective exchange of information and ensuring cooperation between organizations establishing reference substances	136

1. Criteria for determining the need for the establishment of chemical reference substances

The production, validation, maintenance, and distribution of chemical reference substances[1] is a costly and time-consuming undertaking. It is therefore of great importance to limit the work involved by determining in a critical way whether a need for a given substance exists. Requests for new reference substances usually arise because a certain approach to the development of a specification for a new substance or product has been adopted. Methods may have been proposed in a specification that require the establishment of a reference substance for use as a comparative standard and the first matter that should be assessed, therefore, is whether some alternative procedure could be adopted that does not require a comparative standard and that might still be equally satisfactory. For example, an analytical procedure based on a stoichiometric relationship might be as valid, in a given context, as one based on ultraviolet absorption spectrophotometry and would obviate a possible need for a reference substance.

The types of analytical procedure at present used in specifications for pharmaceutical substances and products that may require a chemical reference substance are:

(a) infrared spectrophotometry, whether for identification or quantitative purposes;
(b) quantitative methods based on ultraviolet absorption spectrophotometry;
(c) quantitative methods based on the development of a colour and the measurement of its intensity, whether by instrumental or visual comparison;
(d) methods based on chromatographic separation for identification or quantitative purposes;
(e) quantitative methods (including automated methods) based on other separative techniques that depend upon partition of the material to be determined between solvent phases, where the precise efficiency of the extraction procedure might depend upon ambient conditions that vary from time to time and from laboratory to laboratory;

---

[1] The term *chemical reference substance*, as used here, refers to an authenticated uniform material that is intended for use in specified chemical and physical tests, in which its properties are compared with the properties of a product under examination, and that possesses a degree of purity adequate for its intended use.

(f) quantitative methods, often titrimetric but sometimes gravimetric, that are based on non-stoichiometric relationships;
(g) assay methods based on measurement of optical rotation; and
(h) methods that might require a reference material consisting of a fixed ratio of known components (for example *cis/trans* isomers).

There is a consensus among experts that for certain of the above categories a reference substance is essential. For example, the use of thin-layer chromatography as a means of identification dictates the need for a reference material, because the migration of a substance relative to the solvent front is dependent on the operating conditions: certain of the conditions, such as temperature and composition of the mobile phase, are readily controllable; others, such as the precise thickness and the water content of the layer used and the degree of saturation of the tank, cannot be exactly reproduced. Other examples are non-stoichiometric procedures, such as the iodimetric titration of penicillins and the determination of ascorbic acid by titration with an indophenol.

In other cases, however, differences of opinion exist as to whether a reference substance is essential. It has been proposed, for example, that a reference sample might not be essential for infrared spectrophotometry; instead it might be possible to define certain characteristics of a spectrum or to provide a copy of an "authentic spectrum" that could be used for purposes of comparison. Differences in the mode of presentation of spectra by diverse instruments, differences in resolution between instruments, and problems associated with polymorphism and solvation make such an approach difficult in some instances at the present time. Nevertheless, this approach, implemented where feasible, would significantly reduce the number of reference substances needed and also reduce the extent of use of those substances required for other purposes.

The need for reference substances in ultraviolet absorption spectrophotometry has probably given rise to the greatest controversy. Certain compendia (for example, the *United States Pharmacopeia*) require comparison of observed spectral characteristics of the substance under examination with those of a reference substance similarly treated, while others (for example, the *European Pharmacopoeia*, the *British Pharmacopoeia*, and the third edition of *The international pharmacopoeia*) rely on comparison with quoted extinction values. Both of these methods have advantages, but neither is above criticism. A mere comparison of spectra obtained by an operator using poor technique and inadequately maintained equipment might lead to acceptance of a sample but might not constitute a valid assay. Conversely, the use of inadequate controlled conditions and a quoted extinction value might lead to rejection of a satisfactory sample. It must also be accepted that, despite considerable improvements in the stability, accuracy and precision of ultraviolet spectrophotometers during the past decade, variations between instruments still occur and may undermine the validity of using quoted extinction values.

THE INTERNATIONAL PHARMACOPOEIA AND RELATED ACTIVITIES

These considerations, which also apply in some measure to other instrumental techniques such as infrared spectrophotometry, make it essential that adequate criteria for instrumental performance should be defined. This, in turn, suggests that a further class of reference materials, designed to assist in the calibration of instruments and the standardization of procedures, is also necessary. For example, *The international pharmacopoeia* (third edition, vol. 1, p. 35) prescribes the use of standardized didymium or holmium oxide filters for wavelength calibration and standardized potassium dichromate or potassium nitrate for absorbance calibration of ultraviolet spectrophotometers. In the field of standardization of procedures it is recognized that reference materials may be required to calibrate, for example, apparatus for dissolution testing. Such reference materials as these are, however, outside the scope of this present discussion of chemical reference substances.

2. Evaluation of reference substances

Evaluation of the suitability of a material proposed for use as a reference substance requires careful testing. It is necessary to consider all data obtained by examining the material, employing a wide variety of analytical methods. When taken as a whole they give confidence that the material is suitable for the intended use. Depending on the intended use of the substance, testing can be more or less searching and involve a number of independent laboratories.

In the case of reference substances that are intended for use in the identification tests or in the determination of purity, the examination may be carried out without a unified programme, all analytical data obtained in different laboratories being then considered. If compatible results are obtained in all the collaborating laboratories, a positive decision concerning the suitability of the material can be arrived at. The procedure may be simplified in the case of the evaluation of replacement batches of an existing reference substance.

When it is necessary to assign quantitative values to a reference substance, a collaborative study, following a carefully designed protocol and employing at least three cooperating laboratories, should be undertaken.

3. Chemical and physical methods used in evaluating reference substances

The methods used to establish a proposed material fall into two broad groups: those intended primarily to identify the material and those to establish the purity. With most methods, the percentage purity of a reference substance cannot be expressed as an absolute value if the impurities have not been identified. In such instances, the quoted purity is an estimate based upon the data obtained by use of the various analytical methods employed to establish the purity of the reference substance.

3.1 Methods useful for verifying the identity of reference substances

The identity of a material that is intended to replace an established reference substance of the same molecular constitution may be verified by means of tests that are capable of demonstrating that the characteristic properties of the two specimens are identical. For this purpose, a comparison of their infrared absorption spectra often suffices. Similarly, where a newly proposed reference substance consists of a compound whose structure has been satisfactorily elucidated, its identity may be confirmed by matching the infrared spectra of the material and of an authentic compound. Other highly specific techniques, such as nuclear magnetic resonance spectroscopy, mass spectrometry, or X-ray diffraction crystallography, may also be used for such comparisons.

However, where no authentic specimen of the proposed reference substance is available for comparison and definitive data about its properties are lacking, it may be necessary to verify the identity of the material by applying several analytical techniques currently used to characterize new compounds. Such analytical methods may include elemental analyses, crystallographic studies, mass spectrometry, nuclear magnetic resonance spectroscopy, functional group analyses, infrared spectrophotometry, and ultraviolet spectrophotometry, as well as such other supplementary tests as are necessary and sufficient to establish that the proposed reference material is the required substance.

3.2 Purity requirements for reference substances

The purity requirements for a reference substance depend upon its intended use. A reference substance proposed for an identification test by infrared spectrophotometry does not require meticulous purification, because the presence of a small percentage of impurities in the substance often has no noticeable influence on its infrared spectrum. Similarly, reference substances that are applied in low loadings in thin-layer chromatographic tests need not be highly purified.

On the other hand, reference substances that are to be used in assays should preferably possess a high degree of purity. As a guiding principle, a purity of 99.5% or better is desirable for such reference substances, although in cases where the precision of the analytical procedure for which the reference substance is required is low, such a degree of purity may not be necessary. In making a decision about the suitability of a reference substance, the most important consideration is the influence of the impurity on the attribute measured in the assay. Impurities with physicochemical characteristics similar to those of the main component will not impair the usefulness of a reference substance, whereas even traces of impurities with significantly different properties may render a substance unsuitable as a reference substance.

3.3 Methods used in determining the purity of reference substances

A consideration of the methods to be employed in examining a chemical reference substance should take account of its method of preparation and its intended use. Such analytical methods may be divided into two broad categories — those that depend solely upon an intrinsic thermodynamic property of the system (e.g. phase solubility analysis and differential scanning calorimetry), and those that require comparison with an external standard (e.g. chromatographic or spectrophotometric methods). Methods in the former group allow the measurement of total impurity levels in absolute terms but provide little information regarding the molecular structure of the contaminants.

3.3.1 Methods based on intrinsic thermodynamic properties

3.3.1.1 *Phase solubility analysis.* Phase solubility analysis may be employed to detect contaminating substances, including isomeric species, and to estimate their concentration. The coefficient of variation that can be achieved using this method is about 0.2%. It is applicable to most reference substances and uses relatively simple apparatus. In some instances, phase solubility techniques may permit recovery of highly purified crystals of the main component as well as a concentrated solution of the contaminating substances from which they may be isolated for identification by other methods. These fractions provide significant data bearing upon the acceptability of the reference substance. Phase solubility analysis is time-consuming and its execution demands painstaking attention to detail. It is therefore often regarded as unsuitable for routine use in control laboratories, but it has proved of great value in laboratories engaged in the assessment of reference substances. Some factors that may make the method inapplicable are degradation of the substance during the course of analysis, formation of a solid solution, and polymorphism in the main component. In the rare instance where the ratio of the impurity to the main component is the same as the ratio of their respective solubilities in the solvent system employed, the results may lead to erroneous interpretation.

3.3.1.2 *Differential scanning calorimetry.* Purity estimation by differential scanning calorimetry is based on the determination of the heat of fusion of the sample and the determination of the change in its melting point caused by the impurities present in it. This analytical method can be performed rapidly and is capable of high precision. It is, however, inapplicable if the substance melts with decomposition and this limits its value as a general procedure for purity estimation of reference substances. Like phase solubility analysis, it is also inapplicable where solid solutions are formed.

3.3.2 Methods based on comparison with external standards and other methods

3.3.2.1 *Chromatographic methods.* Methods of analysis based on chromatographic separation are especially useful for detecting and determining impurities in reference substances. Thin-layer chromatography and gas-liquid chromatography are often used, and high-pressure liquid chromatography is finding increasing application. The individual components separated by chromatographic methods may sometimes be recovered for characterization.

Thin-layer chromatography employs apparatus that is simple and cheap, it is easy to carry out and is readily applicable even in the microgram range. It is frequently capable of separating closely related compounds, such as geometric isomers and the members of a homologous series. All the constituents of the chromatographed reference substance occur somewhere on the chromatogram. However, some constituents may remain on the starting line of the chromatogram, some may move with the solvent front, some may migrate at the same rate as the main component, and some may remain undetected. The usefulness of the method may be greatly enhanced by means of two-dimensional chromatography and by employing a number of different solvent systems and a variety of methods of detection. It is probably the most widely used method for assessing chemical reference substances. The method is, however, rarely applicable on a quantitative basis but has great value in tests devised to limit the concentration of the amounts of impurities. Variations that may be encountered in material used as stationary phases, particularly when they are obtained from different suppliers, may sometimes cause marked differences in the migration of substances in the thin-layer chromatogram.

The resolving power of gas-liquid chromatography and of high-pressure liquid chromatography usually exceeds that of thin-layer chromatography. Both the first two methods also have the advantage of being readily applicable on a quantitative basis, but require more complex equipment. The use of high-pressure liquid chromatography, employing a spectrophotometric method of detection, is of especial value in the examination of reference substances destined to be used in connexion with ultraviolet spectrophotometric assays. Gas-liquid chromatographic methods, on the other hand, are of particular value in detecting and determining volatile impurities, including solvent residues in reference substances.

3.3.2.2 *Spectrophotometric methods.* Ultraviolet spectrophotometry is a widely used method for determination of purity. Since it depends upon the presence of a characteristic chromophore, it is capable of detecting impurities that contribute excessively to the absorbance value and may indicate the presence of impurities that have negligible absorbance. However, the utility of the method is limited by the small number of absorption maxima in the ultraviolet range, the large numbers of compounds containing similar characteristic chromophores, and the need for reliance on an external reference standard.

As previously noted, infrared spectrophotometry is of less value for detecting impurities. However, it is sometimes useful, for example in determining the proportion of the geometric isomers. Nuclear magnetic resonance spectroscopy is also useful occasionally for the determination of purity.

3.3.2.3 *Titrimetric methods.* Titrimetric methods provide a valuable means of confirming the identity and purity of a candidate reference substance and have the distinct advantage that they are usually stoichiometric in nature and that the external standard used may be chosen with regard to its suitability as a primary reference material.

3.3.2.4 *Optical rotation methods.* Many reference substances are optically active and the relative proportion of optical isomers is usually determined by an optical rotation method. The quantitative use of these techniques is well established and can yield results of high precision, depending on the solvent and the wavelength chosen for measurement.

3.3.2.5 *Other methods.* Other methods, such as gravimetric analysis, electrophoresis, atomic absorption spectroscopy, polarography, and combustion procedures, may be valuable in the determination of purity. Several of the foregoing methods, as well as other techniques, may be used to determine functional groups or elements. The concentration of impurity in the reference substance may then be calculated, using an assumed atomic or molecular weight for the impurity.

3.3.3 General considerations

Whatever methods are used to evaluate chemical reference substances, it is essential that an accurate assessment of the moisture content and the content of other volatile contaminants be made. This may often be achieved in total terms by drying, under defined conditions that are appropriate to the substance being examined. In certain cases, however, this may not be possible, in which case the water content may be determined by Karl Fischer titration and the content of volatile solvents by gas-liquid chromatography. Without an accurate assessment of these values at the time that other determinations are being made, judgements as to the acceptability of the candidate material will be invalid.

4. Handling and distribution of reference substances

The measures employed in handling, distributing, and using established chemical reference substances must provide for assurance that their integrity will be safeguarded and maintained throughout their period of use.

4.1 Packing and storage

Containers for reference substances should afford protection from moisture, light, and oxygen. From the point of view of the stability of the substances, sealed glass ampoules are the best containers, but they suffer from certain disadvantages, notably the risk of contaminating the substance with glass particles when the ampoules are opened and the difficulty of re-closure. Sealed ampoules are therefore principally used for materials that must be kept in an oxygen-free atmosphere. Certain materials may require even more elaborate protection. Most chemical reference substances, however, are conveniently supplied in re-closable containers, which should be uniform in type and size to facilitate distribution. It is emphasized that the permeability of containers to moisture is an important factor in determining their suitability as containers for reference substances.

The packing of a batch of a reference substance into containers is a small-scale operation for which suitable equipment is not always available to the manufacturer of the substance. Therefore the packing of reference substances is usually undertaken by the authorities responsible for them.

Vibration spatulas and similar devices are available for dispensing substances on a small scale, but these should be used with caution because of the risk of segregation of particles of different size during the filling operation, which may lead to inhomogeneity. Screw-type feeders have also been constructed, but as yet are not commercially available, and so far the packing of reference substances has been done manually.

Several pharmaceutical reference substances have to be packed under nitrogen or in conditions of controlled humidity. The use of a glove-box is of great value in this connexion.

The various stages in packing reference substances should be controlled to avoid contamination of the sample, mislabelling of containers, and other factors that might result in an unsatisfactory reference substance.

Information about suitable storage conditions for reference substances can often be obtained from the manufacturer and should be requested routinely when a new reference substance is established. Theoretically the stability of the substances should be enhanced by keeping them at low temperatures but, for substances that contain water, storage below 0 °C may impair the stability. It should also be remembered that the relative humidity in normal refrigerators or cold-rooms may be high and, unless ampoules or other tightly closed containers are used, the intended improvement in stability by storage in such places may be more than offset by degradation due to the absorption of moisture. Storage at about +5 °C with precautions to prevent such absorption has proved satisfactory for most chemical reference substances.

4.2 Stability and periodic re-evaluation

It should be recognized that a reference substance is an integral part of the drug specification. Thus, if the reference substance deteriorates, this also implies a change in the specification of the drug. It is therefore of the utmost importance that the stability of reference substances should be monitored by regular re-examination and that replacement should be made as soon as a significant change in a property is noted.

The definition of what is a "significant change" differs, however, with the intended use of the reference substance. Degradation products in a substance amounting to several per cent may not impair the usefulness of the material in an infrared identification test. For reference substances that are used in chromatographic tests or in assays, however, even small amounts of impurities may be quite unacceptable. In the establishment of standards for reference substances, consideration must be given to the intended use of the substance and to the performance characteristics of the analytical methods for which it is to be used. It must be recognized, however, that the tolerable degree of degradation will be different from case to case.

Laboratories in charge of collections of reference standards should have a system for regular re-examination of the materials in stock. When sufficient experience has been gained, the frequency of retesting may be modified. In this context, however, it is appropriate to bear in mind that the stability of a specially prepared reference substance may not always parallel that of commercial samples of the same material.

The selection of suitable analytical methods for monitoring the stability of reference substances depends on the nature of the substance. Thin-layer chromatography is used extensively and often simple tests, such as determination of water or pH, are useful for recognizing the onset of degradation.

When quantitative estimation of the degree of degradation is needed, more complicated techniques, such as phase solubility analysis, differential scanning calorimetry, or chromatography coupled with quantitative determination of the separated components, must be used.

Change in the moisture content of reference substances is a phenomenon that is difficult to control. To establish suitable conditions for packing operations and storage that might minimize such changes, it is recommended that, for each substance, data be obtained relating to moisture content and relative humidity.

4.3 Information to be supplied with reference substances

Some centres for reference materials supply extensive documentation with the reference substances, and include directions for use. Other centres supply no information except the name of the substance and of the issuing authority. Such differing practices may result in improper use of the reference substances. It is desirable that recommendations should be made concerning the information to be supplied with reference substances and its manner of expression.

Labels on chemical reference substances should give the following information:

(a) name of the substance;
(b) type of reference substance (e.g. International Chemical Reference Substance, or National Chemical Reference Substance, or Authentic Specimen);

(c) name and address of the issuing authority;
(d) approximate quantity of material in the container; and
(e) batch or control number.

The following information should be given, as necessary, either on the labels or in associated documents:

(i) recommended storage conditions (if special conditions apply, these should be given on the label);
(ii) intended use of the reference substances;
(iii) directions for use (e.g. instructions about drying the material before use and any necessary cautionary statements);
(iv) information about the composition of the reference substance, which is needed for calculation of the results of tests in which the substance will be used; and
(v) a disclaimer of responsibility when reference substances are misused, or stored under inappropriate conditions, or used for other purposes than those intended by the issuing authority.

It is recommended that the analytical data given in the certificates supplied with the reference substances should be restricted to what is necessary for the proper use of the substances in the tests and assays for which they are provided. The full analytical reports, should, however, be available when needed for evaluation of the suitability of the reference substances for uses other than those originally intended. It might also be desirable to give more general information about the reference substances concerned, either on separate leaflets or incorporated in the certificates.

4.4 Expiry of reference substances

The question of whether expiry dates should be assigned to reference substances is of great importance both to the users and to the distributors of the substances. The arguments against expiry dating are that it might lead to the unnecessary discarding of satisfactory materials and that considerable experimental work would first have to be carried out to make the setting of meaningful expiry dates possible.

If it is considered necessary to specify an expiry date in a particular case, the date should be stated on the label. At present, most reference substances are replaced by new batches only when this has been shown to be necessary by re-evaluation. This procedure minimizes unnecessary waste of valuable materials, but in order to make it completely satisfactory it would be necessary to devise effective means of informing analysts in possession of reference substances about any replacement of batches.

4.5 Distribution problems

Distribution of reference substances within a country usually presents no problems. However, when samples are to be sent to other countries, both the sender and the receiver of the goods may encounter difficulties because of the vagaries of postal and customs regulations. At present, distributors of reference substances are wasting a considerable portion of their resources in seeking information concerning the different import regulations in various countries and in filling in the required forms. Means should be sought to reduce such difficulties and barriers to the effective distribution of reference substances.

5. Reference materials calibrated against International Chemical Reference Substances

The establishment of reference materials that have been correlated with the International Chemical Reference Substances may be desirable for various practical reasons, e.g. the latter may not be available in adequate quantities to supply all local needs. Moreover, the availability of such reference materials (for example, on a regional basis) should result in a reduction of the time between ordering and receiving the materials.

The authority to establish a reference substance for national or regional use should be clearly defined by the appropriate drug regulatory body. If an International Chemical Reference Substance exists, it is desirable that all corresponding reference substances should be correlated with it in order to obviate the proliferation of possibly dissimilar reference substances. The first step in establishing such a derived material would be to form an estimate of the amount that might be needed for a period of perhaps three to five years (the duration of storage would depend on the known stability characteristics of the material in question), to define the intended use of the substance, and to determine the extent and nature of testing that is required to evaluate it.

Once the material has been obtained, its identity should first be verified (for example, by infrared spectrophotometry in comparison with the International Chemical Reference Substance) and it should be examined by an appropriate stability-indicating procedure so as to provide a starting point for routine stability monitoring. If the material is to be used as a quantitative assay standard, it and the International Chemical Reference Substance should be subjected to a collaborative test following a strictly defined protocol with the participation of at least three laboratories. From the results so obtained, a value for the content of the assayed component should be assigned. Additionally, the substance should be shown to comply with all the requirements of its specification and it should be confirmed that it is suitable for its intended use.

Once established, the material should be packed in an appropriate way (as nearly as possible in the same way as the corresponding International Chemical Reference Substance) and it should be regularly monitored, in comparison with the primary reference material, to confirm that unacceptable deterioration is not occurring.

6. Means of promoting effective exchange of information and ensuring cooperation between organizations establishing reference substances

During the past few years, there has been an increasing exchange of information between laboratories concerned with the evaluation of reference substances. Cooperation that began on a personal and *ad hoc* basis is now, in some cases, being put on a more formal footing. There is a need, however, for circulating timely notifications of the work to be undertaken. In every instance, this should be done well before making any approach to a pharmaceutical manufacturer for the supply of material. In this way, it would be possible for a manufacturer to set aside a portion of a particular batch, so that sufficient of the proposed reference material would be available for all expected needs. The advantages of this procedure would be: first, that the studies carried out might be shared by collaborating laboratories; secondly, that the same reference material would be used by each issuing authority; thirdly, that if supplies of that material at one laboratory were depleted, appropriate arrangements might be made to share the remaining material from the other laboratories. Finally, there would be considerable benefit to industry since requests for the supply of reference materials would be coordinated and would be reduced in frequency.

In such a cooperative effort, it might also be possible for the manufacturer to pack the reference substance into appropriate standardized containers so that any variation due to storage and transport would be minimized.

From time to time, each laboratory will need to replace a certain number of reference substances. It would be advantageous for each laboratory to review its needs well in advance so as to permit a concerted request to be made to a manufacturer, thus achieving the benefits mentioned above.

General recommendations for the preparation and use of infrared spectra in pharmaceutical analysis[1]

1. Introduction

In pharmaceutical analysis the region of the electromagnetic spectrum used is 4000–600 cm^{-1} (wavelength 2.5–16.7 µm), i.e. the mid-infrared. Spectrophotometric measurements in this region are mainly used for identification purposes. Except for enantiomers, which have identical spectra in solution, the infrared spectrum of any given substance is unique. Polymorphism and other factors,

---

[1] *WHO Expert Committee on Specifications for Pharmaceutical Preparations. Thirty-fourth Report.* Geneva, World Health Organization, 1996 (WHO Technical Report Series, No. 863).

such as variations in crystal size and orientation, the grinding procedure, and the possible formation of hydrates may, however, be responsible for minor, and occasionally substantial, variations in the infrared spectrum of a substance in the solid state. The infrared spectrum is not usually greatly affected by the presence of small quantities of impurities in the substance tested. For identification purposes, the spectrum may be compared with that of a reference substance, concomitantly prepared, or with a reference spectrum.

The terms *absorbance, transmittance, absorptivity* and *absorption spectrum* are defined in *The international pharmacopoeia*. 3rd ed., Vol. 1, pp. 33–34, in the chapter "Spectrophotometry in the visible and ultraviolet regions".

2. Apparatus

Conventional infrared spectrometers disperse the infrared radiation by means of either gratings or prisms. The development of computerized laboratory equipment provides the additional option of using an interferometer coupled to a computer for the reduction of the data, by performing a Fourier transformation of the interferogram, to generate an infrared spectrum. These instruments are called Fourier transform infrared spectrometers (FTIRs). Apart from small differences in the low-frequency cut-off, all of the above types of infrared instruments generate comparable data and can generally be used interchangeably for qualitative analyses. However, each instrument will possess specific signal-to-noise and resolution characteristics.

Spectrophotometers suitable for use for identification tests should normally operate in the range 4000–600 cm^{-1} (2.5–16.7 µm) or in some cases up to 250 cm^{-1} (40 µm). If the attenuated total reflectance technique is to be used, the instrument must be equipped with a suitable attachment consisting of a single or multireflecting element. The attachment and a suitable mounting should permit its alignment in the spectrophotometer for maximum transmission.

3. Method of verification of frequency scale and resolution

The spectrum of a polystyrene film of suitable thickness, normally between 0.03 mm and 0.05 mm, is recorded. This includes maxima at the following frequencies, expressed as wavenumbers in cm^{-1}: 3027, 2851, 2924, 1944, 1871, 1802, 1601, 1583, 1181, 1154, 1069, 1028, 907, 699. Acceptable tolerances are ± 8 cm^{-1} for the range 4000–2000 cm^{-1} and ± 4 cm^{-1} for the range 2000–600 cm^{-1}.

The difference between the percentage transmittance of the absorption minimum at 2870 cm^{-1} and that of the absorption maximum at 2851 cm^{-1} should be greater than 18 and the difference between the percentage transmittance of the absorption minimum at 1589 cm^{-1} and that of the absorption maximum at 1583 cm^{-1} should be greater than 12.

4. Environment

Precautions should be taken to minimize exposure to atmospheric moisture during sample preparation. It is advisable to store the halide salts, the sodium chloride or other similar plates, and all necessary accessories in a desiccator at room temperature over silica gel, and to prepare the samples in an area of controlled temperature and humidity; alternatively, all manipulations should be carried out under an infrared lamp.

5. Use of solvents

The solvent used in infrared spectrophotometry must not affect the cell, which usually consists of a halide salt such as sodium chloride or potassium bromide. Where possible, spectral grade solvents should be used.

No solvent is completely transparent throughout the entire infrared spectrum. Carbon tetrachloride R[1] is practically transparent (up to 1 mm of thickness) over the range 4000–1700 cm^{-1} (2.5–5.9 µm). Dichloromethane R and dibromomethane R are useful solvents. Carbon disulfide IR[2] (up to 1 mm in thickness) is suitable as a solvent up to 250 cm^{-1} (40 µm) except in the 2400–2000 cm^{-1} (4.2–5 µm) and the 1800–1300 cm^{-1} (5.6–7.7 µm) regions, where it has strong absorption. Its weak absorption in the 875–845 cm^{-1} (11.4–11.8 µm) region should be noted. Other solvents have relatively narrow regions of transparency.

6. Preparation of the substance to be examined

To obtain a suitable infrared absorption spectrum, it is necessary to follow the instructions given below for the preparation of the substance. Substances in liquid form may be tested directly or in a suitable solution. The usual methods of preparation for solid substances include dispersing the finely ground solid specimen in mineral oil, incorporating it in a transparent disc or pellet obtained by mixing it thoroughly with previously dried potassium halide and compressing the mixture in a die, or preparing a solution in a suitable solvent. Preparation of the substance for the attenuated total reflectance technique is described separately.

6.1 Method 1

The solid substance should be triturated with dry, finely powdered potassium halide (normally potassium bromide). When hydrochlorides are being examined, potassium chloride should be employed to avoid the risk of halide exchange.

---

[1] R: of reagent-grade quality.
[2] IR: of suitable purity for use in spectrophotometry in the infrared region.

The ratio of substance to halide salt should be about 1 to 200–300, e.g. 1.5 mg in 300 mg of the halide salt in the case of prism instruments, or about 1.0 mg in 300 mg of the halide salt for grating or Fourier transform instruments. The mixture should be carefully ground by means of an agate mortar and pestle for 1 minute. In exceptional cases, the use of a ball mill may be indicated, but the resulting risk of producing polymorphic changes generally outweighs any improvement in resolution. The triturate should then be uniformly spread in a suitable die and compressed, under vacuum, at a pressure of about 800 MPa. As an alternative, potassium halide discs can be prepared by means of a hand-held minipress. The disc thus produced is mounted in a suitable holder.

Several factors, e.g. inadequate or excessive grinding or moisture or other impurities in the halide carrier, may give rise to unsatisfactory discs. Unless its preparation presents particular difficulties, a disc should be rejected if visual inspection shows lack of uniformity or if the transmittance at about 2000 cm^{-1} (5 µm), in the absence of a specific absorption band, is less than 75% without compensation.

The quality of a spectrum is often improved by placing a blank disc of the appropriate potassium halide, of similar thickness to that of the sample disc, in the reference beam.

6.2 Method 2

A small quantity of the finely ground substance should be triturated with the minimum amount of a suitable mineral oil (e.g. Nujol) or other suitable liquid to give a smooth creamy paste; 10 mg of the substance to be examined combined with 1–2 drops of mineral oil is often sufficient to prepare a satisfactory mull. The prepared mull should appear opaque.

A portion of the mull is then compressed between two flat sodium chloride or other suitable halide-salt plates.

If the spectrum of the mineral oil used interferes with regions of interest, an additional dispersion of the substance in a medium such as a suitable fluorinated hydrocarbon oil or hexachlorobutadiene R is prepared, and the spectrum recorded in those regions where the mineral oil shows strong absorption.

6.3 Method 3

A capillary film of the liquid held between two sodium chloride plates or a filled cell of suitable thickness is used.

6.4 Method 4

A solution in a suitable solvent is prepared and a concentration and cell thickness are chosen to give a satisfactory spectrum over a sufficiently wide wave number range. Generally, good spectra are obtained with concentrations of 1–10% w/v for a cell thickness of 0.1–0.5 mm. To compensate for the absorption of the solvent, a cell of matched path-length containing the solvent used is placed in the reference beam or a spectrum of the solvent is obtained so as to permit differentiation between solvent and sample absorptions. Alternatively, the solvent absorbance spectrum versus air may be subtracted from the solution spectrum versus air to obtain the absorbance spectrum of the solute. (When an FTIR instrument is used, the spectrum of the solvent recorded under identical conditions can be subtracted digitally.)

6.5 Method 5

Gases are examined in a cell with windows transparent to infrared radiation and having an optical path-length of about 100 mm. The cell is evacuated and filled to the desired pressure through a stopcock or needle valve by means of a suitable gas-transfer line between the cell and the container of the substance to be examined. If necessary, the pressure in the cell is adjusted to atmospheric pressure with a gas transparent to infrared radiation (e.g. nitrogen R or argon R). To avoid absorption interferences due to water, carbon dioxide or other atmospheric gases, an identical cell that is either evacuated or filled with the gas transparent to infrared radiation is placed in the reference beam.

7. Identification by reference substance

Both the substance to be examined and the reference substance are prepared by means of the same method and the spectrum of each from about 4000 to 600 cm^{-1} (2.5–16.7 μm) is recorded. The concentration of the substance should be such that the strongest peak attributable to it corresponds to a transmittance of about 10%.

If the positions and relative intensities of the absorbance maxima in the spectrum of the substance to be examined are not concordant with those of the spectrum of the reference substance when spectra are obtained by methods 1 or 2, this may be the consequence of differences in crystalline form. To avoid this difficulty, one of the procedures described below may be used for both the substance to be examined and the reference substance:

- Solutions of the reference substance and of the sample, of a suitable concentration, are prepared as described in method 4.
- A small amount (2 or 3 drops) of a concentrated solution in a volatile organic solvent is placed on a blank disc of potassium halide and evaporated to dryness in an oven at 105 °C.
- A small amount (2 or 3 drops) of concentrated solution in a volatile organic solvent is mixed with 300 mg of potassium halide and evaporated to dryness in an oven at 105 °C. Both the reference substance and the substance to be

examined are treated in the same manner and then prepared as described in method 1.
- Both the reference substance and the substance to be examined are recrystallized from a suitable solvent.

8. Identification by reference spectrum

The substance to be examined is prepared exactly as described in the note accompanying the International Infrared Reference Spectrum and the spectrum from about 4000 to 600 cm^{-1} (2.5–16.7 µm) recorded by means of an instrument that is checked frequently to ensure that it meets the standards of performance required. The reference maxima of a polystyrene film should be superimposed on the spectrum of the substance to be examined at about 2851 cm^{-1} (3.5 µm), 1601 cm^{-1} (6.25 µm) and 1028 cm^{-1} (9.73 µm). Other suitable polystyrene bands can be superimposed if interference occurs with the bands of the substance. If these polystyrene maxima are taken into account, the identification is considered to be positive if the principal absorbance maxima in the spectrum of the substance to be examined are concordant with the corresponding maxima in the relevant International Infrared Reference Spectrum. When the two spectra are compared, care should be taken to allow for the possibility of differences in resolving power between the instrument on which the International Infrared Reference Spectrum was prepared and that being used to examine the substance. An International Infrared Reference Spectrum of polystyrene recorded on the same instrument as the collection of the reference spectra should be used for assessing these differences. The greatest variation due to differences in resolving power is likely to occur in the region between 4000 and 2000 cm^{-1} (2.5 and 5 µm). However, if the positions and relative intensities of the absorbance maxima in the spectrum of the substance to be examined are not concordant with those of the reference spectrum when methods 1 or 2 are used, this may be due to differences in crystalline form. Another procedure as described in section 7, will then be indicated in the note accompanying the reference spectrum.

9. Reflectance techniques

9.1 Attenuated total reflectance technique

The attenuated total reflectance (ATR) technique is best adapted to smooth, flexible surfaces, such as various plastics, or to strongly absorbing liquids and solutions, but can also be employed to determine the infrared absorption spectra of solid substances. It is usually necessary to reduce the solid substance to a fine powder, which is then packed directly against the reflecting element of the attachment. Alternatively, an adhesive tape can be used to facilitate the contact, the powdered substance being spread on the adhesive side of the tape to form an almost translucent layer, after which the powdered side of the tape is pressed on to the reflecting element. The backing plate is then attached, or moderate pressure applied by means of a suitable clamp for 1–2 minutes. Finally, the reflecting element is placed in the holder. The tape used in the procedure should preferably contain a natural rubber adhesive. Some plastic materials may be placed directly on to the reflecting element.

Reflective elements are usually made of zinc selenide (refractive index = 2.3) or germanium (refractive index = 4.0). The correct alignment of the attachment in the apparatus should be carefully checked.

9.2 Diffuse reflectance

In this technique, the surface of a sample reflects light in many different directions. The solid substance is reduced to a fine powder with a non-absorbing matrix (potassium bromide or chloride is suitable for this purpose). The mixture is placed directly in the sample cup holder of the diffuse reflectance instrument. The spectrum of the matrix recorded under identical conditions should be subtracted digitally. Some plastic materials can be placed directly in the sample cup holder of the diffuse reflectance accessory.

List of available International Chemical Reference Substances[1]

International Chemical Reference Substances are established on the advice of the WHO Expert Committee on Specifications for Pharmaceutical Preparations. They are supplied primarily for use in physical and chemical tests and assays described in the specifications for quality control of drugs published in *The international pharmacopoeia* or proposed in draft monographs.

Directions for use and the analytical data required for the tests specified in *The international pharmacopoeia* are given in the certificates enclosed with the substances when distributed. More detailed analytical reports on the substances may be obtained on request from the WHO Collaborating Centre for Chemical Reference Substances.

International Chemical Reference Substances may also be used in tests and assays not described in *The international pharmacopoeia*. However, the responsibility for assessing the suitability of the substances then rests with the user or with the pharmacopoeia commission or other authority that has prescribed their use.

It is generally recommended that the substances be stored protected from light and moisture and preferably at a temperature of about +5 °C. When special storage conditions are required, this is stated on the label or in the accompanying leaflet.

---

[1] *WHO Expert Committee on Specifications for Pharmaceutical Preparations. Thirty-fourth Report.* Geneva, World Health Organization, 1996 (WHO Technical Report Series, No. 863).

The stability of the International Chemical Reference Substances kept at the Collaborating Centre is monitored by regular re-examination, and materials that have deteriorated are replaced by new batches when necessary. Lists giving control numbers for the current batches are issued in the annual reports from the Centre and may be obtained on request.

Orders for International Chemical Reference Substances should be sent to:

WHO Collaborating Centre for Chemical Reference Substances
Apoteksbolaget AB
Centrallaboratoriet
S–105 14 Stockholm
Sweden

Telex: 115 53 APOBOL S
Fax: 46 8 740 60 40

International Chemical Reference Substances are supplied only in the standard packages indicated in the following list.

Reference substance	*Package size*
aceclidine salicylate	100 mg
p-acetamidobenzalazine	100 mg
acetazolamide	100 mg
allopurinol	100 mg
2-amino-5-nitrothiazole	25 mg
3-aminopyrazole-4-carboxamide hemisulfate	100 mg
amitriptyline hydrochloride	100 mg
amodiaquine hydrochloride	200 mg
amphotericin B	400 mg
ampicillin (anhydrous)	200 mg
ampicillin sodium	200 mg
ampicillin trihydrate	200 mg
anhydrotetracycline hydrochloride	25 mg
atropine sulfate	100 mg
azathioprine	100 mg
bacitracin zinc	200 mg
beclometasone dipropionate	200 mg
bendazol hydrochloride	100 mg
benzobarbital	100 mg
benzylamine sulfate	100 mg
benzylpenicillin potassium	200 mg
benzylpenicillin sodium	200 mg

Reference substance	*Package size*
bephenium hydroxynaphthoate	100 mg
betamethasone	100 mg
betamethasone valerate	100 mg
betanidine sulfate	100 mg
bupivacaine hydrochloride	100 mg
caffeine	100 mg
carbamazepine	100 mg
carbenicillin monosodium	200 mg
chloramphenicol	200 mg
chloramphenicol palmitate	1 g
chloramphenicol palmitate (polymorph A)	200 mg
5-chloro-2-methylaminobenzophenone	100 mg
2-(4-chloro-3-sulfamoylbenzoyl)benzoic acid	50 mg
chlorphenamine hydrogen maleate	100 mg
chlorpromazine hydrochloride	100 mg
chlortalidone	100 mg
chlortetracycline hydrochloride	200 mg
cimetidine	100 mg
clomifene citrate	100 mg
clomifene citrate Z-isomer (*see* zuclomifene)	
cloxacillin sodium	200 mg
colecalciferol (vitamin D_3)	500 mg
cortisone acetate	100 mg
dapsone	100 mg
desoxycortone acetate	100 mg
dexamethasone	100 mg
dexamethasone acetate	100 mg
dexamethasone phosphoric acid	100 mg
dexamethasone sodium phosphate	100 mg
diazepam	100 mg
diazoxide	100 mg
dicloxacillin sodium	200 mg
dicolinium iodide	100 mg
dicoumarol	100 mg
diethylcarbamazine dihydrogen citrate	100 mg
digitoxin	100 mg
digoxin	100 mg
N,N'-di-(2,3-xylyl)anthranilamide	50 mg
dopamine hydrochloride	100 mg

Reference substance	Package size
emetine hydrochloride	100 mg
4-epianhydrotetracycline hydrochloride	25 mg
4-epitetracycline hydrochloride	25 mg
ergocalciferol (vitamin D_2)	500 mg
ergometrine hydrogen maleate	50 mg
ergotamine tartrate	50 mg
erythromycin	250 mg
estradiol benzoate	100 mg
estrone	100 mg
etacrynic acid	100 mg
ethambutol hydrochloride	100 mg
ethinylestradiol	100 mg
ethisterone	100 mg
ethosuximide	100 mg
etocarlide	100 mg
flucytosine	100 mg
fluorouracil	100 mg
fluphenazine decanoate dihydrochloride	100 mg
fluphenazine enantate dihydrochloride	100 mg
fluphenazine hydrochloride	100 mg
folic acid	100 mg
3-formylrifamycin	200 mg
framycetin sulfate (neomycin B sulfate)	200 mg
furosemide	100 mg
griseofulvin	200 mg
haloperidol	100 mg
hydrochlorothiazide	100 mg
hydrocortisone	100 mg
hydrocortisone acetate	100 mg
(−)-3-(4-hydroxy-3-methoxyphenyl)-2-hydrazino-2-methylalanine (3-O-methylcarbidopa)	25 mg
(−)-3-(4-hydroxy-3-methoxyphenyl)-2-methylalanine	25 mg
ibuprofen	100 mg
imipramine hydrochloride	100 mg
indometacin	100 mg
o-iodohippuric acid	100 mg
isoniazid	100 mg

Reference substance	Package size
lanatoside C	100 mg
levodopa	100 mg
levothyroxine sodium	100 mg
lidocaine	100 mg
lidocaine hydrochloride	100 mg
liothyronine sodium	50 mg
mefenamic acid	100 mg
melting point reference substances	
azobenzene (69 °C)	4 g
vanillin (83 °C)	4 g
benzil (96 °C)	4 g
acetanilide (116 °C)	4 g
phenacetin (136 °C)	4 g
benzanilide (165 °C)	4 g
sulfanilamide (166 °C)	4 g
sulfapyridine (193 °C)	4 g
dicyanodiamide (210 °C)	4 g
saccharin (229 °C)	4 g
caffeine (237 °C)	4 g
phenolphthalein (263 °C)	4 g
metazide	100 mg
methaqualone	100 mg
methyldopa	100 mg
methyltestosterone	100 mg
meticillin sodium	200 mg
metronidazole	100 mg
nafcillin sodium	200 mg
neamine hydrochloride (neomycin A hydrochloride)	0.5 mg
neostigmine metilsulfate	100 mg
nicotinamide	100 mg
nicotinic acid	100 mg
niridazole	200 mg
niridazole-chlorethylcarboxamide	25 mg
norethisterone	100 mg
norethisterone acetate	100 mg
nystatin	200 mg
ouabain	100 mg
oxacillin sodium	200 mg
oxytetracycline dihydrate	200 mg

Reference substance	Package size
oxytetracycline hydrochloride	200 mg
papaverine hydrochloride	100 mg
pheneticillin potassium	200 mg
phenoxymethylpenicillin	200 mg
phenoxymethylpenicillin calcium	200 mg
phenoxymethylpenicillin potassium	200 mg
phenytoin	100 mg
prednisolone	100 mg
prednisolone acetate	100 mg
prednisone	100 mg
prednisone acetate	100 mg
probenecid	100 mg
procaine hydrochloride	100 mg
procarbazine hydrochloride	100 mg
progesterone	100 mg
propicillin potassium	200 mg
propranolol hydrochloride	100 mg
propylthiouracil	100 mg
pyrantel embonate	500 mg
pyridostigmine bromide	100 mg
reserpine	100 mg
retinol acetate (solution)	5 capsules[1]
riboflavin	250 mg
rifampicin	200 mg
rifampicin quinone	200 mg
sodium cromoglicate	100 mg
spectinomycin hydrochloride	200 mg
sulfamethoxazole	100 mg
sulfamethoxypyridazine	100 mg
sulfanilamide	100 mg
sulfasalazine	100 mg
testosterone propionate	100 mg
tetracycline hydrochloride	200 mg
thioacetazone	100 mg
4,4'-thiodianiline	50 mg
L-thyroxine sodium *see* levothyroxine sodium	

[1] Each containing about 9 mg in 250 mg of oil.

Reference substance	Package size
tolbutamide	100 mg
tolnaftate	100 mg
trimethadione	200 mg
trimethoprim	100 mg
trimethylguanidine sulfate	100 mg
tubocurarine chloride	100 mg
vitamin A acetate (solution) *see* retinol acetate (solution)	
vincristine sulfate	9.7 mg/vial
warfarin	100 mg
zuclomifene	50 mg

List of available International Infrared Reference Spectra[1]

International Infrared Reference Spectra are established on the advice of the WHO Expert Committee on Specifications for Pharmaceutical Preparations. Full-scale reproductions of spectra produced from authenticated material on a suitable instrument are supplied for use in identification tests described in the specifications for quality control of drugs published in *The international pharmacopoeia* or proposed in draft monographs.

Precise instructions for the preparation of spectra are given on the label of each reference spectrum. All International Infrared Reference Spectra are distributed together with a document giving further details on the use of such spectra, entitled "General recommendations for the preparation and use of infrared spectra in pharmaceutical analysis".

Orders for International Infrared Reference Spectra should be sent to:

WHO Collaborating Centre for Chemical Reference Substances
Apoteksbolaget AB
Centrallaboratoriet
S–105 14 Stockholm
Sweden

Telex: 115 53 APOBOL S
Fax: 46 8 740 60 40

---

[1] *WHO Expert Committee on Specifications for Pharmaceutical Preparations. Thirty-fourth Report.* Geneva, World Health Organization, 1996 (WHO Technical Report Series, No. 863).

The following International Infrared Reference Spectra are currently available from the Centre:[1]

aceclidine salicylate
acetazolamide
allopurinol
amitriptyline hydrochloride
ampicillin trihydrate

benzylpenicillin potassium
biperiden
biperiden hydrochloride
bupivacaine hydrochloride

caffeine (anhydrous)
chlorphenamine hydrogen maleate
clofazimine
cloxacillin sodium
colchicine
cytarabine

dextromethorphan hydrobromide
diazepam
dicolinium iodide
dicoumarol
diethylcarbamazine dihydrogen citrate
diphenoxylate hydrochloride

erythromycin ethylsuccinate
erythromycin stearate
etacrynic acid
ethionamide
ethosuximide

furosemide

gallamine triethiodide
glibenclamide

haloperidol
hydrochlorothiazide

ibuprofen
imipramine hydrochloride
indometacin
isoniazid

lidocaine
lidocaine hydrochloride
lindane

metronidazole
miconazole nitrate

niclosamide
nicotinamide

noscapine

oxamniquine

papaverine hydrochloride
phenobarbital
phenoxymethylpenicillin calcium
phenytoin
primaquine phosphate
propylthiouracil
protionamide
pyrimethamine

salbutamol
salbutamol sulfate
sulfadimidine
sulfadoxine
sulfamethoxazole
sulfamethoxypyridazine

tiabendazole
trihexyphenidyl hydrochloride
trimethoprim

verapamil hydrochloride

---

[1] Spectra for several other substances are still being validated and are not yet available for distribution.

5.
Basic tests

Collaboration within the basic test programme[1]

Introduction

In its twenty-eighth report, the WHO Expert Committee on Specifications for Pharmaceutical Preparations agreed that the prime objectives of basic (or simplified) tests for pharmaceutical products, which was the subject of preliminary discussions in the Committee's twenty-sixth and twenty-seventh reports, should be as follows:

"(a) to provide simple and readily applicable methods for verifying the identity of active ingredients using a limited range of readily available reagents;

(b) to provide a practicable means for confirming the identity of a drug, where fully equipped laboratories are not available;

(c) to provide a means for rapid verification of the identity in cases where each container of a large consignment has to be identified (full quality assessment of such a consignment is usually carried out only on a mixed sample from various containers); and

(d) to indicate if gross degradation has occurred in certain substances that are known to decompose readily under adverse conditions."

It was noted that basic tests are not, in any circumstances, intended to replace the requirements of pharmacopoeial monographs. The latter give an assurance of quality whereas basic tests *merely confirm* the identity.

The test procedures for pharmaceutical substances elaborated so far are contained in the unpublished document WHO/PHARM/81.506/Rev. 1.[2] The procedures for the *confirmation of the identity* consist of one or more test-tube identification reactions based upon colour, precipitate, or fluorescence, and on data regarding the physical aspects of the substance, its melting characteristics, and frequently the melting point of eutectic mixtures.

The test procedures for the *indication of gross degradation* consist of one or

---

[1] *WHO Expert Committee on Specifications for Pharmaceutical Preparations. Twenty-ninth Report.* Geneva, World Health Organization, 1984 (WHO Technical Report Series, No. 704).

[2] Since this statement was made, two volumes of test procedures have been published and a third is in preparation (see Introduction, page 9).

more simple tests based on the description of physical aspects, solubility, or test-tube reactions. These tests have been developed during the course of stability testing carried out under standardized conditions in air at temperatures of 50 °C and 70 °C and 100% humidity, with light excluded. The tests are intended to provide evidence of degradation of 10% or more.

In addition to the test-tube reactions and melting point determinations, procedures based on thin-layer chromatography have been developed.

Attached is a protocol for guidance in the development and the verification of basic tests.

Protocol for the development and verification of basic tests

1. Development of tests

(a) Tests for each drug substance and the corresponding dosage forms should, whenever possible, be developed together by the same person. Only one person should be asked to develop tests for a specific drug substance and/or dosage form. Where suitable tests are contained in *The international pharmacopoeia* these should be given priority, and the description should not be unnecessarily modified.

(b) In order to secure appropriate distribution of work, each investigator should compile a list of locally available drug substances.

(c) When a proposed test proves to be inadequate in the course of validation in other laboratories, the information will be referred back to the prime investigator who will have the responsibility of devising an alternative test. To this end, all samples used in the course of validation of the tests should be supplied to the prime investigator, where appropriate through WHO. Priority should in each case be given to tests based on test-tube reactions and melting characteristics. The test-tube reactions can involve colour reactions, flurosecence, or precipitations.

The following methods are recommended in order to introduce some homogeneity among the reactions used in basic tests:

Element or active functional group	Principle of the reaction
chloride or hydrochloride	– precipitation with $AgNO_3$ – in order to complete the characterization of the formed silver chloride it is always preferable to separate the AgCl before verifying its dissolution in ammonia (otherwise precipitation of the other bases may occur in alkaline medium)
bound chloride	– ignition with Na_2CO_3 then reaction with $AgNO_3$ after acidification

Element or active functional group	Principle of the reaction
fluoride and bound fluorine	– inhibition of wetting the inner wall of a tube containing a chromic acid/sulfuric acid mixture
sulfate	– precipitation with $BaCl_2$
bound sulfur	– fusion with NaOH or Na_2CO_3, then reaction with $BaCl_2$ after acidification with HCl
heterocyclic sulfur	– heating with Zn and HCl: formation of dihydrogen sulfide detected with lead acetate paper
sodium ion	– precipitation with magnesium uranyl acetate
potassium ion	– precipitation with sodium cobaltinitrite
saturated compounds	– absence of decolorization of bromine (obtained from $KBr + KBrO_3 + HCl$)
reducing compounds	– formation of a red precipitate in a warm solution with potassio-cupric tartrate – formation of a silver mirror in ammoniacal solution with silver nitrate
multiple bonds (double or triple)	– in alkaline medium permanganate changes to brown
glycol	– precipitation of silver iodate produced by the reaction of silver periodate
enolizable ketone	– coloration produced with nitroprusside and NaOH
phenol	– coloration produced with the diazonium salt of the sulfanilic acid in alkaline medium – colorations with a ferric salt (various colorations) are also obtained with the same reagent, such as for: formate and acetate ions, benzoate ion, acetylacetone and enolizable ketones, phenazone, camphocarboxylic acid, colchiceine, phenylpyruvic acid, hydroxyacids, amino acids – coloration produced by the reaction of a primary aromatic amine and hypochlorite
ortho diphenol	– coloration of the molybdate ion in acidic medium
aliphatic amine and amino acid	– coloration with triketohydrindene hydrate (ninhydrin) and pyridine
amino acid	– colored precipitate with cupric ion and NaOH
primary aromatic amine	– coloration with dimethylaminobenzaldehyde in acidic medium – diazocoupling by action of nitrite ion in acidic medium followed by 2-naphthol in alkaline medium – coloration produced with phenol and hypochlorite
aromatic nitro compounds	– reaction with zinc in acidic medium and identification of the amine using one of the reactions described above
ammonium salts or aliphatic amine	– reaction with NaOH, the vapours of the liberated base being detected with pH-indicator paper

BASIC TESTS

Element or active functional group	Principle of the reaction
alkaloid or nitrogenous bases with high molecular weights	– precipitate with potassio-mercuric acetate
ester	– reaction with hydroxylamine, then detection of the formed hydroxamic acid by coloration obtained by adding a ferric salt – odour of ethyl acetate on heating with sulfuric acid and ethanol
complex polyhydroxylated or polyunsaturated structures	– coloration formed with phosphoric acid – coloration formed with sulfuric acid alone, or with the addition of nitrous/nitric acid mixture, molybdate, dichromate, or formaldehyde
xanthine	– heating to dryness of the substance with HCl and hydrogen peroxide, then coloration produced with the reaction of ammonia on the residue
barbiturate	– coloration produced with a cobalt salt in ammoniacal solution

2. Verification of tests

(a) Drug substances: If a pharmacopoeial test is selected no verification is required. In other circumstances verification in one laboratory will suffice.
(b) Dosage forms: Verification must be undertaken, in each instance, in at least four different laboratories selected on a representative regional basis. Tests should be undertaken on locally available solid oral dosage forms, branded or generic, containing the substance in question.

3. Coordination

Responsibility for coordination and monitoring of the programme will reside with WHO, which will pay particular regard to reasonable distribution of work among the various collaborators.

6.
Laboratory services

National laboratories for drug quality surveillance and control[1]

1.	Introduction	154
2.	First-stage laboratory for drug surveillance	155
3.	Medium-size drug control laboratory	157
	3.1 Capability	157
	3.2 Premises	157
	3.3 Staff	158
	3.4 Equipment	158
4.	Scope of activity	160
5.	Factors influencing size and location of a laboratory	161
6.	Implementation of control laboratory projects	161
	6.1 Feasibility study	161
	6.2 Phasing of development	162
	6.3 Programme support	162

1. Introduction

The capacity of a drug regulatory authority to undertake quality surveillance is directly related to the operational capability of the associated national quality control laboratories. The results of laboratory assessment of samples of marketed drugs permit the regulatory authority to evaluate the actual quality of products used in the country and to identify the problem areas. When no independent analytical service is available to the regulatory authority, judgements on the quality of drugs must be based largely on data supplied by manufacturers or importers, which are inherently difficult to challenge.

The importance of a drug control laboratory to the implementation of surveillance as an element of quality assurance in pharmaceutical supply systems has been stressed in Annex 1 of the twenty-seventh report of the WHO Expert Committee on Specifications for Pharmaceutical Preparations.[2] Developing

---
[1] *WHO Expert Committee on Specifications for Pharmaceutical Preparations. Twenty-ninth Report.* Geneva, World Health Organization, 1984 (WHO Technical Report Series, No. 704).
[2] WHO Technical Report Series, No. 645, 1980.

countries are particularly vulnerable to the supply of substandard drugs and, where no testing facilities exist, such problems can be particularly acute. This annex therefore examines the principles that should determine the structure and management of a national drug quality control laboratory where no such facility yet exists.

National authorities have the option of establishing either a central laboratory or a number of smaller laboratories dispersed throughout the country. Even the existence of a single small laboratory, when it is concerned with priority issues and perceptively managed, can offer a deterrent against unscrupulous or negligent manufacturing and trading practices. It is also evident that standards of local manufacturers will tend to rise whenever the possibility of an independent assessment of the quality of their products exists.

The laboratory would at least have the potential to detect products, both raw materials and dosage forms, that have been mislabelled, and to detect adulterated and spurious products. Its capacity to undertake full analyses of products to check their conformity with labelled specifications would be severely limited. Clear priorities would therefore need to be set to ensure that attention is concentrated upon products that are of prime importance to public health programmes, or that are potentially dangerous, unstable, or unusually expensive.

The advice contained in the following paragraphs applies to the organization and staffing of two model laboratories, one of medium size and the other providing minimum facilities for efficient work. The latter is designated as a first-stage laboratory for drug surveillance. Although provision is made for some types of biological testing by the laboratories described here, they are not equipped for the testing of sera and vaccines. No consideration is given to larger-scale drug control laboratories, having regard to the limited resources available for such purposes in most developing countries.

Matters concerning the management and operation of drug control laboratories do not fall within the scope of these recommendations; these aspects will be the subject of a separate WHO document.

2. First-stage laboratory for drug surveillance

This small laboratory has a floor space of 60 m^2. It is staffed by one analyst, 2 technicians, and 1–2 housekeeping staff.

Such a laboratory cannot be effectively maintained as an independent unit. It should be incorporated within another governmental laboratory or be sited within a large regional hospital. This provides access to existing technical and library facilities, utilities, and supply arrangements. It is important, none the less, that the manager should remain organizationally independent in the execution of his duties, and that the laboratory should be accorded an independent budget.

It is estimated that such a laboratory could undertake annually 200–300 full analyses (samples fully tested and evaluated in accordance with quality specifications) or a greater number of partial analyses.

The analyst, who should have a proven ability to work independently, should be university trained in pharmacy or chemistry and should have received practical training in an established drug quality control laboratory for 6 months to two years, as determined by background experience. An institutional training for technicians is desirable in addition to in-service training in the laboratory.

The laboratory premises should be provided with basic utilities (water, drainage, and electricity) and equipped with a hot-water source, a distilled-water still, and a propane gas tank, if a piped gas supply is not available. If the laboratory is to be located in a newly erected building it is best constructed as a basic module that may be subsequently extended.

The laboratory furniture, which should be arranged to provide an efficient but uncongested working space, must include: one double chemical bench with two lateral sinks located in the centre of the module, a fume hood, one laboratory bench for instruments, a table for balances, one storage cabinet for solvents, one refrigerator (with freezer compartment), wall shelves, and writing desk. The bench for instruments and the table for balances are positioned in a separate part of the module to protect the instruments from corrosion.

Important items of laboratory equipment are given in Table 1. No listing of reagents or glassware is provided as such lists are best compiled within the laboratory. Provision should always be made for an adequate reserve of glassware and sundry items. This is of particular importance where difficulties in delivery are anticipated.

Table 1. First-stage laboratory for drug surveillance

Equipment and major instruments	No.	Equipment and major instruments	No.
Analytical balance (four place, mechanical)	1	Disintegration test equipment	1
		Microscope	1
Spectrophotometer (UV/visible, single-beam, manual)	1	Refrigerator (with freezer compartment)	1
pH-meter (with electrodes)	1	Micrometer calipers	1
Karl-Fischer titrator	1		
Melting-point apparatus	1		
Polarimeter (manual)	1	*Optional items*	
Drying oven	1		
Vacuum oven	1	Flame photometer	1
Vacuum pump	1	Osmometer	1
Centrifuge (table-top)	1	Vortex mixer	1
Hot plate with stirrer	3	Constant temperature water-bath	1
Equipment for thin-layer chromatography including:		Ultrasonic cleaner	1
— spreader	1	Refractometer	1
— spotting equipment	1	Shaker (wrist-action)	1
— developing chambers	6	Oxygen flask combustion apparatus	1
— spraying bottles	6		
— UV viewing lamp	1		

3. Medium-size drug control laboratory

3.1 Capability

This laboratory is designed to deal with some 1500 full analyses per year and is equipped to provide for almost all types of test for drug identity and purity, all assays for content and strength based on chemical, instrumental, and microbiological techniques, and various performance tests for dosage forms.

The laboratory has several discrete components, including a chemical unit, an instrumental unit, a microbiological unit, a unit for biological safety tests (e.g. pyrogen testing), a pharmacognostic unit and, if appropriate, a special dosage-form unit. It should also have a library of reference books, manuals, and professional and scientific journals.

3.2 Premises

A floor space of 300–400 m^2 is required. All laboratory rooms should be supplied with running water and drainage, electrical power, and gas (either centrally supplied or from a gas tank). Climatic conditions will determine the need for air-conditioning and heating systems. The supply of water should be of adequate pressure for the use of vacuum aspirators (at least 19 kPa or 20 N/cm^2 are needed), otherwise suitable vacuum pumps should be installed. An arrangement to recirculate water used by vacuum aspirators through a collection tank may considerably reduce total water needs and should be considered if the water supply is scarce or irregular. A sewage treatment installation should also be provided (e.g. a lime pit to neutralize acidic effluents). The building should be constructed of fire-resistant material and the layout of the modules and connecting corridors should be determined not only by working efficiency but also by safety considerations, particularly in areas where inflammable liquids or compressed gases are used or stored. If large quantities of inflammable reagents are to be stored, the space should be planned and constructed in accordance with local fire regulations.

Each unit should be provided with rooms equipped for its specific requirements, including hooded benches in chemical rooms; ample electrical outlets in physicochemical rooms and voltage-stabilizing equipment if the local power supply is variable; movement-damping tables in balance rooms; laminar airflow equipment in microbiological rooms. All rooms should be provided with storage cabinets for reagents, glassware, and samples, wall shelving, and writing desks.

Control of temperature and humidity of at least a part of the laboratory area is imperative in tropical regions. In particular, the room for chromatographic work (primarily thin-layer chromatography) should be thermostatically controlled and in all cases protected from draughts and direct sunlight. Rooms equipped with hoods and extractor fans should receive an inflow of dry, cool air and additional dehumidifiers are required in storage areas for reference materials and samples.

Rabbits used for pyrogen testing should be kept in a room apart from other areas of the laboratory. A separate unit should be provided if other experiments on animals are contemplated. Both the animal house and the animal experimentation rooms should be thermostatically controlled within ±2 °C. In warmer climates the temperature is usually maintained within the range 23–25 °C.

Advice on technical facilities required for microbiological testing is provided in the twenty-second report of the WHO Expert Committee on Biological Standardization.[1]

3.3 Staff

The staffing complement comprises 14–18 persons, including the head of the laboratory, 4–5 analysts, 6–8 laboratory technicians, and 2–4 supporting and housekeeping staff. The ratio of analysts to laboratory technicians must be relatively high in a laboratory carrying out analyses on a wide range of pharmaceutical products. The ratio may be reduced in laboratories involved in repetitive testing of batches of a limited number of products.

The head of the laboratory should be a graduate in pharmacy or chemistry, preferably with a postgraduate degree in pharmaceutical analysis or related subjects and with broad practical experience in the many facets of drug quality assessment. The analysts should be graduates in pharmacy, analytical chemistry, biochemistry, or microbiology, as appropriate to their assigned responsibilities. An institutional training for the technicians is desirable, otherwise provision must be made for in-service training in the laboratory. High ethical standards are mandatory for the head of the laboratory and the analysts.

3.4 Equipment

The general laboratory equipment, together with items required in the chemical unit, are listed in Table 2. Water demineralizers and distillation stills are always needed, but their number or capacity can be reduced if a reliable supply of demineralized or distilled water is available from an outside source.

Major items of equipment required for the instrumental unit and for testing of dosage forms, as well as the equipment required for the microbiological unit are also listed in Table 2. Advice on the required performance of many of these instruments is included in *The international pharmacopoeia*.[2]

It is essential to ensure, before major items of equipment are purchased, that facilities are available for their proper maintenance and repair, preferably by representatives of the manufacturer. Electrical equipment must be compatible

---

[1] WHO Technical Report Series, No. 444, 1970.
[2] *The international pharmacopoeia*, 3rd ed. Volume I. *General methods of analysis*. Geneva, World Health Organization, 1979. Volume 2. *Quality specifications*. Geneva, World Health Organization, 1981.

Table 2. Medium-size control laboratory

General laboratory equipment	No.
Microbalance (five-place)	1
Analytical balance (four-place)	2
Laboratory balance (top-loading)	1–2
Refrigerator (with freezer compartment)	2–3
Water distillation still (10 litres/hour)	1
Water deionizing equipment (10 litres/hour)	1
Drying oven	2–3
Muffle furnace	1
Vacuum oven	1
Heating plates with magnetic stirrers	3–4
Vacuum rotary evaporator	1–2
Water-bath (electrical)	2–3
Automatic titrimeter	1
Shaker (wrist-action)	1
Micro-Kjeldahl equipment	1
Equipment for thin-layer chromatography including	
— spreader	1
— spotting equipment	1
— developing chambers	10
— spraying bottles	6
— UV viewing lamps	3
Laboratory centrifuge (floor model)	1
Ultrasonic cleaner	2
Vortex mixers	2
Heating mantles for flasks (assorted sizes)	6
Variable transformers	5
Vacuum pump (rotary, oil)	2
Micrometer calipers	1
Glove box	1
Sieves (set)	2
Microscope	1–2

Major instruments	No.
IR spectrophotometer (recording, grating)	1
UV/visible recording spectrophotometer	1
UV/visible spectrophotometer	1
Gas chromatograph	1
Polarimeter (manual)	1
Refractometer	1
pH-meters (with electrodes)	2
Melting-point apparatus (electrically heated)	1
Disintegration test equipment	1
Dissolution test equipment (for 6 tablets/capsules)	1

Major instruments (continued)	No.
Penetrometer	1
IR hydraulic pellet press with dies (15 tons/in^2 pressure ≈ W 23 × 10^7 Pa)	1
Agate mortar with pestle	1
Karl-Fischer titrator	1
Oxygen flask combustion apparatus	1

Optional items	No.
Ice machine	1
Solvent recovery apparatus	1
Flame photometer or atomic absorption spectrophotometer	1
Osmometer	1
Vibrospatula	1
High-pressure liquid chromatograph	1
Densitometer for TLC plates	1
Fluorometer (filter)	1
Hardness tester	1
Friability tester	1
Viscosimeter	1

Equipment for microbiology unit	No.
Autoclaves	2
Microscopes (bacteriological)	2
Incubators*	2–3
Centrifuge with refrigeration	1
Membrane filter assembly for sterility tests	
Colony counter with magnifier	1
Laminar flow bench	1
Hot-air sterilizer	1
Spectrophotometer, visible range (simple model)	1
Nephelometer (+ turbidimeter)	1
Refrigerators	2
Deep freezer	1
Large-plate microbiological assay equipment, including zone reader and recorder	1 set
pH-meter	1
Cleaning machines for glassware, especially one for cleaning pipettes	2
Water-baths (thermostatically controlled)	2

* Cooling incubators in countries with tropical climates

with the existing frequency and line voltage. Standard sets of replacement parts required for running repairs, containing such items as gaskets and spare bulbs, should always be retained in stock. Certain types of equipment, including gas-liquid and high-pressure liquid chromatographs and atomic absorption spectrophotometers, require a constant supply of special solvents, reagents, and compressed gases of high purity. It is essential that the availability of these is also ascertained before purchase. It can be helpful in selecting apparatus to seek information on the performance of instruments from other laboratories, particularly within the same region.

Requirements for glassware and general laboratory apparatus will vary from case to case and cannot be specified in general terms. Provision must be made for an adequate reserve. Lists of reagents to be held in stock are included in *The international pharmacopoeia*.

Additional equipment will be required if the basic range of tests is extended. Thus, pyrogen testing necessitates provision of animal housing, restraining harnesses or boxes, and a temperature-recording device with probes. An osmometer is required for testing large-volume parenteral preparations.

4. Scope of activity

The principal responsibilities are as follows:

— to establish, by testing, whether a given sample of a drug, either locally manufactured or imported, conforms to required specifications and whether packaging is adequate;
— to examine pharmaceutical products suspected to be of questionable efficacy or safety, and to demonstrate and document any evidence of deterioration, contamination, or adulteration;
— to check the stability of products under local conditions of storage.

Other responsibilities that may devolve upon the laboratory include:

— evaluating data supplied by manufacturers concerning product performance;
— determining whether the product label provides appropriate and clear instructions for use;
— advising on planned purchases of drugs within the public sector.

These additional activities require qualified staff and library facilities. However, since they are not directly dependent on the use of laboratory facilities, the necessary resources have not been taken into consideration within this annex.

In developed countries, drug-licensing regulations require an independent examination of data supplied by the manufacturer in support of an application for registration of a product. The required pharmaceutical data are detailed in Annex 5 to the twenty-fifth report of the WHO Expert Committee on

Specifications for Pharmaceutical Preparations.[1] When resources are available for such work, review and verification of these data by critical examination of pertinent quality specifications may be included among the responsibilities of a large drug control laboratory or it may be undertaken in a separate laboratory associated with the regulatory authority. No provision for these activities has been made in the laboratories described in sections 2 and 3.

5. Factors influencing the size and location of a laboratory

Many considerations determine the location, size, and organization of a national control laboratory. They include: financial resources; the drug control requirements of the national regulatory authority; the extent of drug usage within the country; and the number of different sources from which products are purchased.

If a country has a decentralized national administrative structure or if communications are poor, it may be necessary to establish provincial or peripheral laboratories.

Careful consideration must also be accorded to organizational and professional links between the control laboratory and other public health services, including food control laboratories, microbiological laboratories, hospital or regional clinical laboratories, and university departments of medicine or pharmacy.

Although it is practicable to institute and run a medium-size control laboratory apart from other laboratory services, economies can be effected by siting it in a complex together with other institutions. This enables the laboratory to retain independence of operation, while sharing common supporting services (e.g. supply units, maintenance crews, and repair shops). It also offers the possibility of using specialized facilities in adjacent laboratories (e.g. bacteriological laboratories for sterility testing) instead of duplicating the same facilities within the drug control laboratory.

6. Implementation of control laboratory projects

6.1 Feasibility study

Before any definitive steps are taken to establish a national laboratory service for drug control, a feasibility study must be put in hand to assess, within the context of prevailing needs and legal and administrative provisions, the precise functions it will serve, the scale of operation, and the projected costs. Provision must be made in the costing for: land and/or buildings, services, furnishings, equipment, consultancy fees, training of staff, and routine maintenance and operational

---

[1] WHO Technical Report Series, No. 567, 1975.

costs. The necessity or practicability of phasing the development of the service should also be examined.

6.2 Phasing of development

The rate of development of any laboratory service is commonly limited by the availability of qualified and experienced personnel and the possibilities for further training. New techniques should never be introduced into routine testing programmes until a high standard of performance is assured. Initially, it is prudent to concentrate on the development of chemical and physical techniques of analysis and testing, and to defer the introduction of microbiological and biological techniques to a later stage.

6.3 Programme support

The calibre of the professional personnel is the ultimate determinant of the standard and value of the laboratory service; they must have a high degree of technical competence, motivation, critical ability, and professional integrity. Inculcation of these qualities can be promoted during in-service training in established laboratories and by engaging consultants of repute in newly established national laboratories.

Training facilities for specialized analytical techniques should be made available in countries where they are already established. Recognizing the great need and the limited resources available within the least developed countries, it is to be hoped that relevant assistance may be forthcoming through bilateral and multilateral aid programmes.

Good laboratory practices in governmental drug control laboratories[1]

1.	General	163
2.	Management and operational issues	164
	2.1 Organizational structure	164
	2.2 Staffing	164
	2.3 Incoming samples	165
	2.4 Analytical worksheet	166
	2.5 Testing	167
	2.6 Evaluation of test results	169
	2.7 Retention samples	169
	2.8 Specifications repertory	170

---

[1] *WHO Expert Committee on Specifications for Pharmaceutical Preparations. Thirtieth Report.* Geneva, World Health Organization, 1987 (WHO Technical Report Series, No. 748).

2.9   Reagents   170
2.10 Reference materials   172
2.11 Instruments and their calibration   172
2.12 Safety in drug control laboratories   173
References   174

1. General

A governmental drug control laboratory is a laboratory maintained by the drug regulatory authority for carrying out the tests and assays required to establish that a drug conforms to the quality specifications claimed for it. Some countries maintain larger establishments described as "drug control centres" or "drug control institutes".

The contribution of a drug control laboratory to a national drug control system was described in the twenty-seventh report of the WHO Expert Committee on Specifications for Pharmaceutical Preparations (1). In most countries the laboratory is responsible for analytical services only, and not for pharmaceutical inspection. However, some aspects of inspection are considered in these guidelines.

A control laboratory can provide effective support for a drug regulatory agency and its inspection services only if the analytical results it provides can be relied upon to describe accurately the properties of the samples it assesses, to permit the correct conclusions to be drawn about the quality of each drug, and to serve as an adequate basis for any subsequent administrative and legal action.

Correct assessment of the quality of a drug sample is dependent on:

— the submission of a representative sample to the laboratory, together with a precise indication of why the test is requested;
— a correctly planned and meticulously executed analysis; and
— a competent evaluation of the results to determine whether the sample complies with the specification.

Precise documentation and efficient routines are required to make each operation as simple and as foolproof as possible.

These guidelines provide advice on the analysis both of dosage forms and of pharmaceutical raw materials; particular consideration is given to developing countries wishing to establish governmental drug control laboratories or having recently done so.

Many of the recommendations are also relevant to drug testing in pharmaceutical production plants, but this is a matter of the repetitive testing of a limited number of pharmaceutical products, whereas governmental control laboratories theoretically have to deal with all drugs on the market and therefore have to use a wider variety of test methods.

2. Management and operational issues

2.1 Organizational structure

The full analysis of a drug sample involves a variety of different tests. In a small laboratory where relatively few analyses are undertaken a single analyst may have to take responsibility for carrying out all the chemical and physicochemical tests and evaluating the results. In large laboratories, on the other hand, the sample may be subdivided between several specialized subunits, each of which carries out the part of the analysis that calls for the particular skills and technology that it possesses. In every case, however, a "lead unit" or focal point must be made responsible for distributing and testing the sample and collating and interpreting the results.

The division of the laboratory into subunits may be based on the main techniques used (e.g. chemical unit, instrumental unit, microbiological unit, unit for biological safety testing) or on the type of product tested (e.g. antibiotics unit, crude drug unit, radiopharmaceuticals unit). Whichever plan is chosen, care must be taken to ensure an even distribution of the workload between units and the precise allocation of responsibilities, particularly in the designation of lead units for particular types of drugs. Units specializing in single assay techniques, such as sterility testing, pyrogen testing or special physical measurements, should be regarded as collaborating units that perform specific tests at the request of the lead unit.

Division of a laboratory into subunits should never be allowed to inhibit communication between the staff involved in testing the same sample. Intercommunication helps the lead unit to piece together all the information on which the quality of the sample is ultimately judged.

Large laboratories need various supporting and coordinating sections, including a central registry and a specifications repertory. The size of these units will depend on the number of samples received and the number of different drugs subjected to testing. The head of the central registry must be a person with wide experience in analysis and will be responsible for receiving all incoming samples and accompanying documents, supervising their delivery to the lead units and keeping a constant check on the progress of analyses and the despatch of completed reports. He or she may also be required to collate and evaluate the test results for each analysis. The specifications repertory section maintains an up-to-date collection of all quality specifications and related documents.

2.2 Staffing

The head of the laboratory, and the heads of the various subunits in larger establishments, should be of high professional standing and have had extensive previous experience in drug analysis and laboratory management in a quality control laboratory in the regulatory sector or in industry. Non-supervisory analysts should be graduates in pharmacy, analytical chemistry, microbiology, or other relevant subjects. Technical staff should preferably hold diplomas in their subjects from technical or vocational schools.

The head of the laboratory must be satisfied that all key members of the laboratory staff have the requisite competence and are given grades matching their responsibilities. To encourage them in carrying out their tasks, all staff should be made aware of the important contribution of drug control to public health. In many countries, national regulations prohibit staff from holding independent posts or consultant assignments.

To reduce the possibility of human error, supervisors should periodically arrange for standard samples to be analysed and, where called for, review the adequacy of existing staffing, management, and training procedures. Error is most likely to occur during non-instrumental operations, and particularly in preparatory work, from carelessness, fatigue, boredom, inadequate training or, sometimes, as a result of staff being given work beyond their level of competence. "Self-checking" procedures should be devised for instrument operators. Regular in-service training programmes should be arranged to update and extend the skills of both professionals and technicians. This not only keeps staff abreast of advances in analytical methods and instrumentation, but also provides opportunities for career development and promotion.

In large laboratories the staffing of the various units should be based not only on their workloads but also on the technical demands of the work involved. In most instances the ratio of technicians to analysts should be 1:3 in a chemical or physicochemical unit, and 2:5 in a biological or microbiological laboratory. The greater the proportion of routine analyses undertaken on products that, *a priori*, are not expected to be substandard, the greater the proportion of technicians that can be effectively employed. Non-routine work, and particularly the review of test methods for newly registered drugs, requires a higher proportion of fully qualified analysts.

2.3 Incoming samples

As an initial step in quality evaluation, each incoming sample and the accompanying documents should be numbered and logged in a central register, which may be a record book, a card file, or data processing equipment. The entry should indicate the date when the sample was received and the lead unit to which it was forwarded. To facilitate the routing and tracing of samples, a list of the lead units assigned to each drug on the market should be kept in the central registry. Any unlisted products can then be assigned on a case-to-case basis by the head of the laboratory.

All persons, and particularly pharmaceutical inspectors, who frequently submit samples should be provided with standard "test request" forms and such a form should accompany each sample submitted to the laboratory. It should provide the following information:

— the name of the institution or inspector that supplied the sample;

- the source of the material;
- a full description of the product, including its composition, brand name, dosage form, concentration or strength, manufacturer, and batch number (if available);
- the size of the sample, and the reason for requesting the analysis.

Other information that is often needed includes the date on which the sample was collected, the size of the consignment from which it was taken, the expiry date, and the pharmacopoeial specification to be used for testing.

When the sample is first received it should be immediately inspected to ensure that the labelling is in conformity with the information contained in the test request. If discrepancies are found, or if the sample is obviously damaged, the fact should be recorded at once on the test request form.

No sample should be examined until the relevant test request has been received. If this is lacking, the sample should be safely stored until all the relevant documentation has been received. In emergencies a request for analysis may be accepted verbally. In this event all details should immediately be placed on record pending the receipt of written confirmation.

Incoming samples and test requests should be numbered consecutively. For each sample a self-adhesive label bearing this registration number should be affixed to the container in such a way as not to obliterate other markings or inscriptions. If a request refers to two or more drugs, to different dosage forms, or to different batches of the same drug, separate registration numbers should be assigned to each. Photocopies of all documentation should accompany each numbered sample when it is forwarded to the lead unit.

2.4 Analytical worksheet

A printed analytical worksheet with space for the following information should be used by the analyst to confirm that the sample has been examined in accordance with the requirements and, when necessary, to provide documentary evidence to support regulatory action:

- the registration number of the sample;
- the date of the test request;
- a description of the sample received;
- the quality specifications to which the sample was tested (including any additional or special methods employed);
- the results obtained, including any calculations necessary;
- the interpretation of the results and final conclusions.

Additional space should be provided to indicate whether and when portions of the sample were forwarded to other units for special tests (e.g. sterility, infrared spectrum), and the date when the results were received. To ease the flow of information between collaborating units a further set of printed forms can be useful. These can be sent out in duplicate from the lead unit with the sample to which they refer. In due course one copy is returned to the lead unit for attachment to the analytical worksheet, while the other is retained in the unit that undertook the work.

A separate analytical worksheet should be completed for each numbered sample. Each completed worksheet should be signed by the analyst responsible, initialled by the supervisor and placed on file for safe-keeping together with any attachments, including calculations and tracings of instrumental analyses. If this information is filed centrally in a registry, a copy of the worksheet should be retained in the lead unit for ease of reference.

It is still the custom in many laboratories for each analyst to keep a complete record of his work in a bound laboratory notebook with numbered pages. Although this has value it is an inconvenient form of documentation in a modern laboratory where results obtained on recording instruments or printed calculations have to be entered into the worksheet. If such a notebook is kept, it should be regarded as a supporting record only.

On the day the sample is received in the unit, the registration number, the date, the name of the product, and a description of the material received should be entered on the analytical worksheet. The information contained in the test request should be checked against the data on the label and the findings recorded, dated, and initialled. Any discrepancies in the documentation, or between the data provided and the appearance of the sample, should also be recorded. Any queries should immediately be referred back to the provider of the sample.

The analyst must then determine what specification is to be used to assess the sample. In many cases, the test request will specify a particular pharmacopoeial monograph or manufacturer's specification and the analyst must find out whether the current version is available. If no precise instructions are given, the specification in the officially recognized national pharmacopoeia should be used or, failing that, the manufacturer's officially approved or other nationally recognized specification. The reference number of the specification should be entered on the worksheet and a photocopy of the document attached.

If no formally approved specification exists, preference should be given to a current monograph in a foreign pharmacopoeia. If no suitable pharmacopoeial monograph can be found, the requirements should be drafted in the laboratory itself on the basis of published information and any other relevant documentation (1, 2). Otherwise, if the general policy of the laboratory permits, the specification contained in the product licence may be requested from the manufacturer. Whatever happens, detailed notes on the specification selected and the methods of assessment used must be entered in the worksheet.

2.5 Testing

If specific tests such as sterility tests, pyrogen tests, or special physicochemical tests need to be carried out by another unit or by a specialized external laboratory, the analyst should prepare the request and arrange for the transfer of the required number of units (bottles, vials, tablets) from the sample. Each of these units should bear the correct registration number.

Testing should be started as soon as possible after the preliminary procedures have been completed. If this is not feasible, the reasons should be noted in the worksheet and the sample placed in a special locked storage cabinet.

Detailed guidance on test methods is contained in the general notices and monographs of official pharmacopoeias. The following principles therefore apply only when no pharmacopoeial requirements are available or when ambiguous results are obtained.

Provided the result is unequivocally positive and the analyst is well acquainted with the technique, replicate chemical and physicochemical tests are not, in general, required for identity tests if based upon colour reactions, precipitation tests, infrared spectra, ultraviolet identification, or thin-layer chromatography, nor are they required for purity tests based on the matching of colour or opacity against standards or on thin-layer chromatography. In some laboratories, however, purity tests are routinely run in duplicate as a check against accidental contamination. Assays to assess strength or level of impurity should always be replicated, however, whether they are based on titrimetry, gravimetry, colorimetry, ultraviolet measurements, gas-liquid chromatography, or high performance liquid chromatography. Replicate measurements should also be made of physical properties such as pH values, optical rotations, refractive indices, and melting temperatures. Whenever replicate measurements are made, the results should be recorded as the arithmetic mean of the estimates.

In other cases, the required number of replicate measurements is defined in the description of the method. This applies to physicochemical tests involving gas-liquid chromatography or high performance liquid chromatography and to biological assays whose results require statistical evaluation.

Whenever ambiguous results are obtained, or when the discrepancies between replicate measurements fall outside acceptable limits, at least two further replicate tests should be run, preferably by a different analyst. Any important discrepancies must be investigated. Aberrant results can be rejected only when they are clearly due to error. Otherwise, the mean values obtained by each analyst should be quoted separately to provide clear confirmation that the sample failed the test.

Errors arise not only because of human failings but also as a result of unsuitable or deteriorated reagents and chemical reference substances, inadequate instrumentation, inappropriate methods (particularly methods that are difficult to reproduce), and variations in the laboratory environment. Comparative estimations on standard samples can frequently help to detect such errors, particularly in cases in which the analyst lacks experience in the method he has used.

All values obtained in each test, including blank results, should immediately be entered on the worksheet, and all graphical data, whether obtained from recording instruments or hand-plotted, should be attached.

2.6 Evaluation of test results

The analyst should review the results as soon as possible after all the tests have been completed to determine whether they are mutually consistent and whether they meet the specification. All conclusions should be entered on the worksheet by the analyst and initialled by the supervisor.

The certificate of analysis issued by the laboratory should be based on the analytical worksheet. It should specify the sample and the registration number, state the specification to which the sample was tested, list and provide the results of all the tests that were performed and state whether or not the sample was found to comply with the requirements. Certificates stating that a sample is not in compliance with the required specification must always be signed by the head of the laboratory.

A sample may be recorded on the worksheet as conforming to specification only if it meets all the relevant requirements. Any discrepancy confirmed by replicate testing should be evaluated in relation to the results of the other tests and the conclusions reached should be discussed with the head of the laboratory before they are entered on the worksheet. This record should then be signed by each of the analysts involved.

In large laboratories responsibility for certifying samples that conform to specification usually lies with the lead unit. However, in the event of non-compliance, the head of the laboratory is ultimately responsible for recommending any regulatory action that is required.

2.7 Retention samples

A retention sample originating from the same consignment as the analytical sample must always be kept in the laboratory—when possible in the original container—for use if the results of the analysis are disputed. This is usually prepared by the lead unit from the sample as received. The sample should therefore be large enough to provide an adequate reserve even when a number of replicate tests are required.

Sometimes, however, the retention sample is prepared by the sampling inspector when the analytical sample is taken. In this case the two samples should be separately packaged and transferred together to the laboratory. The retention sample is then labelled as such and given a registration number before it is forwarded with the analytical sample for storage in the lead unit.

Once all the required tests have been performed, any remaining portions of the sample should be resealed in their original containers. They should then be labelled with the date on which they may be discarded and placed in a locked cabinet in central store, if necessary at low temperature. Samples found to comply with specification should be kept for at least 6 months. Those that do not should be kept for at least one year, or for any longer period specified in current regulations.

2.8 Specifications repertory

Every drug control laboratory must possess the current versions of all the specifications that it needs, whether they are contained in pharmacopoeial compendia or in manufacturers' registration documents. In a large laboratory the specifications repertory is a documentation service with responsibility for updating all the pharmacopoeias—including supplements, addenda, and corrections—used in the laboratory and maintaining a specifications file for all drugs marketed within the country.

The repertory should retain a list of all pharmacopoeias in the laboratory and ensure that adequate numbers of supplements and addenda are ordered. All updatings and corrections should be noted in the principal volumes to prevent obsolete sections being used. Additional or replacement pages for loose-leaf publications should be inserted immediately they are received; pages no longer valid should be removed.

In addition, every laboratory should maintain a file of non-pharmacopoeial quality specifications for drugs tested to specifications established either by the manufacturer or by the laboratory itself. The range of monographs in this file will depend on current legal requirements and on whether or not a published national or regional pharmacopoeia is accorded official status within the country. Each entry should be numbered and dated so that the latest revision can easily be seen. The copy in the repertory file should bear the date of approval by the national registration authority or the lead unit and any other information relevant to the status of the monograph. All subsequent corrections or changes should be entered in these copies and endorsed with the date and the initials of the person making the entry. The master copy should never be released from the repertory; for laboratory use photocopies should be taken.

Manufacturer's specifications are the property of the company and in some countries are made available to governments strictly for registration purposes. In this case the quality control laboratory may need to negotiate their release with manufacturers or even, in some cases, to develop independent specifications. In other countries national laboratories are routinely asked to give their opinion on the specifications for each newly introduced product when it is registered by the drug regulatory authority.

2.9 Reagents

All reagents, including solvents, used in tests and assays must be of appropriate quality. They should be purchased from reputable manufacturers or dealers, preferably in small factory-filled containers suitable for laboratory use. Stocks stored in greater bulk are more vulnerable to contamination and degradation. Appropriate safety regulations should be drawn up and rigorously implemented wherever toxic or flammable reagents are stored or used. Those subject to poison regulations or to the controls applied to narcotic and psychotropic substances should be clearly marked as "Poison" and kept separately from other reagents in locked cabinets. A register of these substances must be maintained by the responsible member of staff. The head of each unit must accept personal responsibility for the safe-keeping of any of these reagents kept in the workplace.

Reagents made up in the laboratory should be prepared according to prescribed procedures and, when applicable, to published pharmacopoeial or other standards. Each label should clearly specify the contents, the manufacturer, the date received, and, as appropriate, the concentration, standardization factor, shelf-life, and storage conditions. Volumetric solutions made up by dilution should be labelled with the name of the manufacturer of the concentrate, the date of preparation, and the initials of the responsible technician.

Responsibility for making up reagents in the laboratory should be clearly assigned. Standardization of procedures is more readily implemented when this work is supervised by one person, even when the same reagents are used in several units. However, the reagents should not be moved unnecessarily from unit to unit and should be transported, whenever possible, in their original containers. When they are subdivided, they should always be transferred into scrupulously clean, fully labelled containers.

Whatever routine precautions are taken to ensure the adequacy of volumetric solutions, they should be checked whenever they are used in a test which indicates that a sample is not in compliance with specifications and the results of the check should be attached to the analytical worksheet.

Distilled water and deionized water should also be regarded as reagents and precautions should be taken to avoid contamination during their supply and distribution. Stocks should be checked at least once a month to ensure that they meet quality requirements: the specific conductance at 20 °C should not be greater than 2.0×10^{-6} ohm^{-1} cm^{-1} and the chloride ion content should meet current pharmacopoeial requirements for purified water.

All reagent containers should be inspected to ensure that seals are intact both when they are delivered to the reagent store and when they are distributed to the units. These inspections should be recorded by initialling and dating the labels. Reagents that appear to have been tampered with should be rejected except in rare instances when their identity and purity can be confirmed by testing. Maintaining stocks of reagents in a central store promotes safety and continuity of supplies, particularly for substances that need to be ordered long in advance of delivery.

In a large laboratory the storage area should provide separate rooms for flammable substances, for fuming acids, including concentrated hydrochloric acid, nitric acid, and bromine, and for ammonia and volatile amines. Self-igniting materials, such as metallic sodium and potassium, should also be stored separately. All storage areas should be located and equipped in accordance with fire regulations. To promote safety and to reduce contamination of the laboratory environment, these reagents should never be stored elsewhere in the laboratory without good reason.

The store should be kept stocked up with the clean bottles, vials, spoons, funnels, and self-adhesive labels required for dispensing reagents from larger to smaller containers. Special equipment may be needed for the transfer of larger volumes of corrosive liquids. The storekeeper should be trained to handle chemicals with the necessary care and safety.

2.10 Reference materials

Details of all the reference materials required should be kept in a central register. In a large laboratory this responsibility should be assigned to a specific person designated as the reference material coordinator. A national drug control laboratory that is required to establish reference materials for other institutions or for drug manufacturers will need to create a separate reference materials unit which will assume all the duties of the coordinator.

The register should contain details not only of all official reference substances and reference preparations, but also of secondary reference materials and non-official materials prepared in the laboratory as working standards. Each entry should be assigned a number and should give a precise description of the material, its source, the date of receipt, the batch designation or other identifying code, the intended use of the material (infrared reference material, impurity reference material for thin-layer chromatography, etc.), the place in the laboratory where it is stored, and any special storage conditions.

In addition to the register, a file should be kept containing full information on the properties of each reference material. In the case of working standards prepared in the laboratory the file should include the results of all tests and checks used to establish the standard and the initials of the responsible analyst.

Its laboratory identification number should be marked on each vial of the material and this must be quoted in the analytical worksheet every time it is used. A new number should be assigned to each new batch of material as soon as it is delivered or prepared. All reference materials should be inspected at regular intervals to make sure that they have not deteriorated and that they are being stored under appropriate conditions.

Further guidance on establishing, handling, and storing reference materials is contained in Annex 1 of the twenty-eighth report of this Committee (*3*).

2.11 Instruments and their calibration

Instruments are subject to wear, corrosion, and mishandling. If they are not in good working order they may give rise to serious analytical errors that may remain undetected unless systematic checks are made.

Whenever possible, regular servicing of instruments by specialist maintenance teams should be arranged. Instruments exposed to high levels of humidity should be resistant to corrosion and adequately protected against mould and fungal growth. Where line voltage is variable, suitable voltage stabilizers should be installed.

Some instruments may need to be protected from extremes of humidity or temperature in a specially designed area. Otherwise, analytical instruments can be either grouped together or dispersed between the various units. The choice will depend on the types of instruments, their fragility, the extent to which they are used, and the skills required to operate them.

Regular calibration of all instruments used to measure the physical properties of substances is essential and specific schedules should be established for each type of instrument, having regard to the extent to which it is used. pH meters should be calibrated at least once a day. The reliability of the wavelength scale of melting-point instruments and spectrophotometers operating in the ultraviolet region should be checked once a week and a full calibration undertaken once a month. Infrared spectrophotometers require calibration every quarter, while refractometers and spectrofluorometers should be serviced half-yearly. Analytical balances should also be serviced at least half-yearly by a qualified balance specialist.

Volume 1 of the third edition of *The international pharmacopoeia* describes the procedure for calibrating refractometers, thermometers used for the determination of melting temperature, and potentiometers for pH determination (4). It also explains the methods for checking the reliability of the scales on ultraviolet and infrared spectrophotometers and spectrofluorometers. A clear description of the standard operating procedure should be placed beside each instrument together with a schedule of the dates on which it is due for calibration.

Whatever routine precautions are taken to ensure the calibration of instruments, they should also be checked whenever they are used in a test which indicates that a sample is not in compliance with specification. The results of the check should be attached to the analytical worksheet.

2.12 Safety in drug control laboratories

Safety depends on the maintenance of exemplary technical standards and laboratory discipline. Safety instructions, both general and specific, should be given to each new member of staff and should be regularly supplemented with written material, poster displays, audio-visual material, and occasional seminars.

General rules for safe working include:

(1) prohibition of smoking, eating, and drinking in the laboratory;
(2) familiarity with the use of fire-fighting equipment, including fire extinguishers, fire blankets, and gas masks;
(3) use of laboratory coats or other protective clothing;
(4) adequate insulation and spark-proofing of electrical wiring and equipment, including refrigerators;

(5) full labelling of all containers of chemicals, including prominent warnings (e.g., "Poison", "Flammable") whenever appropriate;
(6) observation of safety rules in handling cylinders of compressed gases and familiarity with their colour identification codes;
(7) avoidance of solitary work in the laboratory;
(8) provision of first-aid materials and instruction in first-aid techniques, emergency care, and use of antidotes.

Protective clothing should be available, including goggles, masks, and gloves. Rubber suction bulbs should be used on all pipettes and siphons. Staff should be instructed in the safe handling of glassware, corrosive reagents, and solvents, and particularly in the use of safety containers or baskets to avoid spillage from containers. They should also be warned of the danger of violent, uncontrollable or dangerous reactions when mixing specific reagents. They must be instructed in the precautions required when, for example, mixing water and acids, acetone-chloroform and ammonia, or flammable products and oxidizing agents, and they should avoid the use of peroxidized solvents. They must also be instructed in the safe disposal of unwanted corrosive or dangerous products by neutralization or deactivation and of the need for safe and complete disposal of mercury and its salts.

While particularly poisonous or hazardous products must be singled out and appropriately labelled, **it should not be taken for granted that all other chemicals are safe**. All unnecessary contact with reagents, especially with solvents and their vapours, should be avoided. The use of known carcinogens and mutagens should be limited or totally excluded if required by local regulations. Replacement of toxic solvents and reagents by less toxic materials should always be the aim, particularly when new techniques are developed.

References

1. WHO Technical Report Series, No. 645. 1980, Annex 2.

2. WHO Technical Report Series. No. 614, 1977, Annex 1.

3. WHO Technical Report Series, No. 681, 1982, Annex 1.

4. *The international pharmacopoeia*, third edition, volume 1: *General methods of analysis*. Geneva, World Health Organization, 1979.

LABORATORY SERVICES

Sampling procedure for industrially manufactured pharmaceuticals[1]

1. General considerations — 175
    1.1 Purpose of sampling — 175
    1.2 Types of controls — 176
    1.3 Classes and types of materials — 176
    1.4 Parties concerned with sampling procedures — 177
2. Use of terms — 177
    2.1 Sampling operations — 177
    2.2 Samples — 178
    2.3 Quantities of material — 179
    2.4 Personnel — 179
3. General precautions to be taken during sampling operations — 179
4. Packaging and labelling of samples — 180
5. Sampling during pharmaceutical inspections — 181
6. Sampling of pharmaceutical dosage forms in regular surveillance programmes on drug quality during marketing — 182
7. Sampling of pharmaceutical dosage forms for acceptance of consignments — 182
8. Sampling of starting materials — 183
    8.1 General considerations — 183
    8.2 Sampling plans for consignments of starting materials supplied in several sampling units — 184

1. General considerations

Sampling comprises the operations designed to select a portion of a pharmaceutical material for a defined purpose. The sampling procedure must be adapted to the purpose of sampling, to the type of controls intended to be applied to the samples, and to the material to be sampled. The procedure should be described in a written protocol.

1.1 Purpose of sampling

Sampling may be required for different purposes such as: acceptance of consignments; clearance of batches; in-process controls; special controls; inspection for customs clearance, deterioration, adulteration, etc.; or obtaining a retention sample.

---

[1] *WHO Expert Committee on Specifications for Pharmaceutical Preparations. Thirty-first Report.* Geneva, World Health Organization, 1990 (WHO Technical Report Series, No. 790).

1.2 Types of controls

The controls intended to be applied to the sample may be:

(a) checking the identity of a material;
(b) performing complete pharmacopoeial or analogous testing; or
(c) performing special tests.

1.3 Classes and types of materials

The materials to be sampled may belong to the following classes:

(a) Bulk materials, represented by:

   (i) starting materials (including both drug substances and pharmaceutical aids) in solid, liquid, or semi-solid state;
   (ii) vegetable drugs, such as leaves, herbs, flowers, seeds, fruits, roots, rhizomes and bark, in whole or broken state.

   Special care may be needed for certain bulk materials, for example, for those that are very potent, toxic, hygroscopic, or light-sensitive, or require special microbiological precautions.

(b) Intermediates in the manufacturing process.
(c) Drug products (in-process as well as before and after packaging). For finished drug products the sampling procedure must take account of the official and nonofficial tests required for the individual dosage form (for example, tablets, parenteral preparations).
(d) Containers, packaging materials, and labels.

The sampling procedure must take account of the homogeneity and uniformity of the material.

(a) *Homogeneity*. A material is regarded as homogeneous when it is all of the same origin (for example, from the same batch) and as nonhomogeneous when it is of differing origins.
(b) *Uniformity*. A starting material may be considered uniform when samples drawn from different layers do not show significant differences in the quality-control tests. The following materials may be considered uniform unless there are signs to the contrary: organic and inorganic chemicals, purified natural products, various processed natural products like fatty oils and essential oils, plant extracts. The assumption of uniformity is strengthened by homogeneity, i.e. when the consignment is derived from a single batch.

Signs of nonuniformity include differences in shape, size or colour of particles in crystalline, granular or powdered solid substances, moist crusts on hygroscopic substances, deposits of solid material in liquid or semi-liquid products, and stratification of liquid products. Such changes, some of which may be readily reversible, can occur during prolonged storage or exposure to extreme temperatures during transportation.

Dosage forms may be considered uniform when different samples from the same batch comply with the relevant tests for uniformity.

Finally the sampling procedure must take account of the past experience with the material and with the supplier, and of the number of sampling units in the consignment.

1.4 Parties concerned with sampling procedures

Parties concerned with sampling procedures include:

(a) manufacturers, in the context of good manufacturing practice (GMP);
(b) customers, such as governmental or nongovernmental agencies involved in the acquisition of drug products;
(c) drug control authorities, responsible for the clearance of drug products held in quarantine after manufacture or importation, and for the detection of materials that have deteriorated or have been contaminated or adulterated.

These guidelines are intended primarily for drug control authorities and governmental procurement agencies, but the general principles may also be appropriate for the other parties referred to above.

2. Use of terms

The following working definitions or explanations are offered for a number of the terms used in this text.

2.1 Sampling operations

Sampling procedure: the complete sampling operations to be applied to a defined material for a specific purpose. A detailed written description of the sampling procedure is provided as the *sampling protocol.*

Sampling method: section of the sampling procedure dealing with the method prescribed for withdrawing samples.

Sampling plan: description of the number of units or quantity of material that must be collected.

Sampling record: written record of the sampling operations carried out on a particular material for a defined purpose. The sampling record must contain the date and place of sampling, a reference to the sampling protocol used, a description of the containers and of the materials sampled, notes on possible abnormalities, together with any other relevant observations and the name and signature of the inspector.

2.2 Samples

Sample: a portion of a material collected according to a defined sampling procedure. The size of any sample should be sufficient to carry out all anticipated test procedures, including all repetitions. If the quantity of material available is not sufficient for the intended analyses and for the retention samples, the inspector must record that the sampled material is the available sample (see below) and the evaluation of the results must take account of the limitations deriving from the insufficient sample size.

Samples should be stored in accordance with storage instructions for the respective drug; closures and labels should be of such a kind that unauthorized opening can be detected.

Available sample: whatever total quantity of sample material is available.

Final sample: sample ready for the application of the test procedure.

Original sample: sample collected directly from the material.

Pooled sample: sample resulting from the pooling of all or parts of two or more samples of the material.

Random sample: sample in which the different fractions of the material have equal probability of being represented.

Representative sample: sample obtained according to a sampling procedure designed to ensure that the different properties of a nonuniform material are proportionately represented.

Retention sample: sample collected and reserved for future controls. The size of a retention sample should be sufficient to allow at least two confirmatory analyses. In some cases statutory regulations may require one or more retention samples, each of which must be separately packaged and sealed.

Selected sample: sample obtained according to a sampling procedure designed to select a fraction of the material that is likely to have special properties. A selected sample that is likely to contain deteriorated, contaminated, adulterated or otherwise unacceptable material is known as an *extreme sample*.

2.3 Quantities of material

Batch: "a quantity of any drug produced during a given cycle of manufacture."[1]

If the manufacturing process is continuous, the batch originates in a defined period of time during which the manufacturing conditions have not been modified.

Consignment: quantity of a bulk starting material, or of a drug product, made by one manufacturer that is supplied at one time in response to a particular request or order. A consignment may comprise one or more packages or containers and may include material belonging to more than one batch.

Sampling unit: discrete part of a consignment, such as an individual package, drum or container.

2.4 Personnel

Sampling inspector: person responsible for performing the sampling operations. The sampling inspector need not be a qualified analyst. However, everyone called upon to take samples should be trained in the practical aspects of sampling and should have sufficient knowledge of pharmaceutical substances to execute the work effectively and safely. A conscientious approach, with meticulous attention to detail and cleanliness, is essential. The sampling inspector must remain alert to any signs of contamination, deterioration or tampering. Any suspicious signs should be recorded in detail in the sampling record.

3. General precautions to be taken during sampling operations

All operations related to sampling should be performed with care, using proper equipment and tools. Any contamination of the sample by dust or other foreign material is liable to jeopardize the validity of the subsequent analyses.

For the sampling of products at warehouses, the responsible person should have at his or her disposal all the tools needed to open the packages, barrels, containers, etc., including knives, pliers, saws, hammers, wrenches, implements to remove dust (such as brushes), and material to reclose the packages (such as sealing tape), as well as self-adhesive labels to indicate that a part of the contents has been removed from a package or container.

Sampling of uniform starting materials does not require complicated tools.

---

[1] As defined in *Good Practices in the Manufacture and Quality Control of Drugs* (*WHO Official Records*, No. 226, 1975, p. 88).

A variety of pipettes fitted with suction bulbs, cups or beakers, dippers, and funnels are needed for liquids of low viscosity. A glass rod can be used for highly viscous liquids; and spatulas or scoops are needed for powdered and granular solids. A porcelain or stainless steel spoon which can be sterilized by heating is suitable for sampling sterile powders.

Tools for sampling nonuniform materials are more complicated and more difficult to clean. A sampling tube with a shutter at the lower end is used to sample liquids in drums or other large containers. The tube is inserted vertically to the full depth of the drum, the lower end is then closed and the core removed. To sample solids, a slotted tube with a pointed end is used. It is inserted horizontally with the slot downmost and then turned through 180°. When withdrawn, it captures material along its entire length. A double-tubed trier may also be used to remove a portion from the whole length of a large container. Before being sampled, lumped solids must be ground to powder in a mortar.

All tools and implements should be kept scrupulously clean. Before re-use they should be thoroughly washed, rinsed with water or a suitable solvent, and dried. Adequate washing facilities should be provided in warehouses, otherwise inspectors will need to bring separate clean sets of sampling implements for each product.

Sampling from large containers of starting material or bulk products can present difficulties. Whenever possible, this work should be carried out in a separate closed cubicle within the warehouse in order to reduce the risk of contamination by dust of either the sample or the remaining material in the container, or cross-contaminations. For sterile materials, sampling should be carried out under aseptic conditions.

Sampling of drug products in retail containers from outlets such as pharmacies or hospitals in general does not present problems, save that the inspector should ensure that the material taken is sufficient for the intended analyses and for the retention samples, and that all sampling units are derived from the same batch.

4. Packaging and labelling of samples

The container used to store a sample should not interact with the sampled material nor allow contamination. It should also protect the sample from light, air, moisture, etc., as required by the storage directions for the material sampled. As a general rule, the container should be sealed and tamperproof. The container must be properly labelled.

Samples of loose materials, whether solid or liquid, should be placed in one or more clean containers. Liquid samples should be transported in glass bottles closed by screw-tops with inert liners that provide a good vapour-proof (moisture-proof) seal for the contents. Glass screw-top jars are preferable also for solid or semi-solid materials, but metal tins may be used when there is no risk of chemical interaction. In this case the lids should be taped shut. The use of plastic containers is not recommended. Light-sensitive materials should be protected by using amber glass containers or by wrapping colourless glass containers in black paper.

Solid dosage forms, such as tablets or granules, should be protected during transit, either by totally filling the container with the product or by filling any residual space with a suitable material. All containers should be sealed and labelled and all samples from an individual sampling unit of a single consignment should be transported in a single sealed box that is adequately packaged to avoid breakage in transport.

All containers that come apart (e.g. screw-capped jars, metal tins with separate lids) should be labelled on all parts to avoid cross-contamination when they are opened for examination.

If one sample is divided into several sample containers, they should be transported in a single, sealed box, labelled to identify the product, the consignment from which the sample was drawn, the size of the sample, the date and the place of sampling, and the name of the inspector. If the sample is collected in one container only, which is already provided with a tamperproof seal, the label with the necessary information may be attached directly to the container.

Security and adequate storage conditions must be ensured for the rooms where samples are stored.

Supervision of the sampling process should also be provided.

5. Sampling during pharmaceutical inspections

Pharmaceutical inspectors may be called upon to take samples from retail or hospital pharmacies or from industry and wholesalers, either on a routine basis or in a variety of special circumstances, such as:

— following the discovery of products that show signs of possible deterioration, contamination or adulteration;
— when a particular product is suspected of being either ineffective or responsible for adverse clinical reactions;
— when preparations are compounded on the premises.[1]

For deteriorated dosage forms, the sample should consist of one or several retail containers of the product that shows visual signs of deterioration.

When a complaint has been received about a drug product, the sample should include the original container and, if possible, one or more containers with their content of the same product bearing the same batch number.

---

[1] For an individually compounded medicine prepared on a physician's prescription, the whole container with its contents is usually taken.

6. Sampling of pharmaceutical dosage forms in regular surveillance programmes on drug quality during marketing

National drug control authorities hold the responsibility to monitor the quality of all drug products marketed in the territory of their competence. The extent to which routine surveillance, as opposed to assessment of suspect products, should be undertaken will depend upon the capacity of the national quality-control laboratory, the extent to which the quality of products is assessed prior to registration, the extent to which the requirements for good manufacturing practice are implemented, and the number of products that are imported from abroad.

A systematic programme of drug quality surveillance should aim at regular sampling of all marketed products whether registered for sale or compounded in pharmacies. Each product should be assessed at least once every two to three years, but particular attention should be accorded to products that are of prime importance to public health programmes or that are potentially dangerous, unstable, or difficult to formulate properly.

The programme of sampling should be drawn up by the responsible laboratory, if necessary under the guidance of the drug control authority, on a yearly or half-yearly basis. This programme should not only list the products to be sampled during a given period, but should also specify the sampling procedures and the size of the samples to be collected, taking into account the need for retention samples. The programme should determine to what extent each brand of a given product will be sampled and which local authority or inspector will be responsible for each sampling operation, and it should indicate to which laboratory (if more than one exists) each sample should be sent. Such a programme enables the facilities of each laboratory to be used to best advantage.

7. Sampling of pharmaceutical dosage forms for acceptance of consignments

The quality of consignments of finished pharmaceutical products frequently needs to be verified at the time of their importation or purchase. The necessary sampling should be performed in accordance both with an appropriate method and with regard to the presumed homogeneity or nonhomogeneity and uniformity or nonuniformity of the consignments. Thus, a consignment of a product from a single manufacturer labelled with a single batch number is assumed to be homogeneous. This assumption is further strengthened in the case of imported products provided with a batch certificate issued in the country of origin in accordance with the WHO Certification Scheme on the Quality of Pharmaceutical Products Moving in International Commerce.[1]

---

[1] *WHO Expert Committee on Specifications for Pharmaceutical Preparations. Thirty-first Report.* Geneva, World Health Organization, 1990 (WHO Technical Report Series, No. 790), Annex 5.

If these conditions apply and if the size of the batch is reasonable, a single sample for the intended analyses and a single retention sample will suffice. The size of the samples will be determined by the requirements of the analytical procedure according to which the product will be tested. Tests of unit dosage forms for uniformity of weight, volume or content can require a considerable number of units as can tests for sterility. Depending upon the type of the material, the size of the consignment, and the way in which the material is packaged, a sampling unit may be regarded as a box of vials or a box of jars of tablets rather than one of the individual vials or jars. The required number of unit dosage forms is then withdrawn from any individual container in the selected box.

If the consignment consists of one very large batch, or if little experience has been obtained with the product to be sampled, it may be prudent to carry out two independent analyses. Two independent final samples must then be taken from different sampling units. Conversely, when a consignment of moderate size is composed of two or three batches from the same manufacturer, a single sample may suffice, provided that favourable experience has previously been gained with the product and that there is evidence from the expiry date or other information that the batches were produced at approximately the same time.

Pharmaceutical forms supplied in bulk may also need to be examined. These include liquids and semi-solid materials, powdered solids or granulates transported in large containers and intended either for further processing or for direct packaging into final market containers, and unit dosage forms (tablets, capsules) supplied in bulk intended for repackaging into smaller containers.

Unless there is evidence to the contrary, products of this kind labelled with the name of the manufacturer and a single batch number may be assumed to be uniform if they have been produced in accordance with good manufacturing practice and are provided with a certificate issued in the country of origin according to the WHO Certification Scheme. In these circumstances the collection of a single sample sufficient for the intended analyses is adequate.

8. Sampling of starting materials

8.1 General considerations

Drug control laboratories are less frequently involved in the sampling of pharmaceutical starting materials, although they may be called upon to assess the quality of imported consignments. Again, this assessment must be undertaken using samples collected in accordance with an appropriate procedure, because a poorly collected sample may provide misleading information. The sampling procedure must have regard to whether or not the material can reasonably be considered as uniform. A more complex procedure must be employed when there is a suspicion of nonuniformity.

If the material of a consignment can be regarded as uniform, the sample can be taken from any part of the consignment. If, however, the material is not physically uniform, special sampling tools may be required to withdraw a cross-sectional portion of the material. In some instances, however, an attempt can be made to restore the uniformity of the material before sampling. Thus, a stratified liquid may be stirred, or a solid deposit in a liquid may be dissolved by gentle warming and stirring. Such interventions are difficult when the containers are large and they should not be attempted without adequate knowledge of the properties of the contents.

All partially processed natural products both herbal (dried plants and their parts) and mineral, should be treated as intrinsically nonuniform. Special procedures requiring considerable practice are used to prepare representative samples from such consignments, including coning and quartering and the treatment of fines. These procedures are not further described in these guidelines.[1]

8.2 Sampling plans for consignments of starting materials supplied in several sampling units

As already stated, these guidelines are intended primarily for drug control authorities and governmental agencies and are not necessarily appropriate for other parties such as experienced manufacturers with established and time-tested sampling procedures. Manufacturers with limited experience may wish to follow some of these recommendations.

Ideally, each sampling unit should be examined in order to check for intactness or possible damage of the container, and the content should be inspected for uniformity and chemically tested for identity. Uniformity should be tested on selected layer samples at different points of the material without previous intermixing. However, this ideal procedure is not always possible or justified by the purpose of sampling; a number of sampling units should then be randomly selected for sampling. Also it is not prudent to open all containers of products liable to deteriorate under the influence of moisture or oxygen when these are held in a transit warehouse. However, materials in damaged containers or found to be nonuniform must either be rejected or individually sampled for a complete quality control. Unlabelled sampling units must be rejected.

For random sampling, whenever possible each sampling unit is consecutively numbered and the required number of sampling units is then selected at random

---

[1] Sampling procedures for crude natural products are given in several sources, such as: *General control methods for vegetable drugs*. Unpublished WHO document WHO/PHARM/80.502; *The United States Pharmacopeia XXI*, seventh supplement. Rockville, MD, The United States Pharmacopeial Convention Inc., 1988, p. 2859; [*State Pharmacopoeia of the Union of Soviet Socialist Republics*], eleventh edition. Moscow, Medicina, 1987, pp. 267-274.

using tables of random numbers. The number of units depends on different assumptions and three plans in this regard are given below.

Control laboratories of manufacturers are required to analyse and release or reject each received consignment of the starting materials used to produce a drug product. For this purpose they need samples of each sampling unit of a drug substance or a pharmaceutical aid in order to be able to check the identity of the material. These samples subsequently may be pooled in one way or another to perform a full analysis. While for drug substances such a procedure should always be followed, it may be considered not practical or unnecessary for selected pharmaceutical aids.

8.2.1 The "n plan"

The "n plan" should be used with great caution and then only when the material is considered uniform and is supplied from a well-known source. The samples can be withdrawn from any part of the container (usually from the top layer). The "n plan" is based on the formula $n = \sqrt{N}$, where N is the number of sampling units in the consignment. The value of n is rounded up to the next higher integer. According to this plan, original samples are taken from n sampling units selected at random and these are subsequently placed in separate sample containers. The control laboratory inspects the appearance of the material and tests the identity of each original sample according to the relevant specification; if the results are concordant, the original samples are pooled into a final sample from which an analytical sample is prepared, the remaining part being kept as a retention sample. The "n plan" is not recommended for use by control laboratories of manufacturers who are required to analyse and release or reject each received consignment of the starting materials used to produce a drug product.

8.2.2 The "p plan"

The "p plan" may be used when the material is uniform and is received from a source that is well known and when the main purpose is to check the identity. The "p plan" is based on the formula $p = 0.4 \sqrt{N}$, where N is the number of sampling units. According to this plan, samples are taken from each of the N sampling units of the consignment and placed in separate sample containers. These original samples are transferred to the control laboratory, visually inspected and tested for identity (simplified methods may be used), and, if the results are concordant, p final samples are formed by appropriate pooling of the original samples.

8.2.3 The "r plan"

The "r plan" may be used when the material is suspected to be nonuniform and/or is received from a source that is not well known. The "r plan" may also be used for vegetable drugs as starting materials. This plan is based on the formula $r = 1.5 \sqrt{N}$, where N is the number of sampling units. Samples are taken from each of the N sampling units of the consignment and placed in separate sample containers. These original samples are transferred to the control laboratory and tested for identity. If the results are concordant, r samples are randomly selected and individually subjected to testing. If the results are concordant, the r samples are pooled for the retention sample.

The accompanying table gives the values of n, p and r according to the different plans.

Values of n, p or r for N sampling units

Value of n, p or r	Values of N		
	n plan	p plan	r plan
2	up to 4	up to 25	up to 2
3	5–9	26–56	3–4
4	10–16	57–100	5–7
5	17–25	101–156	8–11
6	26–36	157–225	12–16
7	37–49		17–22
8	50–64		23–28
9	65–81		29–36
10	82–100		37–44

7.
International trade in pharmaceuticals

Guidelines for implementation of the WHO Certification Scheme on the Quality of Pharmaceutical Products Moving in International Commerce[1]

1. Provisions and objectives	187
2. Eligibility for participation	188
3. Requesting a certificate	190
4. Issuing a certificate	192
5. Notifying and investigating a quality defect	194
References	194
Appendix 1 Model Certificate of a Pharmaceutical Product	195
Appendix 2 Model Statement of Licensing Status of Pharmaceutical Product(s)	200
Appendix 3 Model Batch Certificate of a Pharmaceutical Product	202
Appendix 4 Glossary and index *[not intended to be a formal part of the Scheme]*	204

1. Provisions and objectives

1.1 A comprehensive system of quality assurance must be founded on a reliable system of licensing[2] and independent analysis of the finished product, as well as on an assurance obtained through independent inspection that all manufacturing operations are carried out in conformity with accepted norms referred to as "good manufacturing practices" (GMP).

---

[1] *WHO Expert Committee on Specifications for Pharmaceutical Preparations. Thirty-fourth Report.* Geneva, World Health Organization, 1996 (WHO Technical Report series, No. 863).
[2] Throughout this document licensing refers to any statutory system of approval required at national level as a precondition for placing a pharmaceutical product on the market.

1.2 In 1969, the Twenty-second World Health Assembly, by resolution WHA22.50, endorsed requirements for "Good practices in the manufacture and quality control of drugs"(*1*) (referred to henceforth as "GMP as recommended by WHO"). These comprise internationally recognized and respected standards that all Member States are urged to adopt and to apply. These requirements have since been revised twice. The first revision was adopted by the Health Assembly in 1975 in resolution WHA28.65 (*2*), and a second revision of the requirements is included in the thirty-second report of the WHO Expert Committee on Specifications for Pharmaceutical Preparations (*3*).

1.3 These standards are fully consonant with those operative within the countries participating in the Convention for the Mutual Recognition of Inspection in Respect of the Manufacture of Pharmaceutical Products, and other major industrialized countries. They also provide the basis for the WHO Certification Scheme on the Quality of Pharmaceutical Products Moving in International Commerce (referred to henceforth as "the Scheme") recommended initially in resolution WHA22.50 (*1*). The Scheme is an administrative instrument that requires each participating Member State, upon application by a commercially interested party, to attest to the competent authority of another participating Member State that:

— a specific product is authorized to be placed on the market within its jurisdiction or, if it is not thus authorized, the reason why that authorization has not been accorded;
— the plant in which it is produced is subject to inspections at suitable intervals to establish that the manufacturer conforms to GMP as recommended by WHO; and
— all submitted product information, including labelling, is currently authorized in the certifying country.

1.4 The Scheme, as subsequently amended in 1975 (*2*) and 1988 (*4*) by resolutions WHA28.65 and WHA41.18, is applicable to finished dosage forms of pharmaceutical products intended for administration to human beings or to food-producing animals.

1.5 Provision for the certification of active ingredients is also included within the scope of the Scheme. This will be the subject of separate guidelines and certificates.

2. Eligibility for participation

2.1 Any Member State intending to participate in the Scheme may do so by notifying the Director-General of WHO, in writing, of:

— its willingness to participate in the Scheme;
— any significant reservations it intends to observe relating to this participation; and

— the name and address of its national drug authority or other competent authority.

2.2 These notifications are subsequently announced in the monthly *WHO pharmaceuticals newsletter*. An updated consolidated list will be published annually in the newsletter and will be available to governments at other times from the Division of Drug Management and Policies, WHO, 1211 Geneva 27, Switzerland. (See also section 3.3.)

2.3 A Member State may opt to participate solely to control the *import* of pharmaceutical products and active substances. This intention should be stated explicitly in its notification to WHO.

2.4 A Member State intending to use the Scheme to support the *export* of pharmaceutical products should first satisfy itself that it possesses:

- An effective national licensing system, not only for pharmaceutical products, but also for the responsible manufacturers and distributors.
- GMP requirements, consonant with those recommended by WHO, to which all manufacturers of finished pharmaceutical products are required to conform.
- Effective controls to monitor the quality of pharmaceutical products registered or manufactured within the country, including access to an independent quality control laboratory.
- A national pharmaceuticals inspectorate, operating as an arm of the national drug regulatory authority, and having the technical competence, experience and resources to assess whether GMP and other controls are being effectively implemented, and the legal power to conduct appropriate investigations to ensure that manufacturers conform to these requirements by, for example, examining premises and records and taking samples.
- The administrative capacity to issue the required certificates, to institute inquiries in the case of complaint, and to notify expeditiously both WHO and the competent authority in any Member State known to have imported a specific product that is subsequently associated with a potentially serious quality defect or other hazard.

2.5 Each Member State assumes the responsibility to determine, through a process of self-evaluation, whether it satisfies these prerequisites. The Scheme contains no provision for external inspection or assessment under any circumstances, either of a competent national authority or of a manufacturing facility. However, should a Member State so wish, it can approach WHO, or a well recognized drug regulatory authority, occasionally to delegate consultants to act as advisers in the course of both national inspections and inspector training activities.

3. Requesting a certificate

3.1 Three documents can be requested within the scope of the Scheme:

— a Certificate of Pharmaceutical Product (product certificate);
— a Statement of Licensing Status of Pharmaceutical Product(s); and
— a Batch Certificate of a Pharmaceutical Product.

3.2 Proposed formats for these documents are provided in Appendices 1, 2 and 3 of these guidelines. To facilitate their use, they are presented in forms suitable for generation by computer. All participating countries are henceforth urged to adopt these formats to facilitate the interpretation of certified information. Requests for the provision of certificates offering more limited attestations – for instance, that the manufacturer complies with GMP or that the product is authorized for "free sale" within the country of export – are discouraged. Similarly, requests should not be made for the certification of information going beyond the scope of the Scheme. When manufacture takes place in a country other than that where the product certificate is issued, an attestation that such manufacture complies with GMP may still be provided as an attachment to the product certificate on the basis of inspections undertaken for registration purposes. The explanatory notes attached to the three documents referred to above are very important. While they are not part of the documents, they should always be attached to them.

3.3 A list of addresses of competent national regulatory authorities participating in the Scheme that are responsible for the registration of pharmaceutical and/or veterinary products, together with details of any reservations they have declared regarding their participation in the Scheme may be obtained from WHO as indicated in section 2.2.

3.4 The competent authority in each country participating in the Scheme should issue guidelines to all agents responsible for importing pharmaceutical products for human and/or veterinary use that operate under its jurisdiction, including those responsible for public sector purchases, to explain the contribution of certification of the drug regulatory process and the circumstances in which each of the three types of documents will be required.

Certificate of a Pharmaceutical Product

3.5 The Certificate of a Pharmaceutical Product (Appendix 1), issued by the exporting country, is intended for use by the competent authority within an importing country in two situations:

— when the product in question is under consideration for a product licence that will authorize its importation and sale;
— when administrative action is required to renew, extend, vary or review such a licence.

3.6 All requests for certificates should be channelled through the agent in the importing country (see section 3. 4) and the product-licence holder or other commercially interested party in the exporting country ("the applicant"). The applicant should submit the following information for each product to the authority issuing the certificate:

— the name and dosage form of the product;
— the name and the amount of active ingredient(s) per unit dose (the International Nonproprietary Name(s), where such exist(s), should be used);
— the name and address of the product-licence holder and/or manufacturing facility;
— the formula (the complete qualitative composition including all excipients); this is particularly important when no product licence exists or when the formulation differs from that of the licensed product;
— product information for health professionals and for the public (patient information leaflets) as approved in the exporting country.

For product information to be attached to the certificate, see section 4.7.

3.7 The certificate is a confidential document. As such, it can be issued by the competent authority in the exporting country ("the certifying authority") only with the permission of the applicant and, if different, of the product-licence holder.

3.8 The certificate is intended to be incorporated into a product-licence application in the importing country. Once prepared, it is transmitted to the requesting authority through the applicant and, when applicable, the agent in the importing country.

3.9 When any doubt arises about the status or validity of a certificate, the competent authority in the importing country should request a copy directly from the certifying authority, as provided for in section 4.9 of these guidelines.

3.10 In the absence of any specific agreement, each certificate will be prepared exclusively in the working language(s) of the certifying authority. The applicant will be responsible for providing any notarized translation that may be required by the requesting authority.

3.11 Since the preparation of certificates imposes a significant administrative load on certifying authorities, the service may need to be financed by charges levied upon applicants.

3.12 Supplementary attestations are obtainable only at the discretion of the certifying authority and with the permission of the applicant. The certifying authority is under no obligation to supply additional information. Requests for supplementary information should consequently be referred to the applicant, and only in exceptional circumstances to the certifying authority.

Statement of Licensing Status

3.13 The Statement of Licensing Status of Pharmaceutical Product(s) (Appendix 2) attests only that a licence has been issued for a specified product, or products, for use in the exporting country. It is intended for use by importing agents when considering bids made in response to an international tender, in which case it should be requested by the agent as a condition of bidding. It is intended only to facilitate the screening and preparation of information. The importation of any product that is provisionally selected through this procedure should be determined on the basis of a Certificate of a Pharmaceutical Product.

Batch Certificate

3.14 A Batch Certificate of a Pharmaceutical Product (Appendix 3) refers to an individual batch of a pharmaceutical product, and is a vital instrument in drug procurement. The provision of a Batch Certificate is usually a mandatory requirement in tender and procurement documents.

3.15 A Batch Certificate is normally issued by the manufacturer and only *exceptionally*, as in the case of vaccines, sera and some other biological products, by the competent authority of the exporting country. The Batch Certificate is intended to accompany and provide an attestation concerning the quality and expiry date of a specific batch or consignment of a product that has already been licensed in the importing country. The Batch Certificate should include the specifications of the final product at the time of batch release and the results of a full analysis undertaken on the batch in question. In most circumstances these certificates are issued by the manufacturer to the importing agent (i.e. the product-licence holder in the importing country), but they must be made available at the request of – or in the course of any inspection made on behalf of – the competent national authority.

4. Issuing a certificate

4.1 The certifying authority is responsible for assuring the authenticity of the certified data. Certificates should not bear the WHO emblem, but a statement should always be included to confirm whether or not the document is issued in the format recommended by WHO.

4.2 When the applicant is the manufacturer of the finished dosage form, the certifying authority should satisfy itself, before attesting compliance with GMP, that the applicant:

(a) applies identical GMP standards to the production of *all* batches of pharmaceutical products manufactured within the facility, *including those destined exclusively for export*;

(b) consents, in the event of identification of a quality defect consonant with the criteria set out in section 5.1, to relevant inspection reports being released, in confidence, to the competent authority in the country of import, should the latter so require.

4.3 When the applicant is not the manufacturer of the finished dosage form, the certifying authority should similarly satisfy itself – in so far as it has authority to inspect the records and relevant activities of the applicant – that it has the applicant's consent to release relevant reports on the same basis as described in section 4.2 (b) above.

4.4 GMP as recommended by WHO assigns to the manufacturer of the finished dosage form responsibility for assuring the quality of active ingredients. National regulations may require that suppliers of active ingredients be identified in the product licence, but the competent authority may have no power to inspect them.

4.5 Notwithstanding this situation, a certifying authority may agree, on a discretionary and voluntary basis, and at the request of a manufacturer, to undertake an inspection of a manufacturer of active ingredients to satisfy specific requirements of a requesting authority. Alternatively, pending the development of specific guidelines for active pharmaceutical ingredients, the certifying authority may be able to attest that the manufacturer is an established supplier of the substance in question to manufacturers of finished dosage forms licensed for marketing under its jurisdiction.

4.6 Whenever a product is purchased through a broker or another intermediary, or when more than one set of premises has been involved in the manufacture and packaging of a product, the certifying authority should consider whether it has received sufficient information to satisfy itself that those aspects of the manufacture of the product for which the applicant is not directly responsible have been undertaken in compliance with GMP as recommended by WHO.

4.7 The certifying authority should officially stamp and date all copies of product information submitted to it in support of an application for a certificate and intended to be appended to the certificate. Every effort should be made to ensure that certificates and all annexed documentation are consonant with the version of the product licence operative on the date of issue. When available, the certifying authority will add a summary basis of approval or any other material that it may deem relevant. Translation by an applicant of these materials into a widely used language, preferably English, shall be deemed to satisfy the provisions of section 3.10.

4.8 Any additional attachment to a certificate submitted by the applicant, such as price lists of products for which bids are offered, should be clearly identified as not forming part of the attestation made by the certifying authority.

4.9 To avert potential abuse of the Scheme, to frustrate attempts at falsification, to render routine authentication of certificates by an independent authority superfluous, and to enable the certifying authority to maintain comprehensive records of countries to which specific products have been exported, each certificate should identify the importing country and be stamped on each page with the official seal of the certifying authority. If requested by the importing country, an identical copy, clearly marked as duplicate, should be forwarded by the certifying authority directly to that country's authority.

5. Notifying and investigating a quality defect

5.1 Each certifying authority undertakes to institute enquiries into any quality defect reported in a product exported in accordance with the provisions of the Scheme, on the understanding that:

— the complaint is transmitted, together with the relevant facts, through the competent authority in the importing country;
— the complaint is considered to be of a serious nature by the latter authority; and
— the defect, if it appeared after delivery of the product into the importing country, is not attributable to local conditions.

5.2 In the case of obvious doubt, a participating national authority may request WHO to assist in identifying an independent quality control laboratory to carry out tests for the purposes of quality control.

5.3 Each certifying authority undertakes to inform WHO and, as far as is possible, all competent national authorities, of any serious hazard newly associated with a product exported under the provisions of the Scheme or of any criminal abuse of the Scheme directed, in particular, to the export of falsely labelled, spurious, counterfeited or substandard pharmaceutical products. On receipt of such notification, WHO will transmit the message immediately to the competent national authority in each Member State.

5.4 WHO stands prepared to offer advice should difficulty arise in implementing any aspect of the Scheme or in resolving a complaint, but it cannot be a party to any resulting litigation or arbitration.

References

1. Quality control of drugs. In: *Twenty-second World Health Assembly, Boston, Massachusetts, 8–25 July 1969. Part 1: Resolutions and decisions, annexes.* Geneva, World Health Organization, 1969: 99–105 (Official Records of the World Health Organization, No. 176).

2. Certification Scheme on the Quality of Pharmaceutical Products Moving in International Commerce. In: *Twenty-eighth World Health Assembly, Geneva, 13–30 May 1975. Part 1: Resolutions and decisions, annexes.* Geneva, World Health Organization, 1975: 94–95 (Official Records of the World Health Organization, No. 226).

3. Good manufacturing practices for pharmaceutical products. In: *WHO Expert Committee on Specifications for Pharmaceutical Preparations. Thirty-second Report.* Geneva, World Health Organization, 1992: 14–79 (WHO Technical Report Series, No. 823).

4. WHO Certification Scheme on the Quality of Pharmaceutical Products Moving in International Commerce. In: *Forty-first World Health Assembly, Geneva, 2–13 May 1988. Resolutions and decisions, annexes.* Geneva, World Health Organization, 1988: 53–55 (document WHA41/1988/REC/1).

Appendix I. Model Certificate of a Pharmaceutical Product

Certificate of a Pharmaceutical Product[1]

This certificate conforms to the format recommended by the World Health Organization (*general instructions and explanatory notes attached*).

No. of Certificate: _____

Exporting (certifying) country: _____

Importing (requesting) country: _____

1. Name and dosage form of product:
_____

1.1 Active ingredient(s)[2] and amount(s) per unit dose:[3]
_____
_____
_____

For complete qualitative composition including excipients, see attached.[4]

1.2 Is this product licensed to be placed on the market for use in the exporting country?[5] yes/no (*key in as appropriate*)

1.3 Is this product actually on the market in the exporting country? yes/no/unknown (*key in as appropriate*)

If the answer to 1.2 is yes, continue with section 2A and omit section 2B.

If the answer to 1.2 is no, omit section 2A and continue with section 2B.[6]

2A.1 Number of product licence[7] and date of issue:
_____

2A.2 Product-licence holder (name and address):

_____

_____

_____

2A.3 Status of product-licence holder:[8] a/b/c (*key in appropriate category as defined in note 8*)

2A.3.1 For categories b and c the name and address of the manufacturer producing the dosage form are:[9]

_____

2A.4 Is Summary Basis of Approval appended?[10] yes/no (*key in as appropriate*)

2A.5 Is the attached, officially approved product information complete and consonant with the licence?[11] yes/no/not provided (*key in as appropriate*)

2A.6 Applicant for certificate, if different from licence holder (name and address):[12]

_____

_____

2B.1 Applicant for certificate (name and address):

_____

_____

2B.2 Status of applicant: a/b/c (*key in appropriate category as defined in note 8*)

2B.2.1 For categories b and c the name and address of the manufacturer producing the dosage form are:[9]

_____

2B.3 Why is marketing authorization lacking?

not required/not requested/under consideration/refused
(*key in as appropriate*)

2B.4 Remarks:[13] _____

_____

3. Does the certifying authority arrange for periodic inspection of the manufacturing plant in which the dosage form is produced?

yes/no/not applicable[14] (*key in as appropriate*)

If no or not applicable proceed to question 4.

3.1 Periodicity of routine inspections (years): _____

3.2 Has the manufacture of this type of dosage form been inspected? yes/no (*key in as appropriate*)

3.3 Do the facilities and operations conform to GMP as recommended by the World Health Organization?[15]

yes/no/not applicable[14] (*key in as appropriate*)

4. Does the information submitted by the applicant satisfy the certifying authority on all aspects of the manufacture of the product?[16]

yes/no (*key in as appropriate*)

If no, explain: _____

Address of certifying authority:

_____

_____

Telephone number: _____ Fax number: _____

Name of authorized person:

_____

Signature:

_____

Stamp and date:

_____

General instructions

Please refer to the guidelines for full instructions on how to complete this form and information on the implementation of the Scheme.

The forms are suitable for generation by computer. They should always be submitted as hard copy, with responses printed in type rather than handwritten.

Additional sheets should be appended, as necessary, to accommodate remarks and explanations.

Explanatory notes

1. This certificate, which is in the format recommended by WHO, establishes the status of the pharmaceutical product and of the applicant for the certificate in the exporting country. It is for a single product only since manufacturing arrangements and approved information for different dosage forms and different strengths can vary.

2. Use, whenever possible, International Nonproprietary Names (INNs) or national nonproprietary names.

3. The formula (complete composition) of the dosage form should be given on the certificate or be appended.

4. Details of quantitative composition are preferred, but their provision is subject to the agreement of the product-licence holder.

5. When applicable, append details of any restriction applied to the sale, distribution or administration of the product that is specified in the product licence.

6. Sections 2A and 2B are mutually exclusive.

7. Indicate, when applicable, if the licence is provisional, or the product has not yet been approved.

8. Specify whether the person responsible for placing the product on the market:

    (a) manufactures the dosage form;
    (b) packages and/or labels a dosage form manufactured by an independent company; or
    (c) is involved in none of the above.

9. This information can be provided only with the consent of the product-licence holder or, in the case of non-registered products, the applicant. Non-completion of this section indicates that the party concerned has not agreed to inclusion of this information.

    It should be noted that information concerning the site of production is part of the product licence. If the production site is changed, the licence must be updated or it will cease to be valid.

[10] This refers to the document, prepared by some national regulatory authorities, that summarizes the technical basis on which the product has been licensed.

[11] This refers to product information approved by the competent national regulatory authority, such as a Summary of Product Characteristics (SPC).

[12] In this circumstance, permission for issuing the certificate is required from the product-licence holder. This permission must be provided to the authority by the applicant.

[13] Please indicate the reason that the applicant has provided for not requesting registration:

(a) the product has been developed exclusively for the treatment of conditions – particularly tropical diseases – not endemic in the country of export;
(b) the product has been reformulated with a view to improving its stability under tropical conditions;
(c) the product has been reformulated to exclude excipients not approved for use in pharmaceutical products in the country of import;
(d) the product has been reformulated to meet a different maximum dosage limit for an active ingredient;
(e) any other reason, please specify.

[14] Not applicable means that the manufacture is taking place in a country other than that issuing the product certificate and inspection is conducted under the aegis of the country of manufacture.

[15] The requirements for good practices in the manufacture and quality control of drugs referred to in the certificate are those included in the thirty-second report of the Expert Committee on Specifications for Pharmaceutical Preparations (WHO Technical Report Series, No. 823, 1992, Annex 1). Recommendations specifically applicable to biological products have been formulated by the WHO Expert Committee on Biological Standardization (WHO Technical Report Series, No. 822, 1992, Annex 1).

[16] This section is to be completed when the product-licence holder or applicant conforms to status (b) or (c) as described in note 8 above. It is of particular importance when foreign contractors are involved in the manufacture of the product. In these circumstances the applicant should supply the certifying authority with information to identify the contracting parties responsible for each stage of manufacture of the finished dosage form, and the extent and nature of any controls exercised over each of these parties.

The layout for this Model Certificate is available on diskette in WordPerfect from the Division of Drug Management and Policies, World Health Organization, 1211 Geneva 27, Switzerland.

Appendix 2. Model Statement of Licensing Status of Pharmaceutical Product(s)

No. of Statement _____

Exporting (certifying) country:
Importing (requesting) country:

Statement of Licensing Status of Pharmaceutical Product(s)[1]

This statement indicates **only** whether or not the following products are licensed to be put on the market in the exporting country.

Applicant (name/address):

Name of product	Dosage form	Active ingredients(s)[2] and amount(s) per unit dose	Product-licence no. and date of issue[3]

The certifying authority undertakes to provide, at the request of the applicant (or, if different, the product-licence holder), a separate and complete Certificate of a Pharmaceutical Product in the format recommended by WHO, for each of the products listed above.

Address of certifying authority:
Telephone/fax numbers:

Name of authorized person:
Signature:
Stamp and date:

This statement conforms to the format recommended by the World Health Organization (*general instructions and explanatory notes below*).

INTERNATIONAL TRADE IN PHARMACEUTICALS

General instructions

Please refer to the guidelines for full instructions on how to complete this form and information on the implementation of the Scheme.

The forms are suitable for generation by computer. They should always be submitted as hard copy, with responses printed in type rather than handwritten.

Additional sheets should be apppended, as necessary, to accommodate remarks and explanations.

Explanatory notes

[1] This statement is intended for use by importing agents who are required to screen bids made in response to an international tender and should be requested by the agent as a condition of bidding. The statement indicates that the listed products are authorized to be placed on the market for use in the exporting country. A Certificate of a Pharmaceutical Product in the format recommended by WHO will be provided, at the request of the applicant and, if different, the product-licence holder, for each of the listed products.

[2] Use, whenever possible, International Nonproprietary Names (INNs) or national nonproprietary names.

[3] If no product licence has been granted, enter "not required", "not requested", "under consideration" or "refused" as appropriate.

The layout for this Model Statement is available on diskette in WordPerfect from the Division of Drug Management and Policies, World Health Organization, 1211 Geneva 27, Switzerland.

Appendix 3. Model Batch Certificate of a Pharmaceutical Product

Manufacturer's/Official[1] Batch Certificate of a Pharmaceutical Product

This certificate conforms to the format recommended by the World Health Organization (*general instructions and explanatory notes attached*).

1. No. of Certificate: _____
2. Importing (requesting) authority: _____
3. Name of product: _____
3.1 Dosage form: _____
3.2 Active ingredient(s)[2] and amount(s) per unit dose: _____

3.2.1 Is the composition of the product identical to that registered in the country of export? yes/no/not applicable[3] (*key in as appropriate*)

If no, please attach formula (including excipients) of both products.

4. Product-licence holder[4] (name and address):

4.1 Product-licence number:[4] _____
4.2 Date of issue:[4] _____
4.3 Product licence issued by:[4] _____
4.4 Product-certificate number:[4,5] _____
5.1 Batch number: _____
5.2 Date of manufacture: _____
5.3 Shelf-life (years): _____
5.4 Contents of container: _____
5.5 Nature of primary container: _____
5.6 Nature of secondary container/wrapping: _____

5.7   Specific storage conditions: _____

5.8   Temperature range: _____

6.   Remarks:[6]

7.   Quality analysis

7.1   What specifications apply to this dosage form? Either specify the pharmacopoeia or append company specifications.[7]

7.1.1   In the case of a product registered in the exporting country, have the company specifications[7] been accepted by the competent authority? yes/no (*key in as appropriate*)

7.2   Does the batch comply with all parts of the above specifications? yes/no (*key in as appropriate*)

7.3   Append certificate of analysis.[8]

It is hereby certified that the above declarations are correct and that the results of the analyses and assays on which they are based will be provided on request to the competent authorities in both the importing and the exporting countries.

Name and address of authorized person:
_____
_____

Telephone number: _____ Fax number: _____

Signature of authorized person: _____

Stamp and date: _____

General instructions

Please refer to the guidelines for full instructions on how to complete this form and information on the implementation of the Scheme.

These forms are suitable for generation by computer. They should always be submitted as hard copy, with responses printed in type rather than handwritten.

Additional sheets should be appended, as necessary, to accommodate remarks and explanations.

Explanatory notes

Certification of individual batches of a pharmaceutical product is only undertaken exceptionally by the competent authority of the exporting country. Even then, it is rarely applied other than to vaccines, sera and biologicals. For other products, the responsibility for any requirement to provide batch certificates rests with the product-licence holder in the exporting country. The responsibility to forward certificates to the competent authority in the importing country is most conveniently assigned to the importing agent.

Any inquiries or complaints regarding a batch certificate should always be addressed to the competent authority in the exporting country. A copy should be sent to the product-licence holder.

[1] Strike out whichever does not apply.

[2] Use, whenever possible, International Nonproprietary Names (INNs) or national nonproprietary names.

[3] "Not applicable" means that the product is not registered in the country of export.

[4] All items under 4 refer to the product licence or the Certificate of a Pharmaceutical Product issued in the exporting country.

[5] This refers to the Certificate of a Pharmaceutical Product as recommended by the World Health Organization.

[6] Indicate any special storage conditions recommended for the product as supplied.

[7] For each of the parameters to be measured, the specifications give the values that have been accepted for batch release at the time of product registration.

[8] Identify and explain any discrepancies from specifications. Government batch release certificates issued by certain governmental authorities for specific biological products provide additional confirmation that a given batch has been released, without necessarily giving the results of testing. The latter are contained in the manufacturer's certificate of analysis.

The layout for this Model Certificate is available on diskette in WordPerfect from the Division of Drug Management and Policies, World Health Organization, 1211 Geneva 27, Switzerland.

Appendix 4. Glossary and index

In order to facilitate understanding, terms used in the guidelines are explained here and/or reference is made to relevant sections. This appendix provides supplementary information and is not a formal part of the Scheme.

For the sake of clarity, all definitions taken from the glossary of "Good manufacturing practices for pharmaceutical products" (*1*) are preceded by an asterisk.

abuse of Scheme
See sections 4.9 and 5.2 of the guidelines.

active ingredients
See sections 1.5, 4.4 and 4.5 of the guidelines.

addresses of competent authorities
See sections 2.2 and 3.3 of the guidelines.

applicant
The party applying for a Product Certificate. This is normally the product-licence holder. Because certain data are confidential for commercial reasons, the competent authority in the exporting country must always obtain permission to release these data from the product-licence holder or, in the absence of a product licence, from the manufacturer.

authentication of certificates
See section 4.9 of the guidelines.

*batch (or lot)
A defined quantity of a starting material, packaging material, or product processed in a single process or series of processes so that it can be expected to be homogeneous. In the case of continuous manufacture, the batch must correspond to a defined fraction of the production, characterized by its intended homogeneity. It may sometimes be necessary to divide a batch into a number of sub-batches, which are later brought together to form a final homogeneous batch.

batch certificate
A document containing information, as set out in Appendix 3 of the guidelines, will normally be issued for each batch by the manufacturer. Furthermore, a batch certificate may exceptionally be validated or issued by the competent authority of the exporting country, particularly for vaccines, sera and other biological products. The batch certificate accompanies every major consignment (see also section 3.14 of the guidelines).

*batch number
A distinctive combination of numbers and/or letters which specifically identifies a batch on the labels, the batch records, and the certificates of analysis, etc.

bulk product
A product that has completed all processing stages up to, but not including, final packaging.

certifying authority
The competent authority that issues product certificates. It must ensure that it possesses the capacities listed in section 2.4 of the guidelines.

charges for product certificates
See section 3.11 of the guidelines.

competent authority
The national authority as identified in the formal letter of acceptance in which each Member State informs WHO of its intention to participate in the Scheme. The extent of its participation should be indicated in the letter of acceptance (see section 2.1 of the guidelines). The competent authority can issue or receive certificates.

WHO makes available on request a continuously updated list of addresses of competent authorities and, when applicable, the specific conditions for participation.

competence and evaluation of national authority
See sections 2.4, 2.5 and 4.2 of the guidelines.

dosage form
The form of the completed pharmaceutical preparation, e.g. tablet, capsule, elixir, suppository.

drug regulatory authority
An authority appointed by the government of a Member State to administer the granting of marketing authorizations for pharmaceutical products in that country.

*finished product
A product that has undergone all stages of production, including packaging in its final container and labelling.

free sale certificate
See section 3.2 of the guidelines.

GMP certificate
See section 3.2 of the guidelines.

importing agents, guidelines for
See section 3.4 of the guidelines.

language of product certificate
See section 3.10 of the guidelines.

licence holder
An individual or a corporate entity possessing a marketing authorization for a pharmaceutical product.

licensee
An individual or corporate entity responsible for the information and publicity on, and the pharmacovigilance and surveillance of batches of, a pharmaceutical product and, if applicable, for their withdrawal, whether or not that individual or corporate entity is the holder of the marketing authorization.

limits of certificate by competent authority
See sections 3.12 and 4.8 of the guidelines.

lot
See *batch*.

*manufacture
All operations of purchase of materials and products, production, quality control, release, storage, shipment of finished products, and related controls.

*manufacturer
A company that carries out at least one step of manufacture. (For the different categories of manufacturer, see Appendix 1, explanatory note no. 8.)

marketing authorization
See *product licence*.

pharmaceutical product
Any medicine intended for human use or administered to food-producing animals, presented in its finished dosage form or as an active ingredient for use in such dosage form, that is subject to control by pharmaceutical legislation in both the exporting state and the importing state.

product
See *pharmaceutical product*.

product certificate
A document containing the information as set out in Appendix 1 of the guide-

lines that is validated and issued for a specific product by the competent authority of the exporting country and intended for use by the competent authority in the importing country or — in the absence of such an authority — by the drug procurement authority (see also section 3.5 of the guidelines).

Transmission of product certificate: see sections 3.8 and 4.9 of the guidelines.

Validity of product certificate: see section 3.9 of the guidelines.

When to request a product certificate: see section 3.5 of the guidelines.

product information
The approved product information referred to in section 4.7 of the guidelines and item 2A.5 of the Product Certificate. It normally consists of information for health professionals and the public (patient information leaflets), as approved in the exporting country and, when available, a data sheet or a Summary of Product Characteristics (SPC) approved by the regulatory authority.

product licence
An official document issued by the competent drug regulatory authority for the purpose of the marketing or free distribution of a product. It must set out, *inter alia*, the name of the product, the pharmaceutical dosage form, the quantitative formula (including excipients) per unit dose (using International Nonproprietary Names or national generic names, where they exist), the shelf-life and storage conditions, and packaging characteristics. It also contains all the information approved for health professionals and the public (except promotional information), the sales category, the name and address of the licence holder, and the period of validity of the licence.

product-licence holder
See *licence holder*.

*production
All operations involved in the preparation of a pharmaceutical product, from receipt of materials, through processing and packaging, to completion of the finished product.

registration
Any statutory system of approval required at national level as a precondition for introducing a pharmaceutical product on to the market.

registration certificate
See *product licence*.

specifications
See Appendix 3, explanatory note 7.

statement of licensing status

See section 3.13 of the guidelines and Appendix 2.

Summary Basis of Approval

The document prepared by some national regulatory authorities that summarizes the technical basis on which the product has been licensed (see section 4.7 of the guidelines and explanatory note 10 of the Product Certificate contained in Appendix 1).

Summary of Product Characteristics (SPC)

Product information as approved by the regulatory authority. The SPC serves as the basis for production of information for health personnel as well as for consumer information on labels and leaflets of medicinal products and for control of advertising (see also *Product information*).

tenders and brokers

See section 4.6 of the guidelines.

WHO responsibility

See section 5.4 of the guidelines.

Reference

1. *WHO Expert Committee on Specifications for Pharmaceutical Preparations. Thirty-second report.* Geneva, World Health Organization, 1992:18–22 (WHO Technical Report Series, No. 823).

World Health Assembly resolution WHA50.3: Guidelines on the WHO Certification Scheme on the Quality of Pharmaceutical Products Moving in International Commerce

The Fiftieth World Health Assembly,

Taking note of previous resolutions on WHO's Certification Scheme on the Quality of Pharmaceutical Products Moving in International Commerce, and particularly resolutions WHA45.29 and WHA49.14;

Having reviewed the revised guidelines on implementation of the Certification Scheme which are the result of field trials in a number of WHO Member States and discussions during the sixth and seventh biennial International Conferences of Drug Regulatory Authorities;[1]

Believing that the adoption of the revised guidelines will provide an

---

[1] WHO Technical Report Series, No. 863, 1996, Annex 10.

important instrument in support of drug registration in the importing country by ensuring access to transparent information on the regulatory status of the pharmaceutical product in the exporting country and the true origin of products to be imported,

1. ENDORSES the guidelines for implementation of the WHO Certification Scheme on the Quality of Pharmaceutical Products Moving in International Commerce and model certification forms annexed to the guidelines;

2. URGES Member States:
   (1) to implement these guidelines, to request WHO-type certificates in the form contained in the guidelines and to issue the certificates in the form proposed, as from 1 January 1998;
   (2) to inform the Director-General of their intent to apply the Scheme and of any significant reservations they intend to express relating to their participation as provided for in article 2.1 of the guidelines.

Guidelines on import procedures for pharmaceutical products[1]

1. Introductory notes

1.1 Public health considerations demand that pharmaceutical products should not be treated in the same way as ordinary commodities. Their manufacture and subsequent handling within the distribution chain, both nationally and internationally, must conform to prescribed standards and be rigorously controlled. These precautions serve to assure the quality of authentic products, and to prevent the infiltration of illicit products into the supply system.

1.2 Within the context of its revised drug strategy, adopted in 1986 by the Thirty-ninth World Health Assembly in resolution WHA39.27, WHO developed "Guiding principles for small national drug regulatory authorities" (1, 2) which established a regulatory approach in line with the resources available within a small national regulatory authority, and were intended to assure not only the quality, but also the safety and efficacy, of pharmaceutical products distributed under its aegis.

1.3 The principles emphasize the need for the effective use of the WHO Certification Scheme on the Quality of Pharmaceutical Products Moving in International Commerce. This constitutes a formal agreement between participating Member States to provide information on any product under consideration for export, notably on its registration status in the country of origin and whether or

---

[1] *WHO Expert Committee on Specifications for Pharmaceutical Preparations. Thirty-fourth Report.* Geneva, World Health Organization, 1996 (WHO Technical Report Series, No. 863).

not the manufacturer complies with WHO's guidelines on good manufacturing practices (GMP) for pharmaceutical products (*3*).

1.4 To be fully effective, the Scheme needs to be complemented by administrative and other safeguards aimed at ensuring that consignments of imported products are in conformity in all particulars with the relevant import licence and that they remain secure within the distribution chain. Storage and transit facilities must be proof against tampering and adverse climatic conditions, and relevant controls must be applied at every stage of transportation.

1.5 Pharmaceutical products containing substances controlled under the international conventions have long been subjected to rigorous border controls. Some of these controls, and particularly those designed to prevent the diversion and illicit interchange of products during transit, are relevant to all pharmaceutical products, and are therefore included in these guidelines. Full details of the special import controls required for narcotic drugs and psychotropic substances are given in the Appendix.

2. Objectives and scope

2.1 The following guidelines, which stem from the above considerations, have been developed in consultation with national drug regulatory authorities, the pharmaceutical industry, the World Customs Organization, and the United Nations International Drug Control Programme.

2.2 The guidelines are directed to all parties involved in the importation of pharmaceutical products, including national drug regulatory authorities, competent trade ministries, customs authorities, port authorities, and importing agents.

2.3 They are intended to promote efficiency in applying relevant regulations, to simplify the checking and handling of consignments of pharmaceutical products in international transit and, *inter alia*, to provide a basis for collaboration between the various interested parties.

2.4 They are applicable to any pharmaceutical product destined for use within the country of import, and are intended to be adapted to prevailing national conditions and legal requirements.

3. Legal responsibilities

3.1 The importation of pharmaceutical products should be effected in conformity with regulations promulgated under the national drugs act or other relevant legislation and enforced by the national drug regulatory authority. National guidelines providing recommendations on the implementation of these regulations should be drawn up by the national drug regulatory authority in collaboration with the customs authority and other interested agencies and organizations.

3.2 All transactions relating to the importation of consignments of pharmaceutical products should be conducted either through the governmental drug procurement agency or through independent wholesale dealers specifically designated and licensed by the national drug regulatory authority for this purpose.

3.3 The importation of all consignments of pharmaceutical products should be channelled exclusively through customs posts specifically designated for this purpose.

3.4 All formalities undertaken on importation should be coordinated by the customs service, which should have the authority to request the services of an official pharmaceutical inspector as occasion demands. When justified by the workload, a pharmaceutical inspector may be stationed full time at one or more of the designated ports of entry.

3.5 The customs authority should have the discretionary powers to request technical advice and opinions from other appropriately qualified persons, should this be warranted by particular circumstances.

4. Legal basis of control

4.1 Subject to the exemptions specified in paragraph 4.4 below, only pharmaceutical products proved by appropriate documentation to be duly licensed for marketing within the importing country should be cleared by customs.

4.2 The national drug regulatory authority should compile comprehensive and frequently updated lists of licensed products and authorized importing agents, and issue notifications of any product licences withdrawn on grounds of safety; the latter should be rapidly communicated and presented in a manner designed to attract attention. All lists and notifications of withdrawal of a product licence should be accessible, preferably through a computerized database, to designated customs posts, authorized importing agents and all drug wholesalers.

4.3 Efficient and confidential channels for communicating information on counterfeit products and other illicit activities should be established between all interested official bodies.

4.4 In countries where no formal system of product licensing has been established, importation of products is most effectively controlled by issuing permits in the name of the national drug regulatory authority to the authorized importing agency or agent. Additional measures that may be taken under these conditions include:

— the provision by the national drug regulatory authority to the customs

authorities, and to the importing agency and agents, of official lists of pharmaceutical products permitted and/or prohibited to be imported;
— the provision by the importing agent of certified information to establish that the product is authorized by licence for sale in the country of export.

4.5 The national drug regulatory authority should reserve discretionary powers to waive product licensing requirements in respect of consignments of pharmaceutical products imported in response to emergency situations and, exceptionally, in response to requests from clinicians for limited supplies of an unlicensed product needed for the treatment of a specific named patient.

5. Required documentation

5.1 As a prerequisite to customs clearance, the importing agency or agent should be required to furnish the customs authority with the following documentation in respect of each consignment:

— certified copies of documents issued by the national drug regulatory authority in the importing country, attesting that:
  (a) the importer is duly authorized by licence to undertake the transaction; and
  (b) the product is duly authorized by licence to be marketed in the importing country;
— a batch certificate issued by the manufacturer, consonant with the requirements of the WHO Certification Scheme, that documents the results of the final analytical control of the batch(es) constituting the consignment;
— a relevant invoice or bill and, when applicable, an authorization for the release of foreign exchange granted by the competent national authority in the country of import;
— any other documentation required by national legislation for customs clearance.

6. Implementation of controls

6.1 A visual and physical examination should be routinely undertaken by the customs authorities, if possible in collaboration with an inspector of the national drug regulatory authority. The size of the consignment should be checked against invoices, and particular attention should be accorded to the nature and condition of the packaging and labelling.

6.2 Arrangements should be made with the inspector of the national drug regulatory authority for the routine sampling and subsequent analysis of exceptionally large and/or valuable consignments and any other consignment that has apparently deteriorated, or that is damaged or of doubtful authenticity.

6.3 When samples are taken for analysis to a governmental or other accredited drug quality control laboratory, the consignment should be placed in quarantine. During this procedure, and throughout the time that the consignment is held in customs, particular care must be taken to ensure that packages do not come into contact with potential contaminants.

6.4 A consignment suspected of being counterfeit should be placed in quarantine pending the analysis of samples and forensic investigation. Time is often saved if materials and reagents needed to undertake simple analytical tests are available at the port of entry.

6.5 Representatives of the manufacturer of the authentic product, and/or the owner of the trademark, and the consignee should immediately be advised of such action.

6.6 National regulations should define the responsibilities of the interested parties and the precise procedures to be followed. In particular, the provisions should identify the agency responsible for coordinating the investigation and bringing prosecutions.

6.7 Counterfeit or other products which have been imported in contravention of the law must be forfeited and destroyed, or otherwise dealt with in accordance with legal procedures.

6.8 The relevant authorities must be indemnified against any consequent legal actions and proceedings.

6.9 National drug regulatory authorities are urged to notify other national authorities of confirmed cases of imported counterfeit pharmaceutical products through the Division of Drug Management and Policies of WHO.

7. Procedures applicable to pharmaceutical starting materials

7.1 In accordance with good manufacturing practices, formal responsibility for the analytical control of starting materials is vested in the manufacturer of the finished pharmaceutical product. Consequently, few countries have introduced formal licensing requirements for active pharmaceutical substances.

7.2 Exceptionally, however, some national authorities now exercise documentary and, in some cases, analytical control of starting materials as a prerequisite to customs clearance.

7.3 Each imported consignment of a pharmaceutical starting material should be accompanied by a warranty (or batch certificate) prepared by the manufacturer as recommended by the WHO Certification Scheme.

8. Storage facilities

8.1 Many pharmaceutical products tend to degrade on storage and some need to be kept in cold storage. All customs posts designated to handle consignments of pharmaceutical products should consequently be provided with secure storage facilities, including refrigerated compartments. If no pharmaceutical inspector is employed on site, these facilities should be inspected periodically by the national drug regulatory authority to ensure that all equipment is maintained in good working order.

8.2 The importing agency or agent should alert the customs authorities in advance of the anticipated arrival of consignments in order that they may be transferred from the international carrier to the designated storage facility with the minimum of delay and, in appropriate cases, without breaking the cold chain.

8.3 Consignments of pharmaceutical products and pharmaceutical starting materials should be accorded high priority for clearance through customs.

8.4 When several different consignments await clearance, the customs authorities should be guided by the drug inspector as to which should be accorded priority.

9. Training requirements

9.1 Performance in implementing the guidelines should be reviewed on an open-ended basis and, if necessary, improved in the light of on-site monitoring and evaluation. Workshops designed to facilitate efficient implementation of the guidelines and to foster collaborative approaches between the various responsible parties should be organized, as circumstances demand, by the national drug regulatory authority in collaboration with the customs authority.

References

1. *WHO Expert Committee on Specifications for Pharmaceutical Preparations. Thirty-first report.* Geneva, World Health Organization, 1990:64–79 (WHO Technical Report Series, No. 790).

2. *The use of essential drugs. Model List of Essential Drugs (Seventh List). Fifth report of the WHO Expert Committee.* Geneva, World Health Organization, 1992:62–74 (WHO Technical Report Series, No. 825).

3. Good manufacturing practices for pharmaceutical products. In: *WHO Expert Committee on Specifications for Pharmaceutical Preparations. Thirty-second report.* Geneva, World Health Organization, 1992:14–79 (WHO Technical Report Series, No. 823).

Glossary

The definitions given apply to the terms used in these guidelines. They may have different meanings in other contexts.

authorization
See Note.

counterfeit product
A pharmaceutical product that is deliberately and fraudulently mislabelled with respect to identity and/or source. Both branded and generic products can be counterfeited, and counterfeit products may include products with the correct ingredients, with the wrong ingredients, without active ingredients, with insufficient quantity of active ingredients or with fake packaging.

drug regulatory authority
The national agency responsible for the registration of, and other regulatory activities concerning, pharmaceutical products.

import authority
The national agency responsible for authorizing imports (e.g. the ministry or department of trade or of imports and exports).

importation
The act of bringing or causing any goods to be brought into a customs territory (national territory, excluding any free zone).

importer
An individual or company or similar legal entity importing or seeking to import a pharmaceutical product. A "licensed" or "registered" importer is one who has been granted a licence or registration status for the purpose. In addition to a general licence or permit as an importer, some countries require an additional licence to be issued by the national drug regulatory authority if pharmaceutical products are to be imported.

licence
See Note.

pharmaceutical product
Any medicine intended for human or veterinary use, presented in its finished dosage form, that is subject to control by pharmaceutical legislation in both the exporting state and the importing state.

registration
See Note.

starting material
Any substance of defined quality used in the production of a pharmaceutical product, but excluding packaging materials.

Note

Because of a lack of uniformity in national legal requirements and administrative practices, the terms "registered", "licenced" and "authorized" have been used in these guidelines as if they were interchangeable. When the guidelines are being used as a basis for drawing up national guidelines, more precise terminology applicable to the country concerned should be used. In some countries, for example, "certificate of drug registration" has been replaced by terms such as "marketing authorization".

Appendix. Special import controls for narcotic drugs and psychotropic substances[1]

In accordance with the requirements of the international drug control treaties (i.e. the Single Convention on Narcotic Drugs, 1961, and that Convention as amended by the 1972 Protocol, and the Convention on Psychotropic Substances, 1971, referred to subsequently as the 1961 Convention and the 1971 Convention), each state must adopt national legislation and administrative regulations, and establish administrative structures to ensure the full implementation of the provisions of these treaties on its territory and cooperation with other states.

Most of the requirements specified in these guidelines on import procedures for pharmaceutical products also apply to the border control of narcotic drugs and psychotropic substances. In addition, detailed information on the control of international trade in narcotic drugs and psychotropic substances can be found in Article 31 of the 1961 Convention and Article 12 of the 1971 Convention respectively. The guidelines provided in this Appendix are intended to facilitate the operation of control at entry points, and can be expanded by taking into account the legislation and administrative regulations in force in each country.

The customs authorities and, if applicable, any other law enforcement authorities assigned to border control should cooperate closely with the competent authorities for the control of narcotic drugs and psychotropic substances

---

[1] "Narcotic drug" means any of the substances listed in Schedules I and II of the Single Convention on Narcotic Drugs, 1961, as amended by the 1972 Protocol, whether natural or synthetic; "psychotropic substance" means any substance, natural or synthetic, listed in Schedule I, II, III or IV of the Convention on Psychotropic Substances, 1971.

designated by the government (subsequently referred to as the competent authorities). It should be noted that, while the competent authorities in some countries are different from the national drug regulatory authority, in others they may be one and the same.

The customs authorities, or any other competent law enforcement authorities, should be well trained and equipped (e.g. with drug identification kits) so that they can distinguish consignments of narcotic drugs and psychotropic substances from other pharmaceutical products. They should be provided with lists of narcotic drugs and psychotropic substances under international control, e.g. the "Yellow List" and "Green List" published by the International Narcotics Control Board, which include, *inter alia*, trade names of pharmaceutical products containing narcotic drugs and psychotropic substances. They may also make use of the *Multilingual dictionary of narcotic drugs and psychotropic substances under international control* (ST/NAR/1/REV.1) published by the United Nations (sales number E/F/S.93.XI.2). Furthermore, they should be provided with lists of narcotic drugs and psychotropic substances whose importation into the country has been prohibited.

Checks conducted during the border control of narcotic drugs and of psychotropic substances listed in Schedules I and II of the 1971 Convention should ensure that each consignment has been duly authorized by the competent authorities of the importing country. The competent authorities express their consent to each import by issuing an import certificate (for narcotic drugs) or an import authorization (for psychotropic substances). When presented with the original of this document, the competent authorities of the exporting country may issue an export authorization permitting the consignment containing narcotic drugs or psychotropic substances to leave the exporting country. In free ports and zones governments should exercise the same supervision and control as in other parts of their territory, provided, however, that they may apply more drastic measures if appropriate.

The competent authorities of the importing country may wish to inform the customs, or any other competent law enforcement authorities, of authorized imports of narcotic drugs and psychotropic substances before the entry of the consignment into the country.

In addition to the other documents referred to in section 5 of the guidelines, the customs authorities should require the importer or importer's agent to provide them with a copy of the respective import authorization (certificate) issued by the competent authorities of the importing country. This document should be compared with the export authorization issued by the competent authorities of the exporting country, a copy of which must accompany each consignment. The authenticity of these documents must be carefully checked. In case of doubt, the competent authorities should be consulted immediately.

Import and export authorizations (certificates) should contain the following information:

— the name of the narcotic drug or psychotropic substance (if available, the International Nonproprietary Name);
— the quantity to be imported/exported, expressed in terms of anhydrous base content;
— the pharmaceutical form and, if in the form of a preparation, the name of the preparation;
— the name and address of the importer and exporter;
— the period of validity of the authorization.

In addition, the export authorization should contain the number and date of the corresponding import authorization/certificate and the name of the competent authority of the importing country by whom it was issued.

The competent authorities of the importing country may wish to specify in the import authorization/certificate the entry point through which the importation must be effected.

During the visual and physical examination of the imported consignment, the quantity of narcotic drugs or psychotropic substances contained in it should be carefully checked. If the quantity exceeds the amount authorized, the consignment should be stopped by the customs and the matter brought to the attention of the competent authorities for the control of narcotic drugs and psychotropic substances in the importing country. If the quantity imported is the same as, or less than, the amount authorized, the quantity should be recorded on the copy of the export authorization accompanying the consignment and communicated to the competent authorities of the importing country.

All consignments containing psychotropic substances included in Schedule III of the 1971 Convention must be accompanied by a separate export declaration. This document should indicate the name and address of the exporter and importer, the name of the substance, the quantity and the pharmaceutical form in which the substance is exported, including, if applicable, the name of the preparation and the date of dispatch.

Pursuant to the recommendations contained in resolutions of the Economic and Social Council of the United Nations, many governments now require import authorizations not only for psychotropic substances in Schedules I and II but also for those in Schedules III and IV of the 1971 Convention. This strengthening of the control requirements has proved to be very useful in preventing attempts to divert psychotropic substances, such as stimulants, sedative hypnotics and tranquillizers, into illicit traffic.

8.
Counterfeit products

Observations and recommendations on counterfeit drugs[1,2]

A counterfeit medicine is one which is deliberately and fraudulently mislabelled with respect to identity and/or source. Counterfeiting can apply to both branded and generic products, and counterfeit products may include products with the correct ingredients, with the wrong ingredients, without active ingredients, with an insufficient quantity of active ingredient or with fake packaging.

Observations

1. Society and all innocent parties in the health care chain are "victims" when counterfeiting occurs and it is important that they work together in an atmosphere of mutual cooperation and trust, rather than criticism, in order to combat the menace.

- Patients are the primary victims because their health and even lives are put at risk when they take medicines without the safeguards which they are entitled to expect from legitimate pharmaceutical production and regulatory control.
- Legitimate manufacturers are victims not only because of direct loss of revenue but because confidence in their products is undermined, leading to loss of sales. The reputation of the company and image of the products are both damaged.
- Governments are victims because their funds are used to purchase medicines of unknown reliability and safety and they are therefore failing in their objective to protect the public health. Governments are also victims because of fiscal revenue losses.
- Health care professionals are the victims through loss of patients' confidence in their services. When the professional is also the supplier (e.g. the pharmacist) financial losses may be incurred through the purchase of fake products.

---

[1] Adapted from WHO document WHO/DMP/CFD/92.
[2] Observations and recommendations made at a joint WHO/International Federation of Pharmaceutical Manufacturers Associations workshop on counterfeit drugs, Geneva, 1–3 April 1992.

2. There is evidence that trade in counterfeit products is facilitated where:

— there is weak drug regulatory control and enforcement;
— there is a scarcity and/or erratic supply of basic medicines;
— there are extended, relatively unregulated markets and distribution chains, in both developing and developed countries;
— price differentials create an incentive for drug diversion within and between established channels;
— there is lack of effective intellectual property protection;
— due regard is not paid to quality assurance.

3. There is inadequate information about the scale of pharmaceutical counterfeiting. The Counterfeiting Intelligence Bureau of the International Chamber of Commerce estimates that 5% of all world trade in 1991 was counterfeit. This is likely to be greater for pharmaceuticals which are in high demand and easily transportable. Estimates from a wide range of countries vary from 0 to over 60% in sectors of the market that are inadequately controlled.

4. There is little consistent information on the source of counterfeits. However, there appears to be a clear correlation between the source of counterfeits and the absence of a strong intellectual property system.

5. Although the exchange of information on counterfeit pharmaceuticals is improving:

- there is a perceived inadequacy on the part of certain regulatory authorities in both developing and developed countries to acknowledge and manage the problem, perhaps because this admits to a failure in their control systems, perhaps because they are unable or unwilling to commit adequate resources to address the issue, or perhaps because of other priorities.
- there is also a perceived reluctance on the part of authentic manufacturers to share information available to them, perhaps because of lack of confidence in the way regulatory authorities address the problem and because of concern about the damage to the legitimate product which may result.

6. Counterfeiting varies from small "cottage industries" in some countries to large international consortia, including some elements of organized crime. Often those dealing in counterfeit medicines are also involved in counterfeiting other products such as spirits, tobacco and perfume. There are signs of generalized corruption, including bribery or threats to politicians, officials, pharmacists and others.

7. Evidence is emerging of links between pharmaceutical counterfeiting and international narcotics rings. There are highly developed laws to address the distribution of narcotic drugs and psychotropic substances, in contrast with the lack of laws or adequate systems to cope with counterfeit drugs. Lessons can therefore be learned from the experience of the International Narcotics Control

Board (INCB) and United Nations International Drug Control Programme (UNDCP) in trying to combat the illicit trafficking of narcotic drugs and psychotropic substances through international controls.

8. There is a general lack of effective regulation and appropriate legal infrastructure to manage the counterfeiting problem in both developed and developing countries, leading to surprising loopholes in the most sophisticated of systems.

9. Conditions are being created for a greater flow of counterfeits between countries as border controls are relaxed or are abolished.

10. While there is a need to avoid unnecessary public alarm, the principle of openness is, in the long term, in the best interest of all parties.

11. Consumer-generated demand for inappropriate products, in a situation where such products are misused or abused, can encourage the availability of counterfeits.

12. Often there are insufficient official resources dedicated to prevention and prosecution in instances of the distribution and sale of counterfeit products.

13. Also in many countries there are insufficient channels available to pharmaceutical companies to pursue effective remedial action.

Recommendations

International level

1. There is a need for greater international awareness and acknowledgement of the hazards to health of counterfeit medicines. Political will is needed to mobilize resources for implementation of effective countermeasures. Without political will and effective regulation, counterfeiting will continue to thrive.

2. Counterfeiting is an international problem, which needs to be addressed by the implementation of international laws. A sound legal framework is provided by the proposed anti-counterfeiting provisions in the draft GATT–TRIPS Agreement (General Agreement on Tariffs and Trade—Aspects of Intellectual Property Rights including Trade in Counterfeit Goods), which is based on effective international trademark protection and is supported by enforceable sanctions and penalties (including imprisonment).

3. Governments should implement appropriate legislation that identifies the import, national transit and export of counterfeit goods into, across and out of their customs territories as a customs offence and should confer upon their customs services the necessary legal powers to seize the goods with a view to forfeiture if they are subsequently found to be counterfeit. Such legislation should provide for customs services to act on an *ex officio* basis, and not only on application by the trademark owner.

4. A mechanism should be established through which organizations with an interest in tackling the problem of counterfeiting can exchange information about the nature and extent of counterfeiting, the movement of counterfeit products and concluded investigations into counterfeit operations. To be fully effective, this information network should include manufacturers, distributors, professional bodies and regulatory agencies.

5. A data bank of cases should be established within a clearing house that maintains a directory of interested organizations and contact points. The medium should also provide technical support for training those involved in the detection of counterfeiting activity.

6. Since investigation of an inquiry may be frustrated by leakage of information it was recognized that, until a given case is concluded, relevant information should be disclosed only to organizations and agencies in a position to assist in its investigation.

National level

1. A legal and administrative framework needs to be in place to define and control the legitimate drug market and the drug distribution system before effective controls can be applied to illicit trade and counterfeiting.

The establishment of a drug regulatory agency with a registration procedure for all products is a prerequisite and the workshop endorsed the recommendations of the WHO Guiding Principles for Small National Drug Regulatory Authorities. Full use should also be made of the WHO Certification Scheme on the Quality of Pharmaceutical Products Moving in International Commerce to establish the true origin of products. Counterfeiting of medicines should be an explicit criminal offence with appropriately severe penalties.

2. Adequate resources must be made available for inspection and enforcement of controls at all stages in the drug distribution chain. Laboratory facilities for carrying out analytical tests on products should be available everywhere, preferably on a national basis or, failing this, through regional or international cooperation.

3. The points through which pharmaceutical products can be imported or exported should be designated. Customs staff at these designated points should be alerted to the significance of pharmaceutical counterfeiting and trained to identify counterfeit material.

There should be targeted inspection of pharmaceutical goods at border points and samples should be taken for analysis where appropriate.

4. Procedures should be established to ensure cooperation and exchange of information between the different branches of law enforcement: police, customs and the national drug inspectorate.

5. A critical examination of the whole legal framework should be made in both developed and developing countries in order to ensure that there are no loopholes which allow pharmaceutical products to be manufactured, imported, exported or distributed outside the controls of good manufacturing practices, product licensing and other regulatory requirements.

6. Pharmaceutical manufacturers, distributors and health care professionals should notify their national customs service of any information that comes into their possession concerning possible import/export shipments of pharmaceutical products suspected to be counterfeit. Whenever possible, specific details should be provided of carrier, likely point of entry/departure, consignor/consignee, probable date of arrival, description of goods involved and details of packaging/labelling to assist customs to target the goods for interception.

7. National laws should provide rights of private action by companies to enforce their trademark rights through seizure of clearly suspected counterfeit shipments. Such rights, which are exemplified by the Trademark and Counterfeiting Act of 1984 of the United States of America can provide additional protection to patients and manufacturers if:

— confidentiality in associated legal proceedings is protected, and
— penalties for their infringement constitute a serious deterrent.

8. Developing countries should study, in particular, the countermeasures adopted in some countries of West Africa, and consider the adoption of similar strategies.

The pharmaceutical industry

1. The national industry associations and the International Federation of Pharmaceutical Manufacturers Associations (IFPMA) should encourage pharmaceutical companies to share information both with drug regulatory agencies and among themselves when instances of counterfeiting are detected. The development of guidelines should be considered.

2. The industry should continue to develop anti-counterfeiting measures such as packaging and labelling which are hard to copy (e.g. use of holograms). This includes the use of both covert and overt devices that are made known to reliable enforcement agencies to facilitate identification.

3. Manufacturers should ensure that they establish suitable security measures to detect and prevent diversion of ingredients, products and packaging material for illegal purposes.

4. The industry, through the IFPMA, should collaborate with the Customs Co-operation Council (CCC) over the preparation of guides and training material for customs officials and inspectors.

5. The industry should be prepared to contribute its expert knowledge on both the packaging and the active ingredient profile of its products in undertaking or assisting in the inspection and analysis of products suspected of being counterfeit.

6. Pharmacists, wholesalers and manufacturers should cooperate with each other and with enforcement authorities to ensure regular sampling and analysis of pharmaceutical products in circulation as a means to identify and deter counterfeiting activities.

Pharmacists

1. The professional bodies should exhort pharmacists to purchase stocks from reputable sources, to report any suspicion that they have been offered or have acquired counterfeit products, to isolate and withhold from sale any suspect products and to cooperate with enforcement agencies.

2. The professional bodies should also establish effective channels for communication and cooperation with enforcement agencies and legitimate manufacturers, and should act to disseminate information about suspected counterfeiting activity to their members.

Wholesalers

1. Products should reach the end-user by the most direct route that is practicable. Distribution of products through a large number of intermediaries and complex transactions should be discouraged. Each facility within the distribution chain must be registered, licensed, inspected and required to maintain complete records of the source from which consignments are purchased.

2. Ideally the dispensing pharmacist should obtain medicines directly from a reputable manufacturer. In practice, a legitimate role exists for the responsible wholesaler. However, there should not normally be more transactions than those between manufacturer and wholesaler, and wholesaler and dispensing pharmacist. Batch documentation should provide details of all transactions relating to the distribution of a given consignment.

3. As a condition of licensing, distributors should employ a suitably qualified person, preferably a pharmacist, to be responsible for documentation and analysis.

4. To facilitate the investigation of suspected counterfeit products and their origin, acquisition and sales records should be available to authorized persons.

Consumers and educators

1. The public should be made aware of the existence of counterfeit pharmaceutical products in order to mobilize the political will for implementation of

effective countermeasures. In countries where medicines are sold outside normal pharmaceutical channels, the public should be encouraged to purchase medicines only from reliable vendors.

2. A programme of education about counterfeit medicines, having regard for national circumstances, should be developed for community leaders, teachers, the media, the police, traditional healers and local health personnel.

3. The industry, professional bodies, regulatory authorities and the international community should ensure that consumers are given appropriate and timely information on the availability of counterfeit products, recognizing the complementary needs to provide relevant consumer information without engendering unwarranted public alarm.

9.
Training

Training programme in drug analysis[1,2]

1. Introduction

The establishment of a new drug control laboratory in a developing country and the subsequent expansion of its activities is dependent on the local availability of properly trained staff. This applies both to the supervisory personnel (including the head of the laboratory) and to the analysts who will perform the tests (either single-handed or with the assistance of technicians).

Staff for drug control laboratories are usually recruited from schools of pharmacy but may also come from institutions specializing in various other branches of science. These graduates have adequate theoretical knowledge to perform standard analytical tasks but need a period of practical in-service training before they can be allowed to work independently.

In large established drug control laboratories, the practical training of newly recruited staff is usually accomplished by their temporary attachment to experienced analysts for periods of apprenticeship. In addition, a new staff member is sometimes required to attend briefing sessions on such matters as the internal organization of the laboratory, analytical documentation and reporting, and safety measures. However, such training is often impracticable in small laboratories and is out of the question when a completely new laboratory is to be established.

The WHO Expert Committee on Specifications for Pharmaceutical Preparations, in its twenty-eighth and twenty-ninth reports, reviewed various aspects of the establishment and expansion of drug control laboratories in developing countries and came to the conclusion that the lack of adequately trained staff for governmental drug control laboratories is a major obstacle in the way of national programmes on improvement of drug quality (1, 2). The Committee is aware that some provision has already been made for individual training of drug analysts from developing countries (2). This arrangement, however, is more suited to the training of supervisory staff or of analysts who already have

---

[1] *WHO Expert Committee on Specifications for Pharmaceutical Preparations. Thirtieth Report.* Geneva, World Health Organization, 1987 (WHO Technical Report Series, No. 748).
[2] A group training course for recent science and pharmacy graduates in the practical and theoretical aspects of regulatory drug analysis.

substantial professional experience and are under consideration for promotion to supervisory positions. The Committee has therefore focused its attention on group training (1, 2) of recent graduates and has further developed the basic ideas presented in the twenty-ninth report of the Expert Committee (2).

The syllabus is designed to train people for the facilities provided in the model governmental drug control laboratories described in section 2 of this report.[1] However, the training provided would enable the participants to adapt readily to the requirements of work in industrial control laboratories.

In order to ensure that the training is of direct relevance to analysts from developing countries, it should be carried out in a well-equipped drug control laboratory in a developing country that has specialists in each discipline on its staff.

2. Course objectives and types of training

2.1 Course objectives

The main objective of the proposed training is to provide basic practical guidance on the analysis of pharmaceutical products. It is not intended to produce highly qualified specialists in the whole field of drug analysis. Special skills can only be acquired through long experience in laboratory work.

As a national drug control laboratory is not usually involved directly in the sampling of pharmaceutical products, sampling has not been included in the curriculum.

2.2 Types of training

Separate courses are proposed for chemical, microbiological, and biological methods of drug control.

The course dealing with chemical methods of analysis is comprehensive and reflects the present preponderance of chemical and instrumental methods among analytical procedures. It does not, however, include instruction on the use of complex instruments, such as nuclear magnetic resonance spectrometers, mass spectrometers, or autoanalysers, these not being provided for in the model laboratories described in section 2 of this report.[1] Instruments, such as polarographs, that are rarely used are discussed only from the theoretical standpoint.

The course on microbiological control emphasizes sterility testing, microbiological spoilage testing, potency tests for antibiotics and other specific drug substances, and the preparation and monitoring of culture media under local conditions. Methods used in the control of natural products are included, as well as the use of microscopic techniques for plant identification.

---

[1] *WHO Expert Committee on Specifications for Pharmaceutical Preparations. Thirtieth Report.* Geneva, World Health Organization, 1987 (WHO Technical Report Series, No. 748): 12–13.

The biological control course is mainly concerned with pyrogen testing and specific safety tests. The testing of biological products such as vaccines and blood products is left out of consideration. Since many of the trainees admitted to the course will have received little formal training in pharmacology, sufficient theoretical knowledge must be provided to enable them to appreciate the objectives and importance of experimental work.

2.3 Educational background of trainees

The courses are intended for recent graduates in science or pharmacy with 3–4 years of education at university level. Among science graduates, preference should be given to those with detailed knowledge of analytical chemistry, biochemistry, or microbiology, but extensive practical experience is not required.

2.4 Training in more than one subject

Trainees desiring to be trained in more than one aspect of analysis should allow an interval of at least 1 year to elapse between courses, in order to ensure that each period of training is complemented by an extended period of practical experience.

3. Duration of training courses

3.1 General

It is envisaged that the courses in chemical control methods and in microbiological control should each last 6 months.

Since training in biological control is more restricted in its scope the syllabus can be completed in 3–4 months.

3.2 Teaching arrangements

The first week of each course provides an introduction to the general principles of quality control and analysis as they relate to procurement and distribution systems for pharmaceutical products.

It also develops a general awareness of all important aspects of quality control and a clear perception of the duties and responsibilities of an analyst. In particular it underscores the importance of instituting good laboratory practices in the interests of both efficiency and safety.

The practical training that follows also provides for discussions on the theoretical aspects of the use of instruments and the applicability and utility of individual methods, which it is recommended should occupy some 10–15% of the time available.

No guidance is given on the sequence of topics or the amount of time to be allocated to each. Detailed schedules can only be prepared locally on the basis of the facilities available.

In each course, the trainee, in addition to becoming familiar with the use of instruments and test methods, is expected to perform independently the full range of tests that he or she will subsequently meet in routine practice. Participants in the chemical drug control course should complete analyses of at least 25 pharmaceutical products, including both dosage forms and drug substances and in accordance with both pharmacopoeial monographs and manufacturer's specifications.

3.3 Course certificate

Trainees who successfully complete the whole course should be awarded a certificate indicating the nature of the course and its duration.

4. Course programmes

4.1 Introductory subjects

- Introduction to a national drug regulatory system and the activities involved in pharmaceutical inspection.
- The reasons for drug quality testing, including in-process quality control (good manufacturing practice requirements) and the analysis of finished products.
- An introduction to the statutory instruments in force locally (e.g. a drug and cosmetics act).
- The role of governmental drug control laboratories in relation to drug surveillance programmes.
- An introduction to the use of regional/national and international pharmacopoeias; selection of requirements and test methods suitable for the product.
- Operation of an analytical laboratory.
- Duties and responsibilities of an analyst.
- Good laboratory practices in governmental drug control laboratories.
- Maintenance of analytical instruments.
- Safety procedures in analytical laboratories.
- Record-keeping; the importance of properly documented laboratory work; maintenance of laboratory notebooks and the preparation of certificates of analysis.
- Reference standards and working standards; their importance and maintenance.
- Storage and care of samples.

4.2 Chemical drug control training programme

	Theoretical subject	Laboratory work
General		
• Checking and calibration of simple laboratory instruments, including analytical balances	+	+
• General quality standards and limit tests (sulfated ash, loss on drying, iron, arsenic, chloride, sulfate, lead, and heavy metals)	+	+
• Testing of packaging material	+	
• Preparation of reagents for the quantitative analysis of pharmaceutical products	+	+
• Evaluation of test results and the concept of statistical evaluation of analytical results	+	
Physical tests		
• Melting point determination and the concept of mixed melting points	+	+
• Viscosity	+	+
• Refractive index	+	+
• Specific optical rotation	+	+
• Relative density	+	+
• Osmolarity	+	+
• Azeotropic distillation	+	
Gravimetric methods (test-tube methods)		
• Assay by the gravimetric method	+	+
Potentiometric techniques		
• Determination of pH	+	+
• Ion-selective electrodes	+	+
Titrimetric and related methods (employing both visual and potentiometric endpoint determination)		
• Acid-base	+	+
• Oxidation-reduction	+	+
• Non-aqueous	+	+
• Complexometric	+	+
• Karl Fischer	+	
• Polarography	+	
• Iodine value	+	+
• Saponification and acid values	+	+
• Nitrogen assay by the Kjeldahl method	+	+
• Oxygen combustion method	+	+
Spectrophotometric techniques		
• UV/visible	+	+
• Infrared	+	+
• Flame photometry	+	+
• Atomic absorption	+	+
• Fluorescence (especially in the analysis of vitamins)	+	+

	Theoretical subject	Laboratory work
Chromatographic techniques		
• Thin-layer	+	+
• Paper	+	+
• Column	+	+
• Gas-liquid chromatography	+	+
• High performance liquid chromatography	+	+
• Electrophoresis	+	
Pharmacognostic testing		
• Organoleptic examinations	+	+
• Microscopic examination of crude drugs	+	+
• Microchemical and phytochemical evaluation (alkaloids, glycosides, saponins, etc.)	+	+
• Physical evaluation (ash value, fluorescence, moisture content of crude drugs, extractive value)	+	+
• Physicochemical and chemical assay of crude drugs and galenicals	+	+
Dosage-form testing		
• General test procedures	+	
• The concepts of bioavailability and bioequivalence	+	+
• Disintegration	+	+
• Dissolution	+	+
• Uniformity of mass	+	+
• Content uniformity of single-dose pharmaceutical products	+	+
• Tablet hardness and friability	+	+
• Assay of preservatives in a parenteral preparation	+	+
• Verification of added colouring matter in tablets and oral liquid preparations	+	+
• Limit tests for particulate matter in large-volume parenterals	+	+
Stability studies		
• Studies of the shelf-life of single-ingredient and multi-ingredient formulations at room temperature and at elevated temperature (accelerated decomposition) under different humidity conditions	+	+
Control of products requiring enzymatic determination		
• Control of pharmaceutical products containing pepsin, trypsin, papain, diastase, and pancreatin	+	+

4.3 Microbiological control training programme

Theoretical basis

- Morphology and fine structure of bacteria, fungi, and viruses; classification and nomenclature of bacteria; cultivation of microorganisms: nutritional

requirements; ingredients, types, and preparations of culture media; physical conditions required for microbial growth; pure cultures and their characteristics; methods of isolating pure cultures; methods of preserving microorganisms.
- Effects of physical agents: pasteurization; sterilization by dry heat, moist heat, radiation and ethylene oxide; filtration; sterility testing.
- Effects of chemical agents; characteristics and classification of disinfectants; their selection and evaluation.
- Antibiotics and other chemotherapeutic agents; history of chemotherapy; classification of antibiotics; general chemical properties; mode of action; antimicrobial spectrum; development of resistance.
- Introduction to general biometry including the fundamentals of probability and significance calculations.
- Assay of antibiotics.
- Microbiological control of preparations not normally required to be sterile.
- Documentation and evaluation of test results.

Laboratory work

- General microbiology

    — Preparation and dispensing of solid and liquid culture media.
    — Sterilization of glassware.
    — Small-scale preparation of sterile liquids.
    — Aseptic transfer of microbial cultures.
    — Microbiological method of testing the efficiency of a laminar-flow hood.
    — Count of microorganisms: plate method and most-probable-number method.
    — Study of the morphology of microorganisms by different staining methods:

        (i) Gram staining;
        (ii) spore staining;
        (iii) capsule staining.

    — Microbial limit tests for pathogenic organisms (*Pseudomonas aeruginosa, Staphylococcus aureus, Escherichia coli,* and *Salmonella.*
    — Sterility test for injectables:

        (i) containing no inhibitor;
        (ii) containing inhibitors (membrane filter method).

    — Isolation of microorganisms from locally available material; their maintenance; maintenance of reference microbial cultures.
    — Microbiological spoilage testing.
    — Testing the effectiveness of antimicrobial preservatives.

- Microbiological assay
  - Assay of antibiotics by the agar diffusion method, using both small plates (Petri dishes) and large plates, by means of the following techniques (including statistical analysis):
  - (i) 2 + 2 and 3 + 3 design for both large and small plates;
  - (ii) 6 × 6 and 8 × 8 Latin-square design for large square plates.
  - Turbidimetric assay of antibiotics, with due attention to the experimental design.
  - Assay of vitamins by both turbidimetric and agar diffusion methods.
  - Bioautographic technique.
  - Determination of the effectiveness of disinfectants (Rideal-Walker coefficient).

4.4 Biological control training programme

Theoretical basis

- General introduction to pharmacology.
- Absorption, distribution, biotransformation, and excretion.
- Dosage forms; different routes of administration and their influence on the biological response.
- Pharmacological classification of drugs, with representative examples.
- Modes of action of drugs with examples: extracellular and intracellular effects, membrane effects, enzyme effects, action on specific receptors, interactions.
- Responses in isolated tissues and intact animals; graded responses (oxytocin on rat uterus, vasopressin on cat blood pressure).
- Nature, source, and effects of pyrogens.
- Determination of dose and solvent for the pyrogen test on rabbits.
- Introduction to general biometry, including the fundamentals of probability and significance calculations.
- Quantal responses: minimum lethal dose (toxicity of stibogluconate sodium), percentage of animals responding to different doses (insulin assay in mice).
- Recording and evaluation of test results.
- Ethical responsibilities in using animals and consideration of alternatives to animal testing.

Laboratory work

- Animal house
  - Selection, handling, and care of laboratory animals; safety considerations; demonstration and instruction.

- Pyrogens
  - Preparation of pyrogen-free glassware, water, and solutions.
  - Test for pyrogens in rabbits.
  - *In vitro Limulus* amoebocyte lysate (LAL) test for the presence of endotoxins.
- Test for local irritation
  - Subcutaneous and intramuscular irritation tests for drugs and implants.
- Test for abnormal toxicity.
- Test to be carried out in mice.
- Histamine-like substances
  - Test of histamine-like substances on cat blood pressure (demonstration only).
- Bioassay.
- Insulin potency in mice.
- Heparin.
- Oxytocin (demonstration only).

References

1. WHO Technical Report Series, No. 681, 1982.

2. WHO Technical Report Series, No. 704, 1984.

Places of training in drug quality control offered by the International Federation of Pharmaceutical Manufacturers Associations[1]

At the Thirty-second World Health Assembly in May 1979 the International Federation of Pharmaceutical Manufacturers Associations (IFPMA) made an offer of training fellowships in drug quality control in the pharmaceutical industry. Places are available for nationals of developing countries who are employed by governmental drug control laboratories (not connected with the manufacture of pharmaceuticals) or pharmaceutical inspection services. The training is carried out in the analytical laboratories or quality control departments of pharmaceutical companies and covers one of three areas:

(a) chemical control
(b) microbiological control
(c) biological control

According to individual circumstances, the training may last three to six

---

[1] Adapted from WHO document PHARM/82.3/Rev. 1.

months. There is a possibility of more limited training for persons from countries interested only in dosage forms of pharmaceuticals, and combined training in all three areas can be arranged where a demand exists. The companies that provide the training operate in a wide geographical area so in many cases training can take place at convenient locations. Candidates for these training fellowships will often be those who work in conditions with limited capital and technical resources—such as for automated equipment—and every effort will be made to tailor the training to individuals needs. The application for training should include as much detail as possible about the facilities and equipment available in the applicant's control laboratory.

The application procedure is as follows: the government proposing a candidate submits a Fellowship Application Form through the WHO Programme Coordinator to the WHO Regional Office, which examines the application, ensures that funds are available, and transmits the proposal to WHO headquarters. No preference should be expressed in the application regarding the identify of the sponsoring company. IFPMA is then requested to identify a suitable training place, after which WHO headquarters transmits the relevant information to the Regional Office for further action.

The IFPMA officer does not cover the travel costs of trainees. These costs have to be financed from WHO Regional Office budgets or from funds allocated by the government concerned. The company with which the candidate is placed will cover all the costs of training and provide an allowance to cover accommodation and living expenses.

IFPMA training in quality control of pharmaceuticals: for nationals of developing countries currently employed by government agencies or academia

Details of the three training areas are given below; in addition managerial topics may be covered, according to the candidate's background and requirements. Examples include: laboratory management and related GMP (good manufacturing practices) requirements; documentation and record keeping; statistical validation of sampling and testing procedures; cost considerations and cost-effectiveness of analytical procedures; method development and validation; environmental and safety aspects of laboratory management.

Chemical control

This covers physico-chemical methods for routine testing of drug substances, excipients, dosage forms and packaging materials. Examples of subjects which might be included in a training programme are:

— Identity tests—for example, chemical, chromatographic and spectrophotometric

- Physical tests, e.g. uniformity of weight, hardness, disintegration, melting points
- Impurity tests, e.g. thin-layer chromatography, gas–liquid chromatography, spectrophotometric
- Dissolution testing
- Assay methods, chemical and instrumental, for batch control and stability monitoring
- Instrumentation: checking and calibration
- Evaluation of test results

Professional qualifications required

Completed education in pharmacy or chemistry with at least basic experience in pharmaceutical analysis; or equivalent knowledge acquired through a long period of practical experience.

Microbiological control

This covers quality control procedures designed to detect microbial contamination in products and in the environment as well as assay methods which use microorganisms for analytical purposes. Examples of subjects which might be included in a training programme are:

- Sterility testing and aseptic techniques
- Determination and classification of bioburden, microscopy
- Microbiological assay methods, e.g. for antibiotics and vitamins
- Challenge tests for effectiveness of preservatives
- Evaluation of results, including statistics
- Microbiological monitoring of production areas and GMP aspects

Professional qualifications required

Completed education in microbiology, pharmacy, medicine or biology with at least a basic theoretical, and if possible practical, knowledge of microbiological testing of drugs; or equivalent knowledge acquired through a long period of practical experience.

Biological control

This covers quality control procedures using animals, cell or tissue cultures, or other biological materials. Examples of subjects which might be included in a training programme are:

- Pyrogen testing
- Testing for abnormal toxicity

- Bioassays of hormones, e.g. insulin, oxytocin
- Evaluation of results, including statistics
- Care and handling of laboratory animals

Professional qualifications required

Completed education in pharmacy, medicine or biology, with at least basic theoretical knowledge of pharmacology, preferably with basic practical experience in pharmacology or in biological testing of drugs; or equivalent knowledge acquired through a long period of practical experience.

Note

Training posts are normally for a period of three to six months, though the length of time will depend on the trainee's experience, motivation, learning capacity and fluency in the language concerned.

Applicants should have detailed knowledge of which facilities and equipment are available in their own country so as to avoid receiving training that would be of no practical use. In particular, trainees should be familiar with:

- the local availability of instrument servicing and maintenance (which instruments companies have local service teams)
- the local supply of spare parts and other materials necessary to run the equipment.

This does not exclude the possibility of training in new techniques that may become feasible.

SELECTED WHO PUBLICATIONS OF RELATED INTEREST

Prices are in Swiss francs*

The international pharmacopoeia, third edition.
Volume 1: general methods of analysis. 1979 (223 pages) 24.–
Volume 2: quality specifications. 1981 (342 pages) 36.–
Volume 3: quality specifications. 1988 (407 pages) 64.–
Volume 4: tests, methods, and general requirements; quality specifications
for pharmaceutical substances, excipients and dosage forms. 1994 (358 pages) 85.–

WHO Expert Committee on Specifications for Pharmaceutical Preparations.
Thirty-fourth report.
WHO Technical Report Series, No. 863, 1996 (vi + 194 pages) 35.–

WHO Expert Committee on Specifications for Pharmaceutical Preparations.
Thirty-second report.
WHO Technical Report Series, No. 823, 1992 (vi + 134 pages) 17.–

International nonproprietary names for pharmaceutical substances.
Cumulative list No. 9.
1996 (xliii + 885 pages) 250.–

The use of essential drugs.
Seventh report of the WHO Expert Committee
(including the revised Model List of Essential Drugs).
WHO Technical Report Series, No. 867, 1997 (vi + 74 pages) 15.–

Basic tests for pharmaceutical dosage forms.
1991 (v + 129 pages) 24.–

Basic tests for pharmaceutical substances.
1986 (205 pages) 34.–

WHO model prescribing information.
Drugs used in anaesthesia. 1989 (53 pages) 11.–
Drugs used in mycobacterial diseases. 1991 (40 pages) 9.–
Drugs used in sexually transmitted diseases and HIV infection. 1995 (97 pages) 25.–
Drugs used in parasitic diseases, second edition. 1995 (146 pages) 35.–
Drugs used in skin diseases. In press

Further information on these and other WHO publications can be obtained from
Distribution and Sales, World Health Organization, 1211 Geneva 27, Switzerland

*Prices in developing countries are 70% of those listed here.

www.ingramcontent.com/pod-product-compliance
Ingram Content Group UK Ltd.
Pitfield, Milton Keynes, MK11 3LW, UK
UKHW051250180426
11947UKWH00020B/1626